NEWCASTLE UNITED
REVIEW 1993

NEWCASTLE UNITED

Published by Sports Projects Limited

ACKNOWLEDGEMENTS

Newcastle United Review 1993
First published in Great Britain in June 1993
by Sports Projects Limited

© 1993 Sports Projects Limited
188 Lightwoods Hill, Smethwick, Warley,
West Midlands B67 5EH.

ISBN 0-946866-10-4

Printed and bound in Great Britain
by Butler & Tanner Limited

Editor: Paul Tully

Photographs: Sports Projects and
Ian Dobson Photography.

Production: Bernard Gallagher, Phil Lees,
Nadine Goldingay, Trevor Hartley, Lisa Vokes
and Scott Anderson.

Key to symbols

❏	Player booked
■	Player sent off
† ‡	Player Substituted
(†25) (‡78)	Time of substitution
# § †† ‡‡	These symbols are also used in friendly games to denote substitutions
61p	Figure in goals column indicates time of goal. If followed by the letter 'p', this indicates a goal scored from a penalty kick.

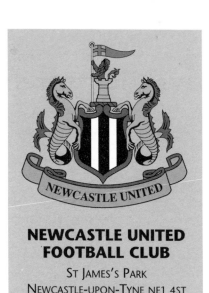

NEWCASTLE UNITED FOOTBALL CLUB

St James's Park
Newcastle-upon-Tyne NE1 4ST

★ ★ ★ ★

PRESIDENT
TREVOR BENNETT

DIRECTORS

CHAIRMAN
SIR JOHN HALL

VICE CHAIRMAN
W. F. SHEPHERD

D. S. HALL

R. JONES

★ ★ ★ ★

CHIEF EXECUTIVE
A. O. FLETCHER

★ ★ ★ ★

GENERAL MANAGER & SECRETARY
R. CUSHING

★ ★ ★ ★

TEAM MANAGER
K. KEEGAN

★ ★ ★ ★

It's the stuff dreams are made of...

THERE was a moment during the 6-0 victory over Barnsley at St James' Park on the evening of April 7th, when Kevin Keegan saw the future reflected bright and clear in the present.

"It was at 5-0," he said, "and watching the team play, and watching the fans with smiles on their faces, I looked at the new stand going up and I thought: 'Yes, perhaps it's the Geordies' turn at last'."

Only in the long-gone years of Milburn, Gallacher and Veitch can today's potential future for Newcastle United be accurately reflected in the past... but those glory days could now be returning.

In the last four decades, there has been little more than fleeting glimpses of success to inspire the United supporters.

There was the Second Division championship in 1965. Followed by failure. There was the 1969 Fairs Cup win. Followed by failure. There was promotion with Keegan as captain in 1984. Followed by failure.

Today, as Keegan said, perhaps it is the Geordies' turn at last: the Geordies' turn for success followed by success. For now there is a real air of achievement at St James' Park, built more on reality than vague hopes.

On the pitch, Keegan and his assistant Terry McDermott plus coach Derek Fazackerley have led a revolution and raised from it a team of inspirational quality.

Off the pitch, the expert leadership of Sir John Hall and his directors has provided the wherewithal for the feats on it,

Quite how a club disabled by a £6m debt can be resurrected into a vibrant, progressive force capable of spending further millions is perhaps a question only the men of miracles can answer.

But after so many years of unfulfilled promise, 1992-93 may be viewed in the future as the most significant landmark in the history of Newcastle United.

And if, in 40 years time, I can write in the 41st edition of the Newcastle United Review about four decades of success, and the continued development and realisation of the Newcastle United dream, I shall think back to Kevin Keegan's words on April 7th 1993.

For this is where it all began...

Paul Tully, May 1993

CONTENTS

CONTENTS

Saturday 15th August 1992 • St James' Park • 3.00pm

NEWCASTLE UNITED 3 SOUTHEND UNITED 2

Half-time 2-0 • Attendance 28,545

Referee John KEY (Sheffield)

Linesmen M.G. ROBINSON, M.J. STODDART

Black and White Striped Shirts, Black Shorts		Goals	Blue Shirts, Blue Shorts		Goals
1	Tommy WRIGHT		1	Paul SANSOME	
2	Barry VENISON		2	John CORNWELL	
3	John BERESFORD		3	Chris POWELL	
4	Paul BRACEWELL	10	4	Keith JONES	
5	Brian KILCLINE		5	Pat SCULLY	
6	Steve HOWEY		6	Spencer PRIOR	o.g.18
7	Steve WATSON		7	Adam LOCKE †	
8	Gavin PEACOCK		8	David MARTIN	57
9	David KELLY		9	Andy SUSSEX ❏ ‡	
10	Lee CLARK	70	10	Ian BENJAMIN	76
11	Kevin SHEEDY		11	Andy ANSAH	

Substitutes | | | *Substitutes* | |

| 12 | Micky QUINN | | 12 | Kevin O'CALLAGHAN (†70) |
| 14 | Mark STIMSON | | 14 | Steve TILSON (‡82) |

BEFORE	P	W	D	L	F	A	pts	AFTER	P	W	D	L	F	A	pts
Newcastle	0	0	0	0	0	0	0	Newcastle	1	1	0	0	3	2	3
Southend	0	0	0	0	0	0	0	Southend	1	0	0	1	2	3	0

FACTFILE

Paul Bracewell scores his first goal for two years in tenth minute of Newcastle debut... United attract England's biggest crowd of the day... Keegan's men off to winning start in only third meeting with Southend... Barry Venison and John Beresford also make United debuts.

United triumph in tough opener

THE CONFLICTING forces of eternal hope and nagging doubt greeted the dawning of Kevin Keegan's first full season in charge of Newcastle United. Hope . . . that Keegan the miracle-worker could once more work his special brand of magic. And doubt . . . that a side which had narrowly escaped relegation only three months earlier could launch a serious bid for promotion to the newly-formed Premier League.

However, the faith inspired by the mere presence of Keegan was sufficient to attract Britain's biggest crowd of the opening Saturday to the shrine. Southend could hardly be regarded as attractive opposition, but no less than 28,545 loyalists sensed enough cause for optimism to turn out on a day of cold, driving rain.

Such a figure was evidence of the so often untapped potential at Newcastle United: a potential which, in the summer, had persuaded Gavin Peacock to stay on Tyneside alongside Lee Clark, whose prodigious young talent was to become such a feature of the campaign.

And there was Paul Bracewell. In May, an FA Cup Final captain for rivals Sunderland; in June, a purchase of pride for Keegan. Suitably, too, it was Bracewell who launched United's drive for glory with a stunning goal after only ten minutes of that opening match.

When Southend only half-cleared a high ball from their penalty area, Bracewell struck an awesome shot high into the left corner of the net. The first expectations were fulfilled.

United's football in an enthralling first half was a harbinger of what was to come; slick, skilful and fast, with the midfield in particular merging into a formidable unit.

Lee Clark, encouragingly, was displaying all of his vision and style and was directly responsible for United's second goal on 18 minutes.

The Wallsend boy cut through the Southend defence like a knife through butter, but pulled his shot across goal, only for Spencer Prior to complete Clark's job for him by slicing the ball horribly into the gaping net.

For all United's dominance, Southend - the previous year's surprise package - were not about to surrender, and 12 minutes into the second half David Martin beat Tommy Wright from 20 yards to halve the deficit.

The nerves jangled but briefly. Within a further 13 minutes Clark, denied the glory of the second goal, collected one that was undeniably his. Steve Watson, destined not to play in the first team again until February in the league, worked a splendid exchange inside the area and released Clark to prod an eight-yard shot through the legs of Sansome and into the Gallowgate End net.

There would be no easy stroll to the tape, however, for Ian Benjamin dribbled round Tommy Wright to peg back the score once again in the 76th minute.

Wright needed to be at his best twice more to keep Newcastle ahead, but the winning start that everyone craved was secured, if anxiously.

The new full-backs, Barry Venison and John Beresford, had served notice of their talents and young Steve Howey, alongside Brian Kilcline in the centre of defence, demonstrated the defensive know-how that had been spotted in the one-time centre-forward by United's perceptive coaches several months before.

That Newcastle had not destroyed Southend at 2-0 up was a cause for some minor concern, but the result was all-important and the result was right. Micky Quinn, watching unused from the bench, must have reflected that his reign as King of Newcastle could be coming to an end.

But for all the optimism generated by a victorious start, Southend had run United close and in so doing provided a salutary lesson that nothing could be taken for granted in this remarkable season.

Wednesday 19th August 1992 • St James' Park • 7.45pm

NEWCASTLE UNITED 2 MANSFIELD TOWN 1

Half-time 1-0 • *Attendance* 14,083

Referee Roger DILKES (Mossley)

Linesmen R. Pearson, K. Thompson

Black and White Striped Shirts, Black Shorts		Goals	Yellow Shirts, Yellow Shorts		Goals
1	Tommy WRIGHT		1	Jason PEARCEY	
2	Barry VENISON		2	Steve PARKIN	
3	John BERESFORD		3	Chris WITHE	
4	Steve HOWEY		4	Steve SPOONER	
5	Brian KILCLINE		5	Kevin GRAY	
6	Kevin SCOTT		6	Paul HOLLAND	
7	Kevin BROCK ‡		7	Gary FORD	
8	Gavin PEACOCK	2, 82	8	Wayne FAIRCLOUGH	
9	David KELLY †		9	Phil STANT	67
10	Lee CLARK		10	Steve WILKINSON	
11	Kevin SHEEDY		11	Steve CHARLES	
	Substitutes			*Substitutes*	
12	Micky QUINN (†70)		12	Paul McLOUGHLIN	
14	Franz CARR (‡45)		14	Nicky CLARKE	

FACTFILE

First meeting in history of Newcastle and Mansfield... United's first appearance in League Cup first round since inaugural year of tournament in 1960... Steve Howey switches to midfield for injured Bracewell... Gavin Peacock double gives United slender first-leg lead.

Gavin Peacock turns to celebrate his opener

Peacock double edges first leg

NEVER since the League Cup's early days had Newcastle United been required to compete in the first round, but in 1992 this was the consequence of the season of struggle just passed.

Thus Mansfield Town, modestly of the Second Division which United had so narrowly avoided, came to peddle their wares at a venue they had never visited in all their 101-year history. The Stags must have wished they had delayed their St James' Park debut another few years when they conceded a goal to Gavin Peacock after only two minutes.

But they were to give a proud and determined performance which would keep the tie on a knife-edge to the very last. Peacock - described by Kevin Keegan as his most important summer signing - showed his predatory instincts when Kevin Sheedy's corner-kick caused havoc in the Mansfield six-yard box.

Big Brian Kilcline flicked on at the far post and though Steve Parkin cleared Peacock's first attempt off the goalline, the United striker headed in at the second.

The 14,083 crowd - less than half the first-day figure four days earlier - settled back in anticipation of the rout which never came.

Initially Town had to resist fierce pressure and goalkeeper Jason Pearcey did well to dive to a Clark shot following fine work in the build-up by Gavin Peacock and John Beresford.

To their credit, though, Mansfield raised the siege and steadily took the game to United, knowing the value of an away goal before the second leg at Field Mill six days later.

The message of menace to come was spelled out loud and clear when former Hereford striker Phil Stant was just wide with a 30th-minute header.

Slowly but surely Mansfield began to realise that attack was the best form of defence.

And after Steve Howey - playing an unfamiliar midfield role - had a goal disallowed and Pearcey saved resourcefully from David Kelly, they put the theory into practice.

Midway through the second half, Steve Wilkinson galloped away down the right and from his low cross, Stant flung himself horizontally almost at ground level to bullet a seven-yard header past Wright.

All the old Cup ghosts resurfaced as United fans shifted uneasily. Would Mansfield add their name to the list of Newcastle United giant-killers which was already uncomfortably long?

Franz Carr, a half-time substitute for Kevin Brock, had looked unlikely to provide the solution to the riddle of how to break down the visitors' stubborn defence. So within three minutes of Stant's equaliser, Kevin Keegan opted for the goalscoring instincts of Micky Quinn, pulling off the out-of-sorts Kelly.

The fingernails were still being bitten when, with eight minutes remaining, Quinn forced the breakthrough which gave United the advantage they so badly needed.

Quinn cleverly found space in the box and though he miscued his 16-yard shot, fortune smiled upon him as the ball first span off a defender then the keeper's legs to leave Peacock in an unmissable goalscoring position.

It was a win: but an unconvincing one. And the rigours of Field Mill beckoned threateningly.

Everyone watches as Gavin Peacock volleys

Saturday 22nd August 1992 • The Baseball Ground • 3.00pm

DERBY COUNTY 1 NEWCASTLE UNITED 2

Half-time 0-0 • *Attendance* 17,522

Referee Vic CALLOW (Solihull)

Linesmen M. ARCH, G. EDGELEY

White Shirts, Black Shorts	Goals	Yellow Shirts, Green Shorts	Goals
1 Steve SUTTON		1 Tommy WRIGHT	
2 Jason KAVANAGH		2 Barry VENISON	
3 Michael FORSYTH		3 John BERESFORD ❏	
4 Mark PEMBRIDGE	83	4 Steve HOWEY	
5 Simon COLEMAN		5 Brian KILCLINE	
6 Darren WASSALL		6 Kevin SCOTT	
7 Tommy JOHNSON		7 Franz CARR	
8 Paul KITSON		8 Gavin PEACOCK	51
9 Marco GABBIADINI †		9 David KELLY	
10 Paul WILLIAMS		10 Lee CLARK	55
11 Paul SIMPSON		11 Kevin SHEEDY	
Substitutes		*Substitutes*	
12 Ted McMINN (†64)		12 Micky QUINN	
14 Andy COMYN		14 Ray RANSON	

BEFORE		P	W	D	L	F	A	pts	AFTER		P	W	D	L	F	A	pts
	Newcastle	1	1	0	0	3	2	3	4	Newcastle	2	2	0	0	5	3	6
	County	1	0	0	1	0	1	0	20	County	2	0	0	2	1	3	0

FACTFILE

Franz Carr makes season's debut - and the first goal... Beresford is United's first booking of the campaign... first victory at Derby in over 20 years... United rise to fourth in first division.

Ram raiders stun Cox's millionaires

FOUR months earlier, a crushing 4-1 defeat at the Baseball Ground had almost condemned Newcastle United to the lowest point in their history - relegation from the Second Division.

On a day of bitter acrimony three men were sent off and United stood on the very trapdoor to oblivion. Two victories in the final two games of the season had brought salvation, but the spectre of Derby was not one easily banished. Thus it was that by a cruel quirk of the fixture computer, United had to return to the scene of that nightmare for their first away game of the new season.

Dauntingly, Derby, under the philanthropic leadership of the mega-rich Lionel Pickering, were in the process of investing several million pounds in their own promotion bid.

Not least among their expensive imports was that arch-tormentor, Marco Gabbiadini, neither forgiven nor forgotten for scoring the goal which deprived United of their last day hopes of promotion in the 1990 play-offs, and sped Sunderland on their way to the first division.

In retrospect, the match at Derby was probably the most crucial of all the early-season games: the ultimate acid test.

And how United responded, exorcising the ghosts of Easter Monday and stunning their former manager Arthur Cox with a display of mesmerising football.

Kevin Keegan has often said that he learned much of what he knows about soccer management from the legendary Bill Shankly and the indomitable Cox - manager at Newcastle in the Keegan Years of 1982 to 1984.

This, though, was the day when the pupil returned to outwit the master.

There was supreme confidence in the way in which United took the game to County from the off in a one-sided first half.

Chances were spectacularly created and narrowly missed as Derby spent much of their time chasing shadows. Kevin Sheedy, indeed, might have had a hat-trick, but the interval arrived with the game goalless.

Was this to be One Of Those Games? Emphatically not. For the breakthrough came six minutes into the second half and four minutes later United led 2-0.

Franz Carr, in sparkling form, supplied the first with a jinking run into the box on the right and a chipped cross perfectly measured for Gavin Peacock at the far post to head high past the stranded Sutton.

The 3,000 United fans fortunate enough to be watching this exhibition were still celebrating Peacock's goal when Lee Clark executed a glorious second in the 55th minute.

Cutting in from the right past two static defenders, Clark saw the gap and rifled in a left-foot drive from 18 yards which caught out Sutton as it sped through his grasp and into the bottom corner of the net.

The first signs of the powerful force which was to sweep to the top of the division were in sharp focus, and it was Clark who orchestrated things, displaying all his vision and skill to take the Man of the Match award.

Tommy Wright, who had safely dealt with the few Derby attacks which found a way past the United back four, was finally beaten by Mark Pembridge's close range header six minutes from time.

The United of old might have trembled and caved in, but this side merely stepped up a gear to control the last few minutes and deny Derby any hint of a point.

Newcastle United grew up on August 22nd, 1992. It was the day they became a team in the strongest sense of the word.

And 19-year-old Lee Clark, so often an onlooker and so nearly a departure, was here to stay.

Tuesday 25th August 1992 • Field Mill • 7.30pm

MANSFIELD TOWN 0 NEWCASTLE UNITED 0

Half-time 0-0 • Attendance 6,725

Referee John BRANDWOOD (Lichfield)
Linesmen J. BIDDLE, S. MATHIESON

Yellow Shirts, Yellow Shorts		Goals	Black and White Striped Shirts, Black Shorts		Goals
1	Jason PEARCEY		1	Tommy WRIGHT	
2	Steve PARKIN		2	Barry VENISON	
3	Chris WITHE		3	Ray RANSON	
4	Gary CASTLEDINE		4	Steve HOWEY	
5	Kevin GRAY		5	Brian KILCLINE	
6	Paul HOLLAND †		6	Kevin SCOTT	
7	Gary FORD		7	Franz CARR	
8	Wayne FAIRCLOUGH		8	Gavin PEACOCK	
9	Phil STANT		9	David KELLY	
10	Paul McLOUGHLIN		10	Lee CLARK	
11	Steve CHARLES		11	Kevin SHEEDY	
	Substitutes			*Substitutes*	
12	Steve WILKINSON (†44)		12	Micky QUINN	
14	Ian STRINGFELLOW		14	Kevin BROCK	

United's first win-less and goalless game... first-ever visit to Field Mill... the draw denies United four-game winning start record in all competitions... Ray Ranson steps in for the injured John Beresford... lowest gate of the season home or away, outside Anglo-Italian Cup.

FACTFILE

Ray Ranson - deputised for John Beresford

Over the first Wembley hurdle

ONE OF the heavier ironies of the first, fabulous two months of the season was that for all the first division opposition United met, second division Mansfield gave them two of their hardest contests.

If Town had rattled United at St James' Park in the Coca-Cola League Cup first round first leg, they positively took Keegan's side by the throat in the return.

In front of 6,725 vociferous fans, Mansfield knocked Newcastle out of their cultured stride and threatened from first to last to grab the single goal that would have secured a famous victory.

That they did not get that goal was down largely to the agility and bravery of United's Northern Ireland international goalkeeper, Tommy Wright.

Doubtless encouraged by their first leg performance, the Stags steadily gained the ascendancy after a quiet opening.

And the Midlands fans were prepared to believe in the fable of David and Goliath as the giants found themselves pinned back inside their own penalty box.

Goliath wobbled, especially at the start of the second half, when Wright saved magnificently three times in a fraught five minutes.

First Phil Stant - scorer of Mansfield's first leg goal - then Steve Wilkinson (twice) were denied by blinding saves from Wright.

Then he did it again in the 68th minute when Steve Parkin came forward from right-back to test his luck - and Wright's agility - from 18 yards.

Perhaps United could point to the absence of calf injury victim John Beresford and the introduction of Barry Venison to the left-back slot for their uncertainty in defence.

But to do so would be to unfairly take from Mansfield the credit on the night that was theirs by right.

Wilkinson was the main tormentor, but, strangely, he was only on the field thanks to a first-half injury to Paul Holland.

United's early threats, when Gavin Peacock and Kevin Sheedy went close, were distant memories as they fought a tooth-and-nail rearguard action.

But as time went by, the fundamental things applied and United restored their balance to come at their brave opponents in the closing stages.

When former Newcastle full-back Chris Withe hauled down the speedy Franz Carr inside the area two minutes from time, United were awarded a penalty; their first under Kevin Keegan.

Peacock stepped forward to apply the coup de grace, only to discover that Jason Pearcey in the Mansfield goal had not read the script.

It was apt that Pearcey should have the honour of saving Peacock's spot-kick. It was apt, too, that Mansfield should not be beaten in a game they could so easily have won.

Kevin Keegan was right when he summed up thus: "That was a good reminder that there are no easy games.

"In the second half, they threw a lot of stuff at us. We battled, had a little bit of luck, and have gone through."

To United went victory and a place in the second round where they would face Middlesbrough. To Mansfield went the glory.

Tommy Wright - a brilliant performance

Saturday 29th August 1992 • St James' Park • 3.00pm

NEWCASTLE UNITED 2 WEST HAM UNITED 0

Half-time 2-0 • *Attendance* 29,855

Referee Bill BURNS (Scarborough)

Linesmen G. BRADBURY, P. KITSON

Black and White Striped Shirts, Black Shorts		Goals		Claret Shirts, White Shorts		Goals
1	Tommy WRIGHT			1	Ludek MIKLOSKO	
2	Barry VENISON			2	Tim BREACKER	
3	Ray RANSON			3	Julian DICKS ■	
4	Liam O'BRIEN ❏			4	Steve POTTS	
5	Kevin SCOTT			5	Alvin MARTIN	
6	Steve HOWEY			6	Matt HOLMES †	
7	Franz CARR			7	Ian BISHOP	
8	Gavin PEACOCK	44		8	Peter BUTLER	
9	David KELLY	45		9	Martin ALLEN	
10	Lee CLARK			10	Clive ALLEN	
11	Kevin SHEEDY			11	Kevin KEEN	
	Substitutes				*Substitutes*	
12	Micky QUINN			12	Mike SMALL (†45) ❏	
14	Kevin BROCK			14	Tony GALE	

BEFORE		P	W	D	L	F	A	pts	AFTER		P	W	D	L	F	A	pts
5	Newcastle	2	2	0	0	5	3	6	4	Newcastle	3	3	0	0	7	3	9
14	West Ham	2	1	0	1	1	1	3	19	West Ham	3	1	0	2	1	3	3

FACTFILE

An almost 30,000 attendance is the country's top of the day... David Kelly opens his season's account after five games... Tommy Wright celebrates his 29th birthday with a clean sheet... Liam O'Brien's first match of the season after a three game ban – and is booked..! Hammers' skipper Julian Dicks is red-carded.

Hammers hit by Gavin and Ned

WATCHING Newcastle dominate and destroy West Ham on this sunny, smiling Saturday, it was easy to make comparison with some of the club's finest sides of the past.

The Hammers may not have borne comparison with some of Upton Park's finest, but their later emergence as genuine promotion contenders underlined how far Newcastle were ahead in terms of skill and teamwork at this early stage of the campaign.

This was a performance to match the artistry of the victory at Derby a week before, and it comfortably brought the third successive League triumph.

The goals were condensed into four euphoric minutes just before half-time but the quality football which delighted the 29,855 crowd was evenly spread over 90 excellent minutes.

Kevin Keegan commented afterwards: "We know we have the best crowd in the country. We just want a team that befits them."

On this day, the best befitted the best, and West Ham had little to offer in reply.

Even without John Beresford, Paul Bracewell and Brian Kilcline, all injured, United were clear winners. And Kilcline's absence, bemoaned at the time, had a hidden bonus, as it cleared the way for Steve Howey to lay claim to the central defensive slot he graced so well thereafter.

Clive Allen, leading the Hammers' line, was rarely given a chance to show his famous goal-poaching touch. But at the other end, Gavin Peacock, David Kelly and Lee Clark led the West Ham defence a merry dance.

Ludek Miklosko had already earned a piece-rate bonus with a string of saves before he was finally beaten by the old one-two which would become a Newcastle United trademark in following games.

In the 44th minute, Peacock showed superb invention to stretch out his right foot to a Howey header and lift the ball gently wide of Miklosko inside the left post. Steve Howey, following it in, was widely credited with the final touch, but video evidence later clearly showed the goal belonged to Peacock.

There was no doubt about the scorer of the second goal three minutes into first-half injury time, David Kelly opening his account for the season in emphatic style.

There may have been a hint of offside against Lee Clark in the build-up, but the flag stayed down for Clark to go on and shoot against the Czech keeper from point-blank range.

Fortune was with United as the ball spun to Kelly on the left side and he thundered a left-foot shot past the recovering Miklosko and Julian Dicks covering on the goalline.

More goals seemed inevitable in the second half, but West Ham survived the barrage without ever looking likely to claw back the deficit.

And there was more than just a touch of frustration about the elbow blow by Dicks on Franz Carr close to the end which earned the West Ham defender a red card from referee Bill Burns.

For the second Saturday in three, United attracted England's top attendance. But they still laid fourth in the table, behind Charlton, Swindon and Leicester who had all played extra games.

West Ham manager Billy Bonds paid fulsome tribute to Newcastle, suggesting the side "played like 11 Kevin Keegans."

It was a significant assessment. And the manager knew exactly what he meant.

Steve Howey – in for Brain Kilcline

Wednesday 2nd September 1992 • St James' Park • 7.45pm

NEWCASTLE UNITED 2 LUTON TOWN 0

Half-time 2-0 • *Attendance* 27,059

Referee John KIRKBY (Sheffield)

Linesmen R. FURNANDIZ, W. NATTRASS

Black and White Striped Shirts, Black Shorts		Goals	Blue and White Shirts, White Shorts		Goals
1	Tommy WRIGHT		1	Andy PETTERSON	
2	Barry VENISON		2	Des LINTON	
3	Ray RANSON		3	Julian JAMES	
4	Liam O'BRIEN		4	Darren SALTON ❏	
5	Kevin SCOTT		5	Trevor PEAKE	
6	Steve HOWEY		6	John DREYER	
7	Franz CARR		7	Steve CLARIDGE	
8	Gavin PEACOCK ❏		8	Scott OAKES	
9	David KELLY	44	9	Phil GRAY	
10	Lee CLARK	35	10	David PREECE	
11	Kevin SHEEDY		11	Jason REES †	
	Substitutes			*Substitutes*	
12	Micky QUINN		12	Marvin JOHNSON	
14	Kevin BROCK		14	Jamie CAMPBELL (†54)	

BEFORE		P	W	D	L	F	A	pts	AFTER		P	W	D	L	F	A	pts
4	Newcastle	3	3	0	0	7	3	9	2	Newcastle	4	4	0	0	9	3	12
21	Luton Town	3	0	1	2	1	5	1	21	Luton Town	4	0	1	3	1	7	1

FACTFILE

*Four straight wins give United their best start in league football for 84 years...
David Kelly scores against his old boss, David Pleat... Lee Clark scores his last
goal for 24 games... a 27,000 plus crowd is bettered only by Manchester United
on the day... United leap from fourth to second in the table.*

The bandwagon keeps on rolling

THE STEAMROLLER that was to crush far better sides than Luton Town had by now gathered sufficient pace to make short work of the struggling Hatters.

David Pleat's team had no answer to Newcastle at full throttle and the only mystery remaining after the comprehensive 2-0 victory was how the score had stayed at that.

It was becoming a Newcastle United speciality to score twice just before half-time and they did it again through Lee Clark and David Kelly to make it four league victories out of four.

If the performance against West Ham sparkled, then this was as if United had not stopped playing between matches.

The delightful, flowing one-touch football was again in evidence and Luton were there for no better reason than that the fixture computer had told them to be.

It was difficult to single out individuals in such a fine team performance, but Lee Clark was in quite majestic form on this balmy evening.

And it was fitting that Clark should strike the first goal in the 35th minute, taking Liam O'Brien's clever pass in his stride to fire in a ferocious 15-yard shot.

Luton goalkeeper Petterson, not for the first time, performed miracles to block the shot. But he was helpless as Clark hurdled over him to slot the rebound between a defender and the near post.

Lee Clark - majestic form

Luton were unable to stem the tide, and when a move of exquisite quality brought the second goal seconds before the interval, the match as a contest was over.

There was pure brilliance about the way Gavin Peacock slid a slide-rule pass inside the full-back for Kevin Sheedy to cut the ball back from the byline on the left.

And there was telepathy in the way David Kelly ghosted into position to sidefoot coolly past Petterson from six yards when Sheedy's low cross arrived.

Speed of thought and execution to rank with the best - and how the fans loved it.

The two-goal cushion gave United *carte blanche* to play as they wished in the second half and if any fault could be levelled at them, it would be that they did not add to their two-goal advantage.

Petterson at times was King Canute against the tide, and no save of his was better than the reaction stop to deny Clark's volley in the 78th minute. By way of a lesson that no game is won until it is lost, Scott Oakes fired a surprise shot against Tommy Wright's right post with 11 minutes remaining.

In truth, that was a rare blip on United's upward graph, and any result but a home win would have made nonsense of natural justice.

By now, the lingering doubts over whether United had what it takes to win things were all but dispelled. And the standing ovation delivered by the 27,059 crowd at the final whistle was ample proof of the strength of passion now surrounding Kevin Keegan's outstanding team.

Saturday 5th September 1992 • Twerton Park • 3.00pm

BRISTOL ROVERS 1 NEWCASTLE UNITED 2

Half-time 1-1 • *Attendance 7,487*

Referee John MARTIN (Alton)

Linesmen P. GRIGGS, K. PIKE

Blue and White Quartered Shirts, White Shorts		Goals	Yellow Shirts, Green Shorts		Goals
1	Brian PARKIN		1	Tommy WRIGHT	
2	Ian ALEXANDER		2	Barry VENISON	
3	Geoff TWENTYMAN		3	Ray RANSON	
4	Steve YATES		4	Liam O'BRIEN	73
5	David WILSON ❏		5	Kevin SCOTT	
6	Lee MADDISON		6	Steve HOWEY	
7	Steve CROSS		7	Franz CARR	
8	Justin SKINNER		8	Gavin PEACOCK ‡	
9	John TAYLOR	2	9	David KELLY ❏	
10	Marcus STEWART		10	Lee CLARK	
11	Tony POUNDER †		11	Kevin SHEEDY ❏	12
	Substitutes			*Substitutes*	
12	Billy CLARK		12	Brian KILCLINE (†77)	
14	Carl SAUNDERS (†72)		14	Paul BRACEWELL (‡14) ❏ †	

BEFORE	P	W	D	L	F	A	pts	AFTER	P	W	D	L	F	A	pts
2 Newcastle	4	4	0	0	9	3	12	2 Newcastle	5	5	0	0	11	4	15
17 Rovers	5	1	0	4	8	13	3	20 Rovers	6	1	0	5	9	15	3

FACTFILE

Fifth consecutive League win equals United club record start of 1908-09... for first time this season United fall behind... Peacock goes off with pulled hamstring and Bracewell is the first United league substitute to be used this season... Liam O'Brien celebrates his 28th birthday with winner... three United players booked.

The Irish eyes are smiling

ONLY once in the first 17 matches of the 1992-93 season did Newcastle fall behind - and that was in the second minute of perhaps the most difficult league game of them all.

When John Taylor of Bristol Rovers crashed a mighty angled drive high past Tommy Wright, United had to get accustomed to the unusual sensation of chasing a game.

But so effectively did they do it that they were level only ten minutes later. And thereafter it was bedlam in Bath.

When the dust had settled on the encounter decided by Liam O'Brien's late winner, the abiding memory was of a monumental performance by United goalkeeper Tommy Wright.

Every great side has a great goalkeeper, and in the unglamorous surroundings of Twerton Park, Wright proved that he had all the credentials to become exactly that. The Wright Stuff, perhaps . . .

Kevin Keegan was moved to describe the Irishman's performance as "world class", adding: "Tommy had no right to make some of those saves."

None was more miraculous than the 84th-minute defiance of gravity which deprived Marcus Stewart of an equalising goal.

Carl Saunders' speculative lob looked destined for the Roman Baths until it plummeted down and onto the top of the left angle of post and bar.

Wright had followed the bizarre flight of the ball and found himself pinned to the left post as the ball rebounded onto the head of Stewart barely six yards out.

The goal was a formality - until Wright, from nowhere, flew across his goal Batman-style to fist the ball around the opposite post for a corner.

Kevin Sheedy and Liam O'Brien may have scored the goals, but the Irish eyes that smiled most at the final whistle belonged to the former barman from Ballyclare.

Not that O'Brien was anything but ecstatic as he celebrated his 28th birthday with the 73rd-minute winner made by yet another Irishman, David Kelly.

Kelly chased a lost cause on the left touchline to keep the ball in play then gallop into the area before clipping a deft cross onto the head of the incoming O'Brien ten yards from goal.

Kevin Sheedy had the new backpass rule to thank for his 12-minute equaliser, the fated Stewart turning a loose ball back to Parkin, who made the fatal mistake of picking it up five yards from his line.

With every Rovers man strung across the goalline, Kelly touched the free-kick to Sheedy who found the tiniest of gaps above the row of heads and bulged the roof of the net.

When Gavin Peacock limped off with a pulled hamstring two minutes later, Paul Bracewell slotted in superbly.

But Rovers gave United's aristocrats no peace, and Bracewell, Sheedy and Kelly were all cautioned in a hectic five-minute spell for time-wasting or dissent.

After O'Brien's goal, Ian Alexander, Geoff Twentyman and Justin Skinner were all denied by the magnificent Wright.

And even following the Stewart save which ranks among the very best memories of this season, Wright again saved splendidly from John Taylor and Carl Saunders.

It had been breathless, but brilliant. Perhaps the only league game so far United had not deserved to win; but a win nonetheless. And five in a row to equal United's best-ever start to a Football League season, set way back in 1908.

But still United were not top of the table. Charlton Athletic, with 16 points from six games, had still to be overhauled.

Saturday 12th September 1992 • St James' Park • 3.00pm

NEWCASTLE UNITED 3 PORTSMOUTH 1

Half-time 2-0 • Attendance 29,885

Referee Philip WRIGHT (Anderton)
Linesmen G. SPOONER, W. GROVES

Black and White Striped Shirts, Black Shorts		Goals	Blue Shirts, White Shorts		Goals
1	Tommy WRIGHT		1	Alan KNIGHT	
2	Barry VENISON		2	Andy AWFORD	
3	John BERESFORD		3	Ray DANIEL	
4	Liam O'BRIEN		4	Alan McLOUGHLIN	
5	Kevin SCOTT		5	Kit SYMONS	
6	Steve HOWEY		6	Stuart DOLING †	
7	Franz CARR		7	Warren NEILL	
8	Micky QUINN	16, 74	8	Martin KUHL	
9	David KELLY †	41	9	Darryl POWELL ‡	
10	Lee CLARK		10	Guy WHITTINGHAM	82
11	Kevin SHEEDY		11	Chris BURNS ❑	
	Substitutes			*Substitutes*	
12	Brian KILCLINE		12	Colin CLARKE (†46)	
14	Alan THOMPSON (†83)		14	Shaun MURRAY (‡46)	

BEFORE		P	W	D	L	F	A	pts	AFTER		P	W	D	L	F	A	pts
2	Newcastle	5	5	0	0	11	4	15	1	Newcastle	6	6	0	0	14	5	18
8	Portsmouth	5	2	1	2	9	8	7	11	Portsmouth	6	2	1	4	10	11	7

FACTFILE

An estimated 3,000 fans are locked out... Micky Quinn replaces injured Gavin Peacock and scores twice against his old club... Barry Venison captains in Peacock's absence... John Beresford returns after missing last four games... It's the first time United top any table for eight years – since September '84.

Newcastle United Review 1993

Quinn makes his mark on Pompey

MICKY Quinn had played precisely 20 minutes of the first six games, and had spent the other 520 minutes sitting on the substitutes' bench watching United demolish all before them.

For the seventh game, at Bristol Rovers, he had not even been substitute. But when leading scorer Gavin Peacock was ruled out of the match against Portsmouth, the forgotten hero's moment had come. It was ironic that Quinn should return to the fold against his former team, and his former manager Jim Smith.

But the old warhorse had lost none of his golden touch, and rattled in two more in a 3-1 victory which for style and quality surpassed all that had gone before.

In fact, Quinn was denied a hat-trick only by an improbable offside decision, and led the United line with flamboyant arrogance.

Not that Quinn was the only Newcastle man that sunny day with something to prove. For Lee Clark, so often ignored and rejected by Jim Smith at Newcastle, came back to haunt the Bald Eagle with a remarkable display.

Clark was everywhere: carving chasms through the Pompey defence, spraying the ball about in midfield, and destroying any last shreds of doubt about his true ability. Smith, to his credit, acknowledged Clark as "outstanding" and said he had "blossomed" hugely since his time at St James' Park two years ago.

Portsmouth were rarely in the hunt as United stormed the barriers before an ecstatic capacity crowd. And once Quinn had converted Clark's pinpoint left-wing cross with a thumping header after 16 minutes, the outcome was never in doubt.

Pompey were dangerous on the break, but spent too much time chasing shadows to stand a chance of pulling back the deficit.

And when David Kelly danced into the area, picking his moment to guide a left foot shot past Alan Knight four minutes before the interval, the partying could begin. By the time Quinn rounded off a move involving Franz Carr and another Pompey old boy, John Beresford, in the 75th minute, there was magic in the air.

Guy Whittingham's late consolation – a fine header high past Tommy Wright – scarcely mattered beyond the goals difference column.

For not only were United's strikers and midfield men on scintillating form, but the Venison-Scott-Howey-Beresford back four was also defending with extreme confidence.

"It was breathtaking at times," purred Kevin Keegan in the afterglow. "You just don't want it to end. We played football that is way beyond this Division.

"That was the dream way to be a manager – just sitting there, watching my team, knowing no side could withstand the pressure of the football we were playing."

Every word of praise was fully earned by this marvellous performance and the critics were not slow to deliver that praise.

In all the 11-match winning start, there was probably no better sustained 90-minute display of sheer quality. And it was supremely apt that on such a day, Charlton Athletic, slipping up at home to Cambridge, should make way for United to hit the top for the first time.

Micky Quinn celebrates his second goal

Wednesday 16th September 1992 • Blundell Park • 7.30pm

GRIMSBY TOWN 2 NEWCASTLE UNITED 2

Half-time 1-2 • Attendance 2,159

Referee Keith HACKETT (Sheffield)

Linesmen I. BILLINGHAM, G. GRANDIDGE

Black and White Striped Shirts, Black Shorts		Goals	Yellow Shirts, Green Shorts		Goals
1	Rhys WILMOT		1	Pavel SRNICEK	
2	Paul FUTCHER		2	Barry VENISON	
3	Gary CROFT		3	John BERESFORD	
4	Andy TILLSON		4	Brian KILCLINE	
5	Peter HANDYSIDE		5	Kevin SCOTT	
6	Jim DOBBIN		6	Steve HOWEY	
7	Tommy WATSON ‡		7	Bjorn KRISTENSEN	
8	David GILBERT		8	Micky QUINN	5
9	Tony REES †	38	9	David KELLY	15
10	Paul GROVES	52	10	Lee CLARK	
11	Neil WOODS		11	Kevin BROCK	
	Substitutes			*Substitutes*	
12	Chris HARGREAVES (†81)		12	Franz CARR	
14	Gary CHILDS (‡81)		14	Darron McDONOUGH	

BEFORE		P	W	D	L	F	A	pts	AFTER		P	W	D	L	F	A	pts
2	Newcastle	0	0	0	0	0	0	0	2	Newcastle	1	0	1	0	2	2	1
3	Grimsby	1	0	0	1	0	4	0	3	Grimsby	2	0	1	1	2	6	1

FACTFILE

United's first defence of trophy won 19 years before... Quinn follows up Portsmouth double with fifth-minute opener... first Cup meeting of Mariners and Magpies other than FA Cup... Grimsby fight back from 2-0 down.

Mariners make it hot for United

THE ANGLO-ITALIAN Cup was destined to be no more than an unwelcome intrusion into the main business of gaining promotion to the Premier League.

Newcastle had spent 19 years as holders; victors over Fiorentina in Italy in May 1973, and never until now asked to defend their modest prize.

Then, United had won it as a first division club against first division clubs; now, they defended it as a first division club in the new age of the Premier League - and against second division Italian clubs.

The Italian part of the Anglo-Italian Cup was still to come, and the qualifying league in England paired United first with Grimsby: scarcely Italian in flavour or climate.

Moreover, a midweek trip to Cleethorpes between two vital League games was scarcely ideal preparation for the visit of Bristol City, but entry was compulsory and United remained diplomatic.

Not that any disillusionment got in the way of the steamroller in the early stages at Blundell Park. Micky Quinn - again replacing the injured Gavin Peacock - took only five minutes to find the target once again.

Kevin Brock's corner was headed on at the near post by Brian Kilcline and Quinn was, as usual, in position to score simply at the far post.

Kevin Brock - **crossed for both goals**

Ten minutes later the same ploy paid dividends again, Brock's corner this time being headed on by Kevin Scott for David Kelly to net from close range.

For the sprinkling of Geordie loyalists in the paltry 2,159 crowd, this was the regular diet on which they had grown fat all season.

But Grimsby had other ideas than surrender, and fought their way back into contention with a spirit that was to pay even greater dividends at St James' Park 38 days later.

Pavel Srnicek, playing his first game of the season, had made three worthy saves before he was finally beaten seven minutes before half-time.

Dave Gilbert's cross bisected United's central defenders and Tony Rees stole in to head past the Czech keeper. The cheer that greeted the goal could scarcely be heard.

In this reserve-game atmosphere, genuine passion was difficult to generate and an always interesting game lost the bite it must surely have had in front of a larger crowd.

When Paul Groves beat Barry Venison to level the scores seven minutes the other side of half-time, United were forced to roll up their sleeves a little further to preserve that proud unbeaten record.

To their credit United did just that and the match threatened to get exciting in the closing stages. Indeed, John Beresford struck Rhys Wilmot's left post from 25 yards; Tommy Watson, similarly, had earlier headed against Srnicek's right post.

Srnicek was there again to deny Neil Woods with a flying save in the 81st minute, and United escaped with their unbeaten record intact. But it was hard to read much significance into so unimportant a match in so unimportant a tournament.

And by the time the United team bus drove away from Blundell Park, thoughts were already turning to the match against Bristol City three days hence.

Saturday 19th September 1992 • St James' Park • 3.00pm

NEWCASTLE UNITED 5 BRISTOL CITY 0

Half-time 2-0 • *Attendance* 29,465
Referee Tom FITZHARRIS (Bolton)
Linesmen G. ATKINS, T. LYNCH

Black and White Striped Shirts, Black Shorts		Goals	Red Shirts, White Shorts		Goals
1	Tommy WRIGHT		1	Keith WELCH	
2	Barry VENISON		2	Andy LLEWELLYN	
3	John BERESFORD		3	Martin SCOTT ❏	
4	Liam O'BRIEN	40	4	David THOMPSON ❏	
5	Kevin SCOTT		5	Matt BRYANT	
6	Steve HOWEY		6	Mark AIZLEWOOD †	
7	Franz CARR †	64	7	Nicky REID ❏	
8	Gavin PEACOCK	45p, 68p	8	Dariusz DZIEKANOWSKI	
9	David KELLY		9	Leroy ROSENIOR	
10	Lee CLARK		10	Wayne ALLISON	
11	Kevin SHEEDY ‡		11	Gary SHELTON	
	Substitutes			*Substitutes*	
12	Micky QUINN (†70)		12	Junior BENT	
14	Kevin BROCK (‡70)	86	14	Terry CONNOR (†15)	

BEFORE		P	W	D	L	F	A	pts	AFTER		P	W	D	L	F	A	pts
1	Newcastle	6	6	0	0	14	5	18	1	Newcastle	7	7	0	0	19	5	21
9	Bristol City	6	2	2	2	11	12	8	12	Bristol City	7	2	2	3	11	17	8

FACTFILE

Gates are closed 25 minutes before kick-off... Andy Cole is sidelined by a knee injury... Kevin Brock is only substitute of the season to score... United get their first league penalty of the season... Newcastle's first 5-0 league win since October 1983... Bristol City's second five-goal defeat of the week.

Team lives up to Kevin's promise

THE BIGGEST isn't necessarily the best, but even if the defeat of Bristol City wasn't quite the best performance thus far, it was good to see United live up to Kevin Keegan's promise that "some team would get a good beating".

Every team was getting a good beating, of course, but poor City must have thought the fates had conspired against them as this became the biggest beating of all.

Two dubious penalties and a freak Franz Carr goal turned a comfortable victory into a runaway and left former Sunderland boss Denis Smith cursing more than just his luck.

This wasn't as consistently brilliant as the show against Portsmouth, but there was still style in abundance; far too powerful for struggling City to match. And when Kevin Keegan described his side after the match as "surely the most entertaining team in the country", he was right on the mark.

Not that the first 40 minutes were, by Newcastle's mighty standards, anything to write home about. City had managed to resist the heavy artillery and something special was needed to break open the floodgates.

The opening goal, when it came, was special indeed – a howitzer from a Liam O'Brien free-kick which dipped viciously over the defensive wall and steamed into Keith Welch's right corner. Five minutes later United had performed the pre-interval double again, David Kelly tumbling under an innocuous challenge in the area and Gavin Peacock applying the sword. A doubtful penalty; but they all count.

Only Welch stood between United and a cricket score at that stage, but City's feeble attack never looked likely to test the Newcastle back four, let alone Tommy Wright.

And the roof fell in on them with two more

United goals in a four-minute blitz midway through the second half.

It would be hard to convince anyone that Franz Carr intended his goal. If he did, it belonged on a 'Best of Brazil' video.

Cutting from the left, Carr aimed a chip in the general direction of the far side of the area and watched in astonishment as the ball arched over Welch and inside the opposite post.

On a day when fortune was totally with Newcastle, such a goal was perhaps not surprising. But Welch must have wondered how many of Denis Smith's black cats he had run over that day. In the 68th minute, it was Captain Peacock's turn to go down in the penalty area and earn another debatable penalty from referee Tom Fitzharris. Peacock himself got up to score again.

At 4-0, the only remaining question was how many, and Kevin Brock, becoming the only substitute of the season to score, made it five when he rifled in Liam O'Brien's crossfield ball.

Superstition, perhaps, had something to do with it all, for Keegan had adopted one or two lucky charms from his Liverpool days.

He had told the groundsman not to change the goalnets as planned, and to water the pitch, despite the day's rain.

Why? "Well, it's just something Shankly used to do," said the sorcerer's apprentice. "If Shanks did it, it must be right."

Bill Shankly also produced an irresistible team at Anfield, of which Keegan was an integral part, and now Newcastle United were threatening to match those standards.

Seven out of seven. And still there was more to come.

Franz Carr - surprising goal

Wednesday 23rd September • St James' Park • 7.45pm

NEWCASTLE UNITED 0 MIDDLESBROUGH 0

Half-time 0-0 • *Attendance* 25,814

Referee David ALLISON (Lancaster)

Linesmen A. REILLY, G. WILKINSON

Black and White Striped Shirts, Black Shorts	Goals	Red and White Shirts, White Shorts	Goals
1 Tommy WRIGHT		1 Ian IRONSIDE	
2 Barry VENISON		2 Chris MORRIS	
3 John BERESFORD		3 Jimmy PHILLIPS	
4 Liam O'BRIEN ❏		4 Alan KERNAGHAN ❏	
5 Steve HOWEY		5 Chris WHYTE	
6 Kevin SCOTT		6 Jamie POLLOCK	
7 Robert LEE †		7 John HENDRIE	
8 Micky QUINN		8 Willie FALCONER †	
9 David KELLY		9 Paul WILKINSON	
10 Lee CLARK		10 Tommy WRIGHT ❏	
11 Kevin SHEEDY		11 Robbie MUSTOE	
Substitutes		*Substitutes*	
12 Franz CARR (†74)		12 Bernie SLAVEN (†58)	
14 Kevin BROCK		14 Jon GITTENS	

FACTFILE

£700,000 Robert Lee makes his United debut... Third-choice keeper Ian Ironside is Boro hero... 95th Tyne-Tees derby ends in first leg stalemate... United's first St James' Park blank sheet of the season... fifth clean sheet in eleven games.

David Kelly gets squeezed out

All out effort draws a blank

FOR ALL the wonderful league form, United's real test would come only when they faced opposition from the Premier League into which they were heading at full speed.

And they didn't come much tougher than Middlesbrough, defiant derby rivals for decades and with an Indian sign over United in recent seasons.

Robert Lee, recruited from Charlton Athletic for £700,000 only two days earlier, made his debut - ironically against the manager, Lennie Lawrence, who had worked with him at Charlton and tried so hard to prise him away to Ayresome Park.

While promotion from division one remained United's priority, the Coca-Cola Cup meeting with Boro set up a battle for local pride as well as the Premier League test of standards.

That pride was clearly evident in United's hell-for-leather opening in which Boro were pushed back and forced to defend desperately.

The hero of the night was destined to be Middlesbrough goalkeeper Ian Ironside, a third choice stand-in for injured Stephen Pears and on-loan Brian Horne.

At the peak of United's early pressure, Ironside pulled off a quite miraculous save to deny David Kelly a ninth-minute goal.

Kelly's close-range header, carefully guided over the keeper, looked a certain winner until Ironside arched backwards to get the slightest of fingertip touches, turning the ball against the bar, his own back, and finally to safety.

Before then, Ironside had saved well from Steve Howey's looping header, and when he was beaten, Liam O'Brien's 25-yarder flew narrowly over.

The lack of a goal allowed Boro to force their way back into contention on equal terms, and their incisive counter-attacking began to stretch and trouble the United defence.

Former Newcastle striker John Hendrie worked a clear sight of goal on one occasion, only for Wright to advance and save.

Late in the first-half, Paul Wilkinson somehow managed to backheel over the bar from close in after a Jimmy Phillips header left him unmarked.

However, as the match ebbed and flowed, United regained the upper hand in the second half. And when Ironside forgetfully picked up a backpass, referee David Allison awarded United a free-kick just seven yards out.

The situation which had paid rich dividends at Bristol Rovers 18 days earlier failed to come up with a goal this time, though, as Boro's goalline defensive wall charged down Kevin Sheedy's shot.

Micky Quinn, in again for Peacock, squeezed one loose ball past Ironside in a desperate scramble, but the ball had not the momentum to cross the line and Chris Morris raced back to clear.

United's last hope of a goal disappeared when the heroic Ironside tipped over an O'Brien special from distance.

It had been frenetic, powerful and rivetting. To use Kevin Keegan's carefully-chosen adjective, superb.

"The game had everything but a goal," he said. "All 22 players and substitutes showed tremendous commitment.

"Two big North-East clubs gave their all tonight, but Middlesbrough came to play a certain way. However, Boro will have to come out more at home. The second leg is evenly balanced with everything to play for."

They were to prove prophetic words. But for now, it was only half-time. The Premier League test had still to be passed.

Saturday 26th September 1992 • London Road • 3.00pm

PETERBORO' UNITED 0 NEWCASTLE UNITED 1

Half-time 0-0 • *Attendance* 14,487

Referee Mike REED (Birmingham)

Linesmen M. CARRINGTON, B. MILLERSHIP

Blue Shirts, White Shorts	Goals	Black and White Striped Shirts, Black Shorts	Goals
1 Ian BENNETT		1 Tommy WRIGHT	
2 Chris WHITE ❏ †		2 Barry VENISON	
3 Ronnie ROBINSON		3 John BERESFORD	
4 Mick HALSALL		4 Liam O'BRIEN	
5 Lee HOWARTH		5 Kevin SCOTT	
6 Steve WELSH		6 Steve HOWEY	
7 Worrell STERLING		7 Robert LEE	
8 Marcus EBDON		8 Micky QUINN †	
9 Tony ADCOCK		9 David KELLY	
10 Ken CHARLERY		10 Lee CLARK	
11 Bobby BARNES ‡		11 Kevin SHEEDY	60
Substitutes		*Substitutes*	
12 Noel LUKE (†32)		12 Kevin BROCK (†79)	
14 Pat GAVIN (‡70)		14 Brian KILCLINE	

BEFORE		P	W	D	L	F	A	pts	AFTER		P	W	D	L	F	A	pts
1	Newcastle	7	7	0	0	19	5	21	1	Newcastle	8	8	0	0	20	5	24
9	Peterboro'	7	3	1	3	9	11	10	11	Peterboro'	8	3	1	4	9	12	10

FACTFILE

United's first league visit to London Road... 7,000 travelling fans watch seventh win in seven in the league... ex-Newcastle 'keeper Ian Bennett plays game of his life... "Biggest game in our history," says Posh boss Chris Turner.

Sheedy's strike makes it eight

NEWCASTLE United fans have always responded to success in large numbers, and the scenes at London Road on a day of warm autumn sunshine were living proof of it.

An estimated 7,000 Tynesiders descended on Peterborough to double their crowd and turn a small corner of Cambridgeshire into a large slice of Geordieland.

Seven league wins out of seven had raised the spirits of the Toon Army even beyond seventh heaven. But while local bookmakers were offering odds on United going through the season unbeaten (40-1 and falling), the realists knew that defeat had to come sooner or later.

Whether Peterborough were the side to do it would depend upon how Newcastle could acquit themselves to their compact little ground.

But by the end of the match United's tally of 21 shots on target against just four from Peterborough told it's own story.

That only one of those 21 shots should count was due to a blinding display from Ian Bennett, a little-known former Newcastle junior who had drifted anonymously away from St James' Park three years before. Bennett, 21, had found his niche at London Road and become something of a hero; and this day was to be one of his most memorable, even in defeat.

The tone of the match was set after just 20 seconds as Robert Lee's snap shot brought the first great save from Bennett. David Kelly struck the bar in the third minute, and when Bennett saved but could not hold a Liam O'Brien 25-yarder, Quinn and Kelly were heartbreakingly close to breaking the deadlock.

United's superiority on their first-ever league visit to Peterborough was almost total, and Kelly (twice) and Lee fell victim to Bennett's brilliance.

It would have been a serious injustice had Peterborough broken away to score, but they almost did just that early in the second half when Terry Adcock found himself clear eight yards out, only for Tommy Wright to take a leaf from Bennett's book, and save brilliantly.

It was, ironically, the prelude to the goal Newcastle so richly deserved but which they must have feared would never come.

The clock had ticked ominously onto the hour mark when Lee picked up the keeper's clearance in midfield and slipped a measured pass between two defenders into the path of Kevin Sheedy, bearing down on goal in the inside-left channel.

The chance was difficult, but Sheedy called upon all his experience to chip across the advancing Bennett and gently into the far corner with a defender chasing the ball into the net.

With the dam at last breached, the 7,000 travelling fans, dancing joyously, waited for the floodgates to open.

But apart from a Lee Clark near-miss and a Robert Lee thunderbolt, Newcastle rarely came close again in the last half-hour; Peterborough, to their credit, came punchdrunk off the ropes to make a real fight of it.

They nearly landed a knockout blow, too, with Ken Charlery going through unchallenged in the final minute, only for Tommy Wright to win the battle of wits with a well-timed block.

Newcastle deserved their victory: of that there was no doubt. But thanks to the extraordinary display by Ian Bennett, it had been a very close run thing.

Kevin Sheedy - winner on the hour

Wednesday 30th September 1992 • St James' Park • 7.45pm

NEWCASTLE UNITED 4 LEICESTER CITY 0

Half-time 2-0 • *Attendance* 14,046
Referee Michael PECK (Kendal)
Linesmen C. BASSINDALE, J. JONES

Black and White Striped Shirts, Black Shorts		Goals	Blue Shirts, Blue Shorts		Goals
1	Pavel SRNICEK		1	Russell HOULT ❏	
2	Bjorn KRISTENSEN		2	Gary MILLS	
3	Mark STIMSON		3	Mike WHITLOW	
4	Liam O'BRIEN †		4	Richard SMITH ❏	
5	Brian KILCLINE ❏		5	Steve WALSH	
6	Alan NEILSON		6	Colin HILL ❏	
7	Kevin BROCK	10	7	Simon GRAYSON	
8	Micky QUINN ❏	44p, 84	8	Steve THOMPSON	
9	David KELLY ‡		9	Bobby DAVISON †	
10	Alan THOMPSON		10	Ian ORMONDROYD	
11	Kevin SHEEDY	59	11	David LOWE	
	Substitutes			*Substitutes*	
12	Peter GARLAND (†68)		12	Mike TROTTER	
14	Matty APPLEBY (‡68)		14	Colin GORDON (†71)	

BEFORE		P	W	D	L	F	A	pts	AFTER		P	W	D	L	F	A	pts
1	Leicester	1	1	0	0	4	0	3	1	Newcastle	2	1	1	0	6	2	4
2	Newcastle	1	0	1	0	2	2	1	2	Leicester	2	1	0	1	4	4	3

FACTFILE

United win handsomely with seven reserves... Quinn's brace takes his tally to five in five games... United overtake Group 2 leaders Leicester... Pavel Srnicek plays his second game of the season.

It's a Foxtrot for United's Reserves

ONE WIT reading out the scoreline after this match announced: "Newcastle Reserves 4, Leicester City 0." And he was right. The manager fielded only four of the side which had won at Peterborough four days earlier, and must have been as pleasantly surprised as everyone else when the 'fringe' men won so convincingly.

Anyone who doubts Leicester's commitment to this cause should look at their tally of three bookings for fouls; not to forget United's two.

But the greater boost was the clear evidence of the strength in depth of the United first-team squad - and the eternal goalgrabbing instincts of Micky Quinn.

Quinn it was who struck twice to ensure that United would partake of two trips to Italy to defend the Cup they had won when it was last contested 19 years earlier.

And even if Keegan and United would have later cause to regret their involvement in the Anglo-Italian Cup, the destruction of Leicester was undoubtedly a high spot.

It was almost as if the first-choice eleven were on show as the football flowed: Srnicek, Kristensen, Stimson, Kilcline, Brock, Neilson and Thompson could have been Wright, Venison, Beresford, Scott, Howey, Lee and Clark.

The 14,000 who had turned out were fully rewarded with a display of genuine style which left City dazed and well beaten.

The first goal arrived after only ten minutes, Brian Kilcline heading down Kevin Sheedy's corner kick for Kevin Brock to shoot low past

Russell Hoult as he fell. Quinn, Kelly and Kristensen all went close as Leicester struggled to turn the tide.

And a minute from half-time, Hoult brought down Kelly to concede a booking and the penalty from which Quinn scored was his fourth goal of the season.

Leicester had needed only a draw to qualify for the final stages, but rarely looked like getting it after Whitlow missed one of their few chances early in the second half.

And when Kevin Sheedy added No 3 on 59 minutes, the game was won and lost.

This time O'Brien was brought down as he weaved past a series of tackles on the edge of the area, and when Brock touched the free-kick to the left, Sheedy curled a simple but superb shot into the left corner from 25 yards.

There was no way back for City and Micky Quinn added the icing to the cake by beating the offside trap and twisting a reverse chip over Hoult in the 84th minute.

Keegan had gambled on attracting criticism for his decision to rest seven first-team players.

But no-one could be critical of such a controlled display and the manager himself said: "I was very proud of them.

"I gave the other lads the chance to show what they can do and they have made the most of it. This performance goes down with our best so far this season."

Such a display from a largely reserve side served to reinforce the aura of invincibility surrounding United after 13 games unbeaten since the season's start.

Another good result at Brentford on the Sunday following would equal United's record run of 16 games without defeat in all competitions.

Man-of-the Match Micky Quinn

Sunday 4th October 1992 • Griffin Park • 3.00pm

BRENTFORD 1 NEWCASTLE UNITED 2

Half-time 0-1 • *Attendance* 10,131
Referee Allan GUNN (South Chailey)
Linesmen B. FIRMIN, R. HARRIS

Red and White Striped Shirts, Black Shorts	Goals	Yellow Shirts, Green Shorts	Goals
1 Gerry PEYTON		1 Tommy WRIGHT	
2 Brian STATHAM ❏		2 Barry VENISON	
3 Chris HUGHTON		3 John BERESFORD	
4 Keith MILLEN		4 Liam O'BRIEN	
5 Jamie BATES		5 Kevin SCOTT ❏	
6 Simon RATCLIFFE		6 Steve HOWEY	
7 Micky BENNETT		7 Robert LEE	
8 Detsi KRUSZYNSKI †		8 Gavin PEACOCK	64
9 Kevin GODFREY ‡		9 David KELLY	10
10 Gary BLISSETT	78	10 Lee CLARK	
11 Neil SMILLIE		11 Kevin SHEEDY	
Substitutes		*Substitutes*	
12 Billy MANUEL (†61)		12 Micky QUINN	
14 Marcus GAYLE (‡68)		14 Brian KILCLINE	

BEFORE		P	W	D	L	F	A	pts	AFTER		P	W	D	L	F	A	pts
1	Newcastle	8	8	0	0	20	5	24	1	Newcastle	9	9	0	0	22	6	27
19	Brentford	8	2	2	4	9	10	8	19	Brentford	9	2	2	5	10	12	8

FACTFILE

First live TV game of season... first of 11 Sunday games in 1992-93... United equal club record of 16 games unbeaten in all competitions... first visit to Griffin Park for 45 years... Quinn dropped to make way for fit-again Peacock.

Bees stung by buzzing Magpies

A DAY of firsts: Kevin Keegan's first match in the capital as a manager, and United's first match of the season live on television.

And even if United didn't dazzle the TV audience as they had dazzled their own fans all season, their skill and strength was still too much for the first division newcomers.

Brentford offered every bit as much spirit and endeavour as Newcastle, but were left far behind when it came to soccer skills.

Once David Kelly had opened the scoring in the tenth minute, The Bees were up against it and with only the occasional minor scare, United saw out the match in relative comfort.

Only when Gary Blissett found a rare gap in United's back line to score 12 minutes from time did a mild flutter or two set in.

But by then Gavin Peacock had celebrated his return after a three-match absence with a 64th-minute diving header after Robert Lee had shot against the crossbar.

Keegan, not surprisingly awarded the Manager of the Month accolade a few days before, could afford a smile of contentment when Kelly settled the early nerves on a cool, blustery day.

Steve Howey's long, high ball sprang the Brentford offside trap - if dubiously - and Kelly ran on to take all his options into careful consideration before planting an angled shot inside Gerry Peyton's near post.

Once again United's midfield dominated, with Liam O'Brien and Lee Clark in top form and Kevin Sheedy adding vital balance on the left side.

Gavin Peacock would have added a second soon after Kelly's opener, but for a goalline clearance from Brian Statham. Then Lee Clark fired into the side-netting from a good position.

As on several occasions already this season, United were indebted to goalkeeper Tommy Wright for keeping the ship on an even keel.

Ten minutes from half-time, Blissett ran around Kevin Scott to collect his own lob and blast in a tremendous volley which brought an even better save from the diving Wright.

Neil Smillie proved Brentford's main threat with a series of thrusting runs down the left which gave Barry Venison an uncomfortable afternoon.

But it was Kevin Godfrey who almost levelled the scores on the hour, burrowing deep into the box to aim for the bottom corner only to see Wright get down quickly to tip behind.

However, these were rare moments of concern as United controlled the majority of the second half.

Yet they needed a second goal to kill off Brentford - and it arrived in the 64th minute when John Beresford picked out Robert Lee from the left in a good position eight yards out.

Lee turned skilfully to drive a shot against the bar and there was Peacock throwing himself forward to head the bouncing ball into the gaping net.

Four times United appealed justifiably for penalties, and only referee Allan Gunn knows why he didn't award one in particular for a foul on Kelly.

Before Blissett's goal, United missed further chances through Peacock and Kelly, and were noticeably less comfortable after the deficit was halved.

They might have rued their profligacy more had Brian Statham not hesitated horribly when clean through on Wright in the final minutes.

But United were now five points clear at the top with nine straight league wins. And the second part of the Premier League test with Middlesbrough was just around the corner.

Wednesday 7th October 1992 • Ayresome Park • 7.45pm

MIDDLESBROUGH 1 NEWCASTLE UNITED 3

Half-time 0-1 • *Attendance* 24,390

Referee Joe WORRALL (Warrington)

Linesmen I. BLANCHARD, A. STREETS

Red and White Shirts, White Shorts	Goals	Black and White Striped Shirts, Black Shorts	Goals
1 Ian IRONSIDE		1 Tommy WRIGHT	
2 Chris MORRIS		2 Barry VENISON	
3 Jimmy PHILLIPS ❏		3 John BERESFORD ❏	
4 Alan KERNAGHAN		4 Liam O'BRIEN	78
5 Chris WHYTE		5 Kevin SCOTT	
6 Andy PEAKE ‡		6 Steve HOWEY	
7 Bernie SLAVEN		7 Robert LEE	
8 Robbie MUSTOE		8 Gavin PEACOCK	
9 Paul WILKINSON	56	9 David KELLY	39, 88
10 Tommy WRIGHT		10 Lee CLARK	
11 John HENDRIE ❏ †		11 Kevin SHEEDY †	
Substitutes		*Substitutes*	
12 Jamie POLLOCK (†28)		12 Micky QUINN (†73) ❏	
14 Jon GITTENS (‡75)		14 Brian KILCLINE	

United's first win at Ayresome Park since 1964... Kelly double sets up third-round trip to Chelsea... club record 17th game unbeaten... 12th victory in 15 games in 1992-93... Quinn's ninth game in 15 on the subs' bench - and he's a hero... O'Brien hits a derby 'rocket'.

David Kelly - first double of the season

Ayresome bogey smashed at last

THERE WERE almost three decades worth of ghosts to banish and a major point to prove when United went to Middlesbrough for the second stage of the Coca Cola League Cup duel.

The point to prove was that, in a triumphant Football League campaign, United were truly of Premier League standard. And the ghosts had gathered in the 28 years since United last won at Ayresome Park: 2-0, in the 1964-65 Second Division championship season.

The goalless first leg draw had been merely a prelude to a night when Newcastle proved to themselves and everyone else that their rightful place was at the very top.

From first to last, Kevin Keegan's super-confident side took the game to Middlesbrough, knocking the ball around in midfield and at the back, and striking Commando-style when the chances arrived. Every man played his part, but no-one could argue against the choice of David Kelly as the evening's star performer.

Tirelessly he worked, skilfully he teased the Boro defence. And, aptly, he claimed two of the three goals which wrecked Middlesbrough and sent United into the third round.

Kelly it was who struck an opening goal of splendid invention in the 39th minute, and Kelly it was who rounded off victory two minutes from time following a move of stunning precision. And sandwiched between Kelly's goals was a quite magnificent strike from Liam O'Brien which bore comparison with Bobby Charlton at his very best.

Paul Wilkinson's shock equaliser for Boro - left unmarked for a 56th-minute header - was ultimately irrelevant, though for 20 minutes it gave the home side second wind.

Long before Kelly hit the first goal United had rocked boro back on their heels and but for a temporary suspension of the law of gravity in the 12th minute, Kevin Sheedy would have been the first name on the scoresheet.

Quite how Sheedy's close-range shot from a narrow angle glanced off the inside of the near post and curled past the far post defies scientific explanation. But when Tommy Wright's long clearance deceived the Boro defence to release David Kelly six minutes before the break, the first goal was on it's overdue way.

Showing great composure, Kelly used his chest to control the ball and open up an angle against the advancing Ironside which was just enough for a low left-foot drive under the keeper's body and into the net.

Wilkinson was the Middlesbrough danger-man and after outwitting Steve Howey to shoot just wide, he rose unchallenged to head Jamie Pollock's cross high past Tommy Wright.

But showing marvellous resilience, United once again took the initiative rather than depend upon the away goals rule to go through.

Micky Quinn, a 73rd-minute substitute for Sheedy, inevitably had a hand in the goal which finally tipped the scales United's way in the 78th minute.

After an intricate passing movement outside the box, Quinn calmly rolled the ball back into the path of Liam O'Brien whose thunderous right-foot drive from 25 yards swept around the diving Ironside and low inside the right post. It was a stunning goal of fulminating power and one to rank alongside the best of the season.

Though Jon Gittens almost scrambled an 85th-minute goal for the Teessiders, United were walking on water and mercilessly tore Boro apart again to add the third and clinching goal two minutes from time.

Robert Lee sent Lee Clark surging into space on the right and Clark produced the perfect low cross for Kelly to touch home from six yards.

The ghosts had been laid, and the point proven. Newcastle United had passed the Premier League test.

Saturday 10th October 1992 • St James' Park • 3.00pm

NEWCASTLE UNITED 1 TRANMERE 0

Half-time 1-0 • *Attendance* 30,137

Referee Ian CRUIKSHANKS (Hartlepool)
Linesmen T. HEILBRON, D. OLIVER

Black and White Striped Shirts, Black Shorts	Goals		Blue Shirts, White Shorts	Goals
1 Tommy WRIGHT			1 Eric NIXON	
2 Barry VENISON			2 Dave HIGGINS ❏	
3 John BERESFORD			3 Ged BRANNAN ❏	
4 Liam O'BRIEN			4 Dave MARTINDALE †	
5 Kevin SCOTT			5 Steve MUNGALL	
6 Steve HOWEY			6 Steve VICKERS	
7 Robert LEE			7 John MORRISSEY	
8 Gavin PEACOCK			8 John ALDRIDGE	
9 David KELLY	37		9 Chris MALKIN ‡	
10 Lee CLARK			10 Neil McNAB ❏	
11 Micky QUINN			11 Pat NEVIN	
Substitutes			*Substitutes*	
12 Franz CARR			12 Kenny IRONS (†74)	
14 Mark STIMSON			14 Steve COOPER (‡76)	

BEFORE		P	W	D	L	F	A	pts	AFTER		P	W	D	L	F	A	pts
1	Newcastle	9	9	0	0	22	6	27	1	Newcastle	10	10	0	0	23	6	30
5	Tranmere	9	5	3	1	16	8	18	7	Tranmere	10	5	3	2	16	9	18

FACTFILE

Ten out of Ten on tenth day of tenth month... Keegan gets September Manager of Month award... Tranmere have not a single shot on target... Kelly takes over as leading scorer... Keegan takes squad on golf break to Isle of Man after match.

Kelly keeps up the perfect start

BOOKMAKERS are not generous folk by nature, and their offer of 40-1 on United going through the League season undefeated was absurdly low.

But the mere fact they were prepared to consider such a feat was testimony to the level of esteem United had reached in their storming start to the campaign.

When Tranmere came next before the firing squad in League match No 10, the Merseysiders were just beginning to launch their own promotion challenge.

They should have been a major threat, but the statistic of not a single Rovers shot on target in the 90 minutes - despite John Aldridge - is ample proof of United's right to victory on the day.

Not that this victory was anything less than a hard battle, settled by one piece of dazzling quality eight minutes before half-time.

Rovers' rear-guard action was beginning to frustrate the lock-out 30,000 crowd when Liam O'Brien worked a superb wall-pass with Micky Quinn then chipped back perfectly from the right corner of the six-yard line for David Kelly to fling himself in at the far post to head into the open net.

O'Brien throughout demonstrated the sort of form which he had so often promised since his £300,000 move from Manchester United in 1988.

With Kevin Sheedy absent through injury, Gavin Peacock moved into the midfield role with Quinn keeping the striking role he took up for the last 17 minutes at Middlesbrough.

Quinn may not have the finesse of others, but his mere presence induced an attack of the jitters in Tranmere whenever the ball arrived in their area.

And while Rovers keeper Eric Nixon was kept more than busy, his opposite number Tommy Wright would have seen more action at the top of Everest.

The match was a personal triumph, too, for Steve Howey, who kept the much-vaunted Aldridge out of the picture from first to last.

The closest the ex-Liverpool striker came was when he slid in agonisingly close to Malkin's deflected shot inches from the Leazes End goalline.

Yet for all their dominance, wasteful finishing prevented United from killing off Tranmere, and ensured a nervous finish.

A win it was, though, and it meant that Kevin Keegan had now gathered in more points from ten games than his predecessor Ossie Ardiles had done the previous season from 29 games.

And how the supporters were gathering round the flame. An estimated 7,000 fans were locked out with the gates shut an hour before the kick-off against Tranmere.

Records were tumbling, too. Already the previous club record of seven successive victories had gone; as had the five-game winning start record.

One more victory would equal Spurs' record First Division winning start to a season of 11, set in 1960-61, though Reading's all-time record of 13 in the third division of 1985-86 was three games away.

And two more victories against Sunderland and Grimsby Town would match the League record of 14 successive victories shared by Manchester United (1904-05), Bristol City (1905-06) and Preston (1950-51).

It was all heady stuff, and thoughts now turned to Roker Park eight days hence - a ground on which United had not won since 1956.

But for now it was Ten out of Ten. Top of the class. And the mid-term report was: Couldn't do better.

Sunday 18th October 1992 • Roker Park • 12.00pm

SUNDERLAND 1 NEWCASTLE UNITED 2

Half-time 0-1 • *Attendance* 28,098

Referee Stephen LODGE (Barnsley)

Linesmen M. SWIFT, S. WILLIAMS

Red and White Striped Shirts, Black Shorts		Goals	Yellow Shirts, Green Shorts		Goals
1	Tim CARTER		1	Tommy WRIGHT	
2	John KAY		2	Barry VENISON	
3	Anton ROGAN		3	John BERESFORD ❏	
4	Gary OWERS	o.g.12	4	Liam O'BRIEN ❏	76
5	Gary BENNETT		5	Kevin SCOTT	
6	Kevin BALL		6	Steve HOWEY	
7	Shaun CUNNINGTON		7	Robert LEE	
8	Don GOODMAN		8	Gavin PEACOCK	
9	Peter DAVENPORT		9	David KELLY	
10	Brian ATKINSON		10	Lee CLARK	
11	David RUSH †		11	Kevin BROCK	
	Substitutes			*Substitutes*	
12	Gordon ARMSTRONG(†66)70		12	Micky QUINN	
14	John COLQUHOUN		14	Brian KILCLINE	

BEFORE		P	W	D	L	F	A	pts	AFTER		P	W	D	L	F	A	pts
1	Newcastle	10	10	0	0	23	6	30	1	Newcastle	11	11	0	0	25	7	33
19	Sunderland	10	3	2	5	7	14	11	19	Sunderland	11	3	2	6	8	16	11

United lay Roker Park bogey... first win there since 1956... new record sixth consecutive away league victory... and new record 15th successive away league game without failing to score... O'Brien free-kick special wins the day... Both number 4s score for United with Gary Owers' own goal.

'Zico' O'Brien's magical moment

IF ONE image above all remains burned into the memory as a symbol of all this season stood for, it will be that of Liam O'Brien wheeling away in ecstacy as his winning free-kick swerved and dipped into the Sunderland net at Roker Park.

As a simple statistic, O'Brien's stunning goal secured United's 11th consecutive victory of the league campaign. But its implications went far deeper than that. In one fell swoop, the 36-year myth of Newcastle's inability to beat the old enemy in their own backyard was swept away.

It clinched the most treasured scalp of all, leaving far behind, in terms of emotion and pride, the technically greater victory at Middlesbrough 11 days earlier. And it symbolised everything good about Newcastle United in this astonishing, unprecedented run of glory.

In terms of performance, the 2-1 victory at Roker did not rate above the majority of those early-season displays which established a ten-point lead at the top of the table.

But Tyne-Wear derbies are rarely classics and the tension inherent in this one ensured that it would not prove the exception. It was more of a test of character, and the final scoreline meant that verdict too went to United, whose smooth inter-passing game was altogether too much for Malcolm Crosby's distinctly ordinary side.

From the moment when United carved open the Sunderland defence to take a 12th-minute lead the writing was on the wall for Roker.

John Beresford began the crossfield move which ended with Robert Lee turning in a low cross from the right which eluded keeper Tim Carter and was turned into his own net by Gary Owers in his last-ditch bid to stop Kevin Brock applying the finishing touch. David Kelly beat the offside trap shortly after only to fire wide,

but Sunderland were nothing if not determined and gave United one or two nasty frights.

Owers, eager to atone for his own goal, hit the top of the bar from a free-kick and Gary Bennett headed a 37th-minute 'goal' which a less observant referee might have awarded.

But Stephen Lodge, who handled the derby cauldron coolly and confidently, had spotted Bennett's subtle push on Kevin Scott.

United still exerted a grip on the second half without being able to add the killer second goal.

And when Sunderland's Newcastle-born substitute Gordon Armstrong took advantage of hesitancy among the Newcastle defenders to drive in the equaliser 20 minutes from time, it seemed the winning run would be at an end.

But six minutes later Brian Atkinson chopped down David Kelly just outside the box, and Liam O'Brien stepped up to work his magic.

This time the lead would not be sacrificed, and United played out the game largely in their opponents' half.

Gavin Peacock chipped over when a goal looked on, then Lee Clark measured a tremendous chip from wide on the left which brought an even better tip-over save from Carter.

At the end, the dancing mass of Newcastle fans in the Roker End were celebrating much more than a victory. United's superiority in the First Division was not in question.

And the private war of Tyne v Wear was at last finally settled. Kevin Keegan's storm-troopers had taken the enemy fortress.

Kevin Brock celebrates United's opener

Saturday 24th October 1992 • St James' Park • 3.00pm

NEWCASTLE UNITED 0 GRIMSBY TOWN 1

Half-time 0-0 • *Attendance* 30,088

Referee Paul HARRISON (Lancaster)

Linesmen B. LOWE, M. RILEY

Black and White Striped Shirts, Black Shorts	Goals	Yellow Shirts, Red Shorts	Goals
1 Tommy WRIGHT		1 Dave BEASANT	
2 Barry VENISON ❏ †		2 John McDERMOTT	
3 John BERESFORD		3 Gary CROFT	
4 Liam O'BRIEN		4 Paul FUTCHER	
5 Kevin SCOTT		5 Mark LEVER	
6 Steve HOWEY		6 Jim DOBBIN	89
7 Robert LEE		7 Tommy WATSON	
8 Gavin PEACOCK		8 David GILBERT	
9 Micky QUINN		9 Paul GROVES	
10 Lee CLARK		10 Clive MENDONCA	
11 Kevin BROCK ‡		11 Neil WOODS	
Substitutes		*Substitutes*	
12 Brian KILCLINE (†64)		12 Tony REES	
14 Paul BRACEWELL (‡76)		14 Mark SMITH	

BEFORE	P	W	D	L	F	A	pts	AFTER	P	W	D	L	F	A	pts
1 Newcastle	11	11	0	0	25	7	33	1 Newcastle	12	11	0	1	25	8	33
17 Grimsby	11	3	3	5	13	15	12	15 Grimsby	12	4	3	5	14	15	15

FACTFILE

Jim Dobbin's last-minute goal ends winning run... United miss out on joint all-time league record of 14 successive victories, plus club record 12-match unbeaten run within a season... one minute away from setting new club record 12-match unbeaten league run from start of a season.

All good things come to an end

NO-ONE seriously believed that Newcastle would go through the entire season undefeated, but even less believed that the record would go to modest Grimsby Town. The Mariners came to Tyneside in 17th position with only three wins from 11 games and little to suggest that they would be anything but a statistic along United's all-conquering way.

The expected capacity crowd gathered in anticipation of a slaughter which never came, as Grimsby more than matched the league leaders and deservedly stole the game with a last-minute goal from Jim Dobbin.

For some reason United's touch was absent on the day. Whatever the reason - over-confidence or casualness perhaps - passes went astray, shots missed the target, even simple, basic control was a major problem.

But Grimsby won more than United lost.

They knew exactly how to handle Newcastle and amidst the debris of exploded dreams, Kevin Keegan was man enough to admit it.

"That's the biggest hammering we've had since I came here," he said. "We were fortunate it was only 1-0. Right from the first few minutes our touch wasn't as good as it has been."

"The writing was on the wall early on."

The absence of eight-goal top scorer David Kelly with a wrenched knee was only a partial excuse for United's lacklustre showing, and Keegan preferred to pay tribute to Grimsby for their ambition and style on the day.

"If we were going to lose, I wanted it to be against a good side - and that's what Grimsby are," he added.

Micky Quinn stood in for Kelly but the cohesion which had torn apart other sides all season was conspicuous by its glaring absence throughout the team.

Ironically, the goalkeeper United failed to beat was their former big-money signing Dave Beasant, farmed out on loan to Grimsby from Chelsea after a rough spell at Stamford Bridge.

Beasant was rarely troubled other than from a Lee Clark shot which took a sharp deflection and brushed the wrong side of a post.

Tommy Wright was the busier keeper, and had to show the class of an international more than once. But even Wright knew little of the excellent Dobbin's 31st-minute drive against the bar during a goalmouth mélée.

The draw, fortunate as it would have been, looked certain, and would have established a new club record of 12 unbeaten games at the start of a league season.

But the victory which would have equalled the all-time Football League record of 14 successive victories was never likely.

And even the draw was snatched away from United in the 89th minute when Dobbin once more drove forward and crashed a 20-yard shot into the top left corner of Wright's net.

Leaving St James' that afternoon, it was difficult to believe that such an enthralling run had ended so tamely, and so suddenly.

"We were chasing an impossible dream. Instead of making history, we are history," concluded Keegan.

But Newcastle United were still nine points clear of second-placed Charlton, and a less impossible dream was still very much on.

Gavin Peacock looks for a way to goal

Wednesday 28th October 1992 • Stamford Bridge • 7.45pm

CHELSEA 2 NEWCASTLE UNITED 1

Half-time 0-0 • *Attendance* 30,193

Referee Keith COOPER (Pontypridd)

Linesmen J. WIFFEN, A. WILLIAMS

Blue Shirts, Blue Shorts	Goals	Black and White Striped Shirts, Black Shorts	Goals
1 Kevin HITCHCOCK		1 Tommy WRIGHT	
2 Gareth HALL		2 Alan NEILSON	
3 Frank SINCLAIR	58	3 John BERESFORD	
4 Andy TOWNSEND		4 Liam O'BRIEN	
5 David LEE		5 Kevin SCOTT ❏	
6 Mal DONAGHY		6 Steve HOWEY	
7 Graham STUART ❏ †		7 Robert LEE	77
8 Robert FLECK		8 Gavin PEACOCK	
9 Mick HARFORD ❏	82	9 Micky QUINN	
10 Eddie NEWTON		10 Lee CLARK	
11 Dennis WISE ❏		11 Kevin BROCK	
Substitutes		*Substitutes*	
12 Graeme LE SAUX (†79)		12 Brian KILCLINE	
14 Joe ALLON		14 Paul BRACEWELL	

FACTFILE

Old boy Harford dumps United out of League Cup... Robert Lee scores first goal for Newcastle... young Alan Neilson steps in for injured Venison... biggest away crowd of season for United... 16th season in succession without passing League Cup third round.

Alan Neilson - in for his third appearance of the season

Old boy ends Wembley dream

MORE THAN once in the early stages of the season, Kevin Keegan had described United's football as "Premier League".

The few remaining doubters had been convinced by the excellent Coca-Cola Cup second round victory at Middlesbrough, but Middlesbrough paled against the task set United by the draw for the third round.

Chelsea, at Stamford Bridge particularly, were very different. A formidable power in front of their own intimidating fans, with the class of Townsend, Fleck and Wise. And Mick Harford.

This was the acid test for United; moreso after the shock defeat by Grimsby at St James' Park.

The match attracted a crowd of 30,193 - almost twice Chelsea's home average; thousands of whom had travelled from Tyneside for an awkward midweek journey to 'the smoke'.

And not one of them could have been disappointed by this memorable, intriguing encounter: or by the standard of both sides.

If United spent more time defending than they were accustomed to, the way in which Kevin Scott & Co protected Wright's goal was of the highest quality.

Andy Townsend was close with a long shot. Harford, once of Newcastle, headed over the crossbar. And Frank Sinclair came even closer, turning a fine header against the bar.

But United gave as good as they got. Robert Lee's header was blocked close to the line, and Kevin Brock's power drive was superbly saved by Hitchcock.

Level at half-time, United found themselves under immediate pressure on the resumption and Lee Clark produced a crucial goalline clearance from David Lee's close-range header.

As Chelsea turned up the heat, United finally cracked. Dennis Wise picked out Sinclair's run from a quick free-kick and the full-back's header did the rest.

A lesser side than United might have buckled, but slowly they forced their way back; steadily they pushed the Londoners back into their own half.

· Thirteen minutes from time John Beresford, the pick of United's side, delivered a searching cross from the left and Robert Lee powered in to guide a perfect downward header past Hitchcock's right hand.

A replay, surely. Chelsea would have nothing left to give.

But they did. With only eight minutes remaining, United's guard slipped fatally and the full cruelty of football was visited upon them.

Having half-cleared one left-wing cross, United failed to pick up Mick Harford's blindside run and, unseen until too late, he came in at the far post to head Wise's second delivery powerfully inside Wright's left post.

It was a harsh reminder that top sides could pull something out of the bag at just the right moment.

Even so, Liam O'Brien almost produced something else in the dying seconds but Hitchcock superbly saved his long-range special and United were out.

Defeat, perhaps. But yet another character test had been passed by Newcastle United.

Liam O'Brien - denied late on

Saturday 31st October 1992 • Filbert Street • 3.00pm

LEICESTER CITY 2 NEWCASTLE UNITED 1

Half-time 2-0 • *Attendance* 19,687

Referee Kevin BREEN (Liverpool)

Linesmen R. HODGETTS, G. RODERICK

Blue Shirts, Blue Shorts		Goals	Black and White Striped Shirts, Black Shorts		Goals
1	Kevin POOLE		1	Tommy WRIGHT	
2	Gary MILLS		2	Alan NEILSON	
3	Nicky PLATNAUER		3	John BERESFORD	
4	Richard SMITH		4	Liam O'BRIEN	67
5	Steve WALSH		5	Kevin SCOTT	
6	Colin HILL ❑		6	Steve HOWEY	
7	David OLDFIELD		7	Kevin BROCK †	
8	Steve THOMPSON ‡		8	Gavin PEACOCK	
9	Bobby DAVISON †	15	9	David KELLY	
10	David LOWE	3	10	Lee CLARK	
11	Phil GEE		11	Kevin SHEEDY ■	

	Substitutes			*Substitutes*	
12	Simon GRAYSON (†84)		12	Brian KILCLINE (†81)	
14	Ian ORMONDROYD (‡90)		14	Paul BRACEWELL	

BEFORE		P	W	D	L	F	A	pts	AFTER		P	W	D	L	F	A	pts
1	Newcastle	12	11	0	1	25	8	33	1	Newcastle	13	11	0	2	26	10	33
7	Leicester	13	6	3	4	16	15	21	3	Leicester	14	7	3	4	18	16	24

FACTFILE

Leicester bounce back from 7-1 Cup hiding at Sheffield Wednesday... two early blunders cost United the game... Kevin Sheedy is sent off in injury time and becomes the only United player suspended from domestic games all season... United behind at interval for first time this season.

Sheedy dismissal caps dismal day

WHILE the Newcastle strikers had claimed the lion's share of the glory in the first weeks of the season, the defence had been quietly playing its considerable part.

With only eight goals conceded in 12 league games, United boasted the meanest defence in the first division. But in the first 15 nightmarish minutes at Filbert Street on the last day of October, that reputation collapsed in tatters.

City ripped through at will, scoring twice, and coming close on several further occasions. The nerves exposed by Grimsby and Chelsea were raw and vulnerable. That United stemmed the tide and battled manfully back spoke volumes for their character, but ultimately the mountain was too high to climb.

Liam O'Brien produced a typical free-kick goal midway through the second half, but the second, point-saving goal just would not come.

And when Kevin Sheedy was sent off in the final minute for an awful lunge at substitute Simon Grayson, the nightmare was complete.

Barry Venison was again absent and replaced by Alan Neilson, though no direct blame could be attached to the youngster, who did as much as anyone to steady the ship after the two-goal tidal wave.

John Lowe could have taken advantage of Neilson's short backpass in the first minute, but two minutes later he netted with a clever overhead kick after Steve Walsh was left unmarked to flick on a corner.

David Kelly was denied by City keeper Kevin Poole and Steve Howey's header was cleared off the line by Nicky Paltnauer.

But United's hopes of a quick equaliser were dashed when Howey's casual pass and Kevin Scott's hesitation let in South Shields-born Bobby Davison to stride clear and comprehensively beat Tommy Wright.

In such a situation, attack was the best form of defence, and attack United did. But inevitably they left gaps at the back, and as a result the chances flowed thick and fast.

City defender Hill denied David Kelly one of those chances by hauling him down on a clear run; only a yellow card resulted. And Kelly was close with two more instinctive efforts: one wide, one saved.

Platnauer should have put City 3-0 up after Brock's slip, but in a game of many openings, Leicester retained their 2-0 lead at half-time.

As the size of the task grew in direct proportion to the ticking clock, United pushed more men forward. The skilled football was there, but tinged with too much urgency.

However, when Gavin Peacock was brought down 25 yards from goal in the 67th minute, O'Brien stepped up to strike a phenomenal free-kick which might have been travelling yet had the net not got in the way.

For all their pressure, United lacked the poise to cut open the Leicester defence and too many promising moves broke down at the vital moment. Frustration had eaten into United hearts by the time Sheedy committed his act of folly deep into injury time.

But the greater concern was that the Newcastle United balloon had exploded. Three out of three...

Stop that! Liam O'Brien makes it 2-1

Wednesday 4th November 1992 • St Andrews • 8.00pm

BIRMINGHAM CITY 2 NEWCASTLE UNITED 3

Half-time 2-3 • *Attendance* 14,376

Referee Keith HACKETT (Sheffield)

Linesmen A. BLACK, G. STONES

Blue Shirts, Blue Shorts	Goals	Black and White Striped Shirts, Black Shorts	Goals
1 Les SEALEY		1 Tommy WRIGHT ‡	
2 Paul HOLMES		2 Barry VENISON	
3 John FRAIN		3 John BERESFORD	
4 David RENNIE ‡		4 Liam O'BRIEN	
5 Martin HICKS		5 Kevin SCOTT	31
6 Trevor MATTHEWSON o.g.38		6 Steve HOWEY	
7 Ian RODGERSON		7 Franz CARR	
8 Paul TAIT		8 Gavin PEACOCK	7
9 David SPEEDIE	9	9 David KELLY	
10 Simon STURRIDGE		10 Lee CLARK	
11 Graeme POTTER †	33	11 Kevin SHEEDY †	
Substitutes		*Substitutes*	
12 Louie DONOWA (†76)		12 Brian KILCLINE (†90)	
14 Darren ROWBOTHAM (‡36)		14 Kevin BROCK (‡45)	

BEFORE	P	W	D	L	F	A	pts	AFTER	P	W	D	L	F	A	pts
1 Newcastle	13	11	0	2	26	10	33	1 Newcastle	14	12	0	2	29	12	36
10 B'ham City	13	5	4	4	11	17	19	14 B'ham City	14	5	4	5	13	20	19

FACTFILE

Brave Brock stands in for injured Tommy Wright - and keeps second half clean sheet with concussion!... United end three-match losing run... all five goals scored in first half... Stan Seymour dies in Birmingham hotel after game.

Crocked Brock is hero of the hour

IT IS difficult to imagine a victory being won out of such adversity as that claimed by Newcastle at St Andrews as they ended the three-match losing run which had threatened to undermine that magnificent start.

Goalkeeper Tommy Wright, carrying a leg injury from the third minute, had to be replaced at half-time by substitute Kevin Brock.

Brock, too, was injured at the start of the second half and played out the rest of the match with severe concussion.

Through the storm, United, three times ahead and 3-2 up at the interval, protected Brock with a superb display of controlled possession football which denied City the advantage fate had apparently delivered.

Birmingham were limited to only two David Speedie attempts on goal in the second 45 minues, and United emerged from a remarkable match with three points to end all talk of a League collapse.

On this most bizarre of football nights every Newcastle man was a hero: not least the enigmatic Franz Carr, who was directly responsible for the first and third United goals.

After only eight minutes, Carr beat the offside trap with a finely-judged ball which set Gavin Peacock free on Les Sealey's goal.

When Sealey parried his first shot, Peacock had sufficient poise to take stock and squeeze the rebound past two defenders by now covering the goalline. Speedie, that arch-tormentor of United, headed a Paul Holmes cross low past the already struggling Wright within two minutes to set the tone of the game.

It was end-to-end, but on 31 minutes United led again, this time with the help of more than a slice of good fortune.

David Kelly, without knowing too much about it, got in the way of Simon Sturridge's attempted clearance and set up Kevin Scott to slide the ball home in a six-yard box scramble.

Amazingly, Birmingham again levelled within two minutes, teenager Graham Potter going clear to slide the ball under Wright.

Two such body blows might have persuaded a lesser side than Newcastle that this was not to be their night.

But the pendulum swung again as United, showing commendable resilience, took the lead once more in the 38th minute.

Liam O'Brien and David Kelly combined to send the speedy Carr in on goal, and this time Trevor Matthewson, desperately trying to cover, carried Carr's shot over the line with him.

Psychologically boosted, United could have had a fourth before half-time but Gavin Peacock shot at Sealey from an excellent position and Matthewson redeemed his own goal by blocking Lee Clark's follow-up effort.

Kevin Brock, a spare-time cricketer, spent the interval brushing up on his fielding technique as Kevin Keegan handed him Tommy Wright's green jersey.

Perhaps Brock should have donned a cricket helmet, too, for after just four minutes he received a bad kick on the head diving at Potter's feet and spent the remaining 41 minutes not sure whether he was opening bat or wicketkeeper.

It should have signalled a crisis. But in a monumental display of composure, United denied Birmingham more than a fleeting glimpse of Brock's goal and spent most of the second half encamped in City's half.

Carr, Kelly and Sheedy might all have scored; by contrast, only Speedie threatened for Birmingham, and that with a couple of weak headers.

On a night when all the fates seemed set against them, United defied all the slings and arrows of outrageous fortune and took another giant step towards the promised land.

Sunday 11th November 1992 • St James' Park • 3.00pm

NEWCASTLE UNITED 0 SWINDON TOWN 0

Half-time 0-0 • Attendance 28,091
Referee Trevor WEST (Hull)
Linesmen S.M. ASTIN, D. CHARLTON

Black and White Striped Shirts, Black Shorts	Goals	Red Shirts, Red Shorts	Goals
1 Pavel SRNICEK		1 Nicky HAMMOND	
2 Barry VENISON		2 David KERSLAKE	
3 John BERESFORD ❏		3 Kevin HORLOCK	
4 Liam O'BRIEN		4 Glenn HODDLE	
5 Kevin SCOTT		5 Colin CALDERWOOD	
6 Steve HOWEY ❏		6 Shaun TAYLOR	
7 Franz CARR		7 Micky HAZARD	
8 Gavin PEACOCK		8 Nicky SUMMERBEE ❏	
9 David KELLY		9 Craig MASKELL †	
10 Lee CLARK		10 Martin LING	
11 Kevin SHEEDY		11 David MITCHELL ❏	
Substitutes		*Substitutes*	
12 Micky QUINN		12 Steve WHITE (†86)	
14 Brian KILCLINE		14 Austin BERKLEY	

BEFORE		P	W	D	L	F	A	pts	AFTER		P	W	D	L	F	A	pts
1	Newcastle	14	12	0	2	29	12	36	1	Newcastle	15	12	1	2	29	12	37
2	Swindon	15	8	3	4	28	21	27	2	Swindon	16	8	4	4	28	21	28

FACTFILE

Top two stalemate... United stay nine points ahead at the top... Hoddle and Hazard shine for Swindon... Pavel Srnicek keeps a clean sheet in his first league game... second successive home blank for United... first league draw of the season.

Hazard warning as Swindon shine

SWINDON were already one of United's main promotion rivals by the time they brought their Sunday Best to St James's Park for the live TV cameras.

Inspired by the cultured and still very capable Glenn Hoddle, the Wiltshire side would maintain that threat throughout the campaign.

And Newcastle felt the full force of their ambitions as they were forced to defend for most of a tense but rivetting encounter.

It was a game for the connoisseur rather than the cavalier; first United producing early pressure, then Swindon edging back and for the remainder of the match taking a majority share of the possession.

Perhaps United's hell-for-leather opening backfired once the steam ran out after a hectic but goalless first 15 minutes. But steadily the initiative slipped away.

It might have been a very different story had Lee Clark not been denied by the left post from 20 yards, and had goalkeeper Hammond not improbably blocked a close-in volley from Kevin Sheedy.

When Sheedy then beat Hammond only to see Nicky Summerbee clear off the line, the nagging feeling emerged that this was to be a blank-sheet day. That nagging feeling became a sharp pain as Hoddle's side asserted their superiority and heralded the shift in fortunes with a shot by Summerbee which was kept out only by the legs of Pavel Srnicek.

Chances fell to Martin Ling, Shaun Taylor and player-manager Hoddle, only to go begging. And through it all, one player shone like a beacon. Micky Hazard, Sunderland-born and of proud pedigree, proved that even at 32 he still had the temperament and talent to rise to the big occasion.

The Hazard Warning was not to be ignored, for he repeatedly stifled United's midfield probings and set up his own forwards with astute, incisive passing. It was a performance which prompted Hoddle - a former Spurs colleague of Hazard's - to say: "That was as good as I've ever seen Micky Hazard play."

The tactical battle made for absorbing television, and if Swindon striker Dave Mitchell - once on loan at United - had not missed a glorious opening created by David Kerslake, Town might have left Tyneside with a Grimsby-sized smile.

United's best chance on the break followed a defensive error when David Kelly forced the ball past Hammond only for Colin Calderwood to clear off the line.

In the final analysis, however, defences were on top and Kevin Keegan summed it up thus: "For all the possession they had, they didn't destroy us."

The United boss added: "It was the hardest match we've had at home this season, and I'm not disappointed with a draw.

"We had to work hard to stop them, and I think it was a fair result."

This was United's first league draw of the season - in the 15th game - and maintained the nine-point lead over Swindon, who edged above Tranmere, West Ham, Millwall and Charlton. The pack was chasing.

Franz Carr on the wing

Wednesday 11th November 1992 • Stadio Porta Elisa • 1.30pm

AS LUCCHESE 1 NEWCASTLE UNITED 1

Half-time 1-0 • *Attendance* 744
Referee Ron GROVES (Weston-Super-Mare)
Linesmen ROSSIGNOLI, SPRILLI

Red and Black Striped Shirts, White Shorts	Goals	Yellow Shirts, Green Shorts	Goals
1 QUIRONI		1 Pavel SRNICEK	
2 Di FRANCESCO		2 Barry VENISON	
3 VIGNINI		3 John BERESFORD ❏	
4 DELLICARRI		4 Paul BRACEWELL	
5 MONACO †		5 Brian KILCLINE	
6 BARALDI		6 Steve HOWEY	
7 Di STEFANO ‡		7 Franz CARR †	
8 GIUISTI		8 Gavin PEACOCK	
9 PACI		9 Bjorn KRISTENSEN ‡	60
10 RUSSO	29	10 Lee CLARK	
11 RASTELLI		11 Kevin SHEEDY	
Substitutes		*Substitutes*	
14 BIANCHI (†45) ❏		12 Micky QUINN (†60)	
16 BALDINI (‡55)		14 Kevin BROCK (‡78)	

BEFORE	P	W	D	L	F	A	pts	AFTER		P	W	D	L	F	A	pts
ENGLISH GROUP A								ENGLISH GROUP A								
Newcastle	0	0	0	0	0	0	0	4	Newcastle	1	0	1	0	1	1	1

Lowest crowd in Newcastle history - only 744 turn up... stand-in Bjorn Kristensen scores his final goal for United... Beresford's fifth booking of the season... Mick Quinn's final game before joining Coventry.

FACTFILE

Benny does the Italian job

THE ITALIAN football public had two ways of approaching the Anglo-Italian Cup: stay at home, or go to the pizzeria.

No-one bothered to find out which of the two options the supporters of Lucchese chose on this dull Wednesday afternoon, though one thing was for certain: they didn't opt for a day at the match.

The vast audience of 744 which huddled in the shadows of the 9,000-capacity stadium in Lucca even included a couple of dozen Tyneside diehards who enjoyed the chance to meet the team and directors rather than the match itself.

It might have been a synchronised swimming marathon for all the passion this Group A fixture roused.

Kevin Keegan fielded a strong side with only Paul Bracewell, Bjorn Kristensen and Brian Kilcline additions to the starting line-up against Swindon.

Lucchese, fifth from bottom of the Italian Serie B, were decidedly ordinary but in a practice-match atmosphere a serious will-to-win was always missing.

The game rarely rose above the mundane, and it was 20 minutes before a decent chance disturbed the slumbering spectators.

It fell to Kristensen but the Danish international, with only keeper Quironi to beat, lost control of the bouncing ball at the vital moment and the opportunity was gone.

Kevin Sheedy volleyed wide and Kristensen, picked out at the far post by Franz Carr, chested the ball wide from only two yards.

Lucchese had threatened little, but stole the lead in their first serious attack in the 29th minute.

John Beresford uncharacteristically sliced a loose ball across his own area and Russo, 12 yards out, saw his shot deflected by Barry Venison, wrong-footing Pavel Srnicek and finishing up in the opposite corner.

Boos from United fans later in the season after the home draw with Bristol Rovers attracted some adverse comment, but there were boos from the small United contingent in Lucca.

Newcastle raised the tempo in the second half and Sheedy had a shot blocked by Di Francesco.

But United were clearly in need of extra punch in attack and Keegan set about correcting the imbalance by sending on substitute Micky Quinn for Carr.

Ironically, Quinn was waiting on the touchline by the dug-out when the equaliser arrived, suddenly and surprisingly.

Steve Howey played a ball into the area and when Gavin Peacock headed on, Kristensen moved in among the static defenders to beat Baraldi to the ball and score easily from six yards.

The equaliser lifted the match from poor to ordinary, and Quironi denied Clark with a leaping save.

But Srnicek was still the busier goalkeeper, advancing to thwart Rastelli then diving to hold onto a low shot from the Lucchese scorer, Russo.

Clark, again, may have snatched a late win but for Quironi's agility but genuine excitement was in short supply.

And there were at least three more Anglo-Italian ties to crowd the already busy fixture list.

A last farewell before flying to Italy

Saturday 14th November 1992 • Upton Park • 3.00pm

CHARLTON ATHLETIC 1 NEWCASTLE UNITED 3

Half-time 0-2 • *Attendance* 12,495

Referee Ian BORRETT (Harleston)
Linesmen L. CABLE, M. STOBBART

Red Shirts, White Shorts	Goals	Black and White Striped Shirts, Black Shorts	Goals
1 Bob BOLDER		1 Pavel SRNICEK	
2 Stuart BALMER		2 Barry VENISON	
3 Scott MINTO		3 John BERESFORD	
4 Alan PARDEW		4 Liam O'BRIEN	
5 Simon WEBSTER		5 Kevin SCOTT	
6 Linvoy PRIMUS		6 Steve HOWEY	63
7 John ROBINSON ‡		7 Robert LEE	
8 John BUMSTEAD †		8 Gavin PEACOCK	3, 35
9 Carl LEABURN		9 David KELLY	
10 Garry NELSON	49	10 Lee CLARK	
11 Colin WALSH		11 Paul BRACEWELL	
Substitutes		*Substitutes*	
12 Darren PITCHER (†70)		12 Brian KILCLINE	
14 Alex DYER (‡79)		14 Franz CARR	

BEFORE		P	W	D	L	F	A	pts	AFTER		P	W	D	L	F	A	pts
1	Newcastle	15	12	1	2	29	12	37	1	Newcastle	16	13	1	2	32	13	40
6	Charlton	16	7	5	4	20	13	26	8	Charlton	17	7	5	5	21	16	26

FACTFILE

United are Charlton's last visitors to Upton Park, 15 months after being their first visitors... Peacock double sets up seventh away win from eight... Howey gets his first goal of the season... Robert Lee's father Reg sponsors the game.

Peacock double paves the way

FIFTEEN months before, in August 1991, Newcastle had been Charlton's first visitors to their temporary home at Upton Park. On a dismal day, Ossie Ardiles' United lost badly, 2-1.

On this November day, Newcastle were Charlton's final visitors to Upton Park before the London club returned to its spiritual home at The Valley.

But if Charlton's long-exiled supporters expected to go home on a high note, they were to be severely disappointed as United hit peak form once again.

The difference between the Newcastle sides of August 1991 and November 1992 was symbolised by these two matches against Charlton.

Gone now was the uncertainty and lack of confidence which had beset the side under Ardiles.

Here instead was class, power and style in abundance, and Charlton had no answer to the league leaders.

From the third minute United led: and if Gavin Peacock later admitted that he knew little of the goal he scored, it also speaks volumes for his deadly goal instinct.

Peacock was blocked from a clear view of David Kelly's cross by two defenders and the goalkeeper, but instinctively threw himself forward to turn the ball into the net.

"I connected with something and the ball ended up in the net," Peacock said, modestly, afterwards.

However, there was no doubt about what Peacock connected with in the 35th minute when he put United 2-0 up.

Robert Lee, playing for the first time against the team with which he became a London hero, got down the right to cross low for Peacock to pivot and volley a goal of clinical creation and execution.

There was more than one Charlton connection in United's ranks, of course, for Peacock's father, Keith, a reserve team coach with The Robins, is part of the Athletic furniture.

Charlton were nothing if not determined, and pegged one goal back in the 49th minute when Carl Leaburn headed John Robinson's cross down in the area for Garry Nelson to beat Srnicek.

For 15 minutes United wobbled as Charlton saw their chance and went for the jugular. But the back line of Venison, Scott, Howey and Beresford held firm; and it was the excellent Howey who restored the two-goal advantage on 64 minutes. When Clark moved up the right wing, Howey waited his moment for the surge into the area and even knocked David Kelly out of the way in his determination to reach the ball. Howey connected with a downward header, Bolder dived and was beaten, and the contest was over.

The poise with which United controlled the final stages was a harsh lesson for Charlton, who lacked the guile to upset the Newcastle defence again.

After the exertions of a midweek trip to Italy, this was the real test of character for Kevin Keegan's side.

And once more the test was passed with flying colours.

Robert Lee - winning return

Saturday 21st November 1992 • St James' Park • 3.00pm

NEWCASTLE UNITED 2 WATFORD 0

Half-time 0-0 • *Attendance* 28,871

Referee John KEY (SHEFFIELD)

Linesmen G. BRADBURY, R. FURNANDIZ

Black and White Striped Shirts, Black Shorts		Goals		Yellow, Red and Black Shirts, Red Shorts		Goals
1	Pavel SRNICEK		1	Perry SUCKLING	
2	Barry VENISON		2	Trevor PUTNEY	
3	John BERESFORD		3	Jason DRYSDALE	
4	Liam O'BRIEN		4	Keith DUBLIN	
5	Kevin SCOTT		5	David HOLDSWORTH	
6	Steve HOWEY †		6	Barry ASHBY	
7	Robert LEE ‡	57	7	Andy HESSENTHALER ❏	
8	Gavin PEACOCK	51	8	Lee NOGAN †	
9	David KELLY		9	Paul FURLONG ‡	
10	Lee CLARK		10	Ken CHARLERY	
11	Paul BRACEWELL		11	Gerard LAVIN ■	
	Substitutes			*Substitutes*	
12	Brian KILCLINE (†67)		12	Gary PORTER (†62)	
14	Franz CARR (‡77)		14	Roger WILLIS (‡11)	

BEFORE		P	W	D	L	F	A	pts	AFTER		P	W	D	L	F	A	pts
1	Newcastle	16	13	1	2	32	13	40	1	Newcastle	17	14	1	2	34	13	43
14	Watford	17	6	5	6	25	27	23	14	Watford	18	6	5	7	25	29	23

FACTFILE

United open up 11-point lead... Watford midfielder Gerard Lavin is sent off... top scorer Peacock's 11th goal of the season - and he misses penalty... but Lee gets his first United league goal from Peacock's penalty rebound.

Hornets hit by inspired Clark

LEE CLARK'S emergence as a genuine talent did not surprise anyone who had watched his development between mid and late teens.

But it defied the doubts and reservations of managers like Jim Smith who had voiced disquiet over Clark's alleged lack of pace.

Smith, manager at Newcastle when Clark was beginning to prove his abilities as a youngster, had already been made to eat his words as Lee tore apart Smith's Portsmouth team two months earlier.

Now Watford felt the full force of the Lee Clark phenomenon as United clocked up their 11th league victory of the season and opened up an 11-point lead at the top of Division One.

Watford, limited in ambition and ability, were never seriously in the hunt as United took a vice-like grip from the start.

But fighting an enforced rearguard action, the Hornets held their fort for the first 45 minutes and might have taken a bizarre lead midway through the half.

Pavel Srnicek made one of the finest saves of the season when a long free-kick glanced wickedly off the head of Liam O'Brien and zipped towards the top corner.

Against that, an apparently endless series of United attacks: a penalty appeal for a pull on Gavin Peacock; a Robert Lee shot kicked off the line to deny him his first league goal for Newcastle; Perry Suckling making many fine saves on an inspired day for him.

Watford's threat - such as it was - had already diminished when it was evaporated totally in first-half injury time by two moments of madness from young Gerard Lavin.

Lavin, in reckless style, kicked the ball away to receive a yellow card from referee John Key, then, within minutes, encroached at a United free-kick and was promptly given early rights to the bath salts.

Six minutes after the interval Watford's house was blown down by a goal of exquisite quality.

Liam O'Brien and Robert Lee teamed up to send John Beresford overlapping on the left. Beresford's cross found Lee Clark who capped his superb performance with a marvellous back-heel to Paul Bracewell in space.

Bracewell's firmly-struck cross reached Gavin Peacock and this time Suckling was reduced to the role of spectator.

Within a further six minutes, the lead was doubled, though the second goal depended upon a degree of generosity from Mr Key.

When David Kelly dummied across a Lee Clark throw-in, the ball struck the hapless Lee Nogan on the hand.

Mr Key, who had refused an earlier more obvious penalty, awarded this one - and Robert Lee claimed his elusive first goal in the league: though he didn't take the spot-kick.

Peacock did, and his driven shot was superbly pushed out by Suckling as he dived to his left. But Lee was first to react and from a tight angle struck the ball unerringly into the roof of the net before Suckling had a chance to regain his feet or his ground.

Peacock joked later: "Rob hadn't had a touch for a while so I thought that if I played the penalty off the keeper's hand at the correct angle it would fall for him. And it worked."

United could afford to smile thus with 11 points to spare above Swindon in second place.

And with Lee Clark here, there and everywhere, anything seemed possible.

Pavel Srnicek - brilliant save from deflection

Tuesday 24th November 1992 • St James' Park • 7.45pm

NEWCASTLE UNITED 0 ASCOLI 1

Half-time 0-0 • *Attendance* 9,789

Referee Robert BOGGI (Salerno)

Linesmen G. ATKINS, W. NATTRASS

Black and White Striped Shirts, Black Shorts	Goals	Yellow Shirts, Yellow Shorts	Goals
1 Pavel SRNICEK		1 Marco BIZZARRI	
2 Barry VENISON ❑		2 Osvaldo MANCINI	
3 Alan NEILSON		3 Carlo PASCUCCI	
4 Liam O'BRIEN ❑		4 Massimo CACCIATORI ❑	
5 Brian KILCLINE		5 Salvatore FUSCO	
6 Kevin SCOTT		6 Giovanni BOSI	
7 Steve WATSON †		7 Claudio PIERANTOZZI ❑ †	
8 Andy HUNT ‡		8 Angelo CIOFFI	
9 David KELLY ■		9 Oliver BIERHOFF	63
10 Alan THOMPSON		10 Michele MENOLASCINA	
11 Kevin SHEEDY		11 Giovanni SPINELLI ‡	
Substitutes		*Substitutes*	
12 Franz CARR (†45)		12 Rosario PERGOLIZZI (†57)	
14 Ray RANSON (‡65)		14 Benito CARBONE (‡58)	

BEFORE		P	W	D	L	F	A	pts	AFTER		P	W	D	L	F	A	pts
ENGLISH GROUP A									ENGLISH GROUP A								
4	Newcastle	1	0	1	0	1	1	1	4	Newcastle	2	0	1	1	1	2	1

FACTFILE

David Kelly sent off on eve of his 27th birthday... on night of violence, Ascoli coach Cacciatori is restrained by Keegan... United left bottom of the group... Bierhoff goal settles outcome... Keegan fields five reserves.

Night of shame and shambles

KEVIN KEEGAN got it right when he said after this fraught and angry fiasco: "This kind of thing always seems to happen when you put the English and Italian temperaments together."

'This kind of thing' was a night of violence which culminated in the dismissal of United striker David Kelly for a dreadful foul on Michele Menolascina ten minutes from time.

'This kind of thing' was the incredible touch-line brawl which followed the Kelly incident, in which Keegan himself had to forcibly restrain Ascoli coach Massimo Cacciatori from grabbing Kelly; and in which police had to intervene to restore order.

'This kind of thing' was the series of shocking tackles perpetrated largely by the Italians yet largely unpunished by Italian referee Robert Boggi.

"They were getting away with tackles that were banned here two years ago," said Keegan, adding: "You keep thinking you've seen everything in football, then something like that happens."

What little football there was on the night scarcely thrilled the sparse 9,789 crowd who, by their desertion, delivered their own damning verdict on this tournament.

The game, for what it was worth, was won by a 63rd-minute goal by Oliver Bierhoff, Ascoli's German striker, who turned well to lift a ten-yard shot past Pavel Srnicek.

Andy Hunt - first appearance of the season

United dominated the first half with Andy Hunt and Alan Thompson both close to beating keeper Bizzarri. Liam O'Brien and David Kelly were also thwarted by Bizzarri though moments of genuine quality from Keegan's under-strength team were few.

The only enduring memory of this tie will be the unsavoury one which followed Kelly's red-card offence. Defiantly, Keegan refused to fine the Republic of Ireland striker for his indiscretion, explaining: "He thought their player was going to kick him.

"He'd been clattered that many times he thought the lad was going to do him again."

On his 'peacekeeper' intervention, Keegan said: "Their coach had 'gone' when he went past me. I don't know what he was thinking. If I ever get like that, shoot me. Just get a gun and shoot me. I've never seen anything like it."

With the exception of one 11-year-old boy who emerged from the Milburn Stand paddock to lend his weight to the scrimmage, there was no crowd trouble.

Had the United fans become involved on any grand scale, the consequences could have been far-reaching: and on that basis, one had to doubt whether the Anglo-Italian Cup was worth the risk.

Thankfully, United's players escaped serious injury but in the final analysis, this night above all others called into question the very nature of the tournament.

Keegan said as much.

"We had an English referee when we played Lucchese and an Italian one here. There's no consistency," he complained.

"I think we have to look long and hard at the future of the competition."

Kelly's sending-off - and a booking for Liam O'Brien - happily did not count in the Football League. Kelly was spared the need to go to Bari by a one-match suspension.

But for the record, on a night of disgrace, dishonours were even.

Saturday 28th November 1992 • St James' Park • 3.00pm

NEWCASTLE UNITED 4 CAMBRIDGE UNITED 1

Half-time 1-0 • Attendance 27,991
Referee Ian HENDRICK (Preston)
Linesmen U. RENNIE, M. STODDART

Black and White Striped Shirts, Black Shorts		Goals
1	Pavel SRNICEK	
2	Barry VENISON	
3	John BERESFORD	
4	Liam O'BRIEN	
5	Kevin SCOTT	
6	Brian KILCLINE	
7	Robert LEE	
8	Gavin PEACOCK	90
9	David KELLY	26, 55, 86p
10	Lee CLARK	
11	Alan THOMPSON	
Substitutes		
12	Franz CARR	
14	Alan NEILSON	

Blue Shirts, Blue Shorts		Goals
1	John VAUGHAN	
2	Andy FENSOME ■	
3	Alan KIMBLE ❑	
4	Paul RAYNOR ❑	
5	Mike HEATHCOTE	
6	Danny O'SHEA	
7	Michael CHEETHAM	
8	Gary ROWETT †	
9	Steve CLARIDGE	82
10	Gary CLAYTON	
11	Chris LEADBITTER ‡	
Substitutes		
12	Devon WHITE (†58)	
14	John FRANCIS (‡63)	

BEFORE		P	W	D	L	F	A	pts
1	Newcastle	17	14	1	2	34	13	43
19	Cambridge	18	4	6	8	19	33	18

AFTER		P	W	D	L	F	A	pts
1	Newcastle	18	15	1	2	38	14	46
20	Cambridge	19	4	6	9	20	37	18

FACTFILE

David Kelly grabs United's first hat-trick of season after Gavin Peacock hands over late penalty... Cambridge's former Newcastle loan defender Andy Fensome is sent off... Howey's absence means Lee Clark is last remaining ever-present... Alan Thompson makes his debut for the season.

Kelly gets three... thanks to Gavin

DAVID Kelly had kept his head down as the Ascoli storm broke around him, but he re-emerged on a high note to take United to three more points against Cambridge.

Kelly hit United's first hat-trick of the season with a virtuoso display against another of the division's no-hopers.

And even if the man they call 'Ned' had to rely upon the Christian generosity of Gavin Peacock for his third goal, there was no denying Kelly's right to the glory and the match-ball.

With four minutes remaining and Newcastle 2-1 ahead after Cambridge's shock 82nd-minute goal, Robert Lee was brought down in the area by Michael Cheetham.

Newcastle needed the goal to reopen the two-goal margin; but as Peacock collected the ball in readiness for the spot-kick, the crowd bayed long and hard for Kelly to be given the kick.

Peacock heeded the advice, did the decent thing, then offered a silent prayer as 'Ned' stepped up the crash the ball high past John Vaughan.

Gavin is a religious sort and perhaps someone up there liked him for what he did, for within a further four minutes he netted the fourth goal - and nudged one goal ahead of Kelly in the scorers' list again.

The late fun and games were preceded by a one-sided match in which Newcastle remained serenely in control until Steve Claridge disturbed the calm eight minutes from time.

Kelly had broken Cambridge's early resistance in the 26th minute, again thanks to Peacock.

Peacock's measured chip brought a deft header from the former West Ham striker which dropped just inside the far post with Vaughan stretching in vain.

Of his three goals, Kelly's second was undeniably the best: a difficult low shot as he leaned backwards to a Lee Clark flick which had held up awkwardly on a deflection.

At 2-0 it seemed a cakewalk, but Claridge broke through from deep to shoot past Pavel Srnicek and sound an alarm bell or two.

However, Newcastle were able to go up a couple of gears; and even argue amiably over who should score the third goal.

Perhaps it was all too much for Cambridge's former Newcastle loan man, Andy Fensome, who launched himself crudely at young Alan Thompson and ended up preparing the bathwater for his team-mates.

There was still time for Peacock's goal and some mutual congratulations before the leading stars in the penalty incident explained their thoughts.

Said Peacock: "I was going to take it but David was on a hat-trick and I was under pressure to give it to him.

"I was pleased for him. If the roles had been reversed I hope he would have done the same. That's one he owes me."

And Kelly added: "I don't care who is leading scorer as long as we go up."

Going up seemed ever more likely as United once more underlined the vast chasm in class between themselves and the great majority of the rest of the first division.

Kelly gets the congratulations

Saturday 5th December 1992 • Meadow Lane • 3.00pm

NOTTS COUNTY 0 NEWCASTLE UNITED 2

Half-time 0-0 • *Attendance* 14,840
Referee Bob NIXON (West Kirby)
Linesmen A. ASHLEY, G. LEE

Black and White Striped Shirts, Black Shorts	Goals	Yellow Shirts, Green Shorts	Goals
1 Steve CHERRY		1 Pavel SRNICEK	
2 Charlie PALMER		2 Barry VENISON	
3 Meindert DIJKSTRA		3 John BERESFORD	
4 Dean THOMAS		4 Liam O'BRIEN	
5 Robbie TURNER		5 Kevin SCOTT	
6 Chris SHORT ■		6 Steve HOWEY	
7 Kevin WILSON ‡		7 Robert LEE	
8 Mark DRAPER		8 Gavin PEACOCK ❑	86
9 Tony AGANA		9 David KELLY ❑	
10 Kevin BARTLETT		10 Lee CLARK	
11 David SMITH †		11 Kevin SHEEDY	47
Substitutes		*Substitutes*	
12 Steve SLAWSON (†77)		12 Brian KILCLINE	
14 Don O'RIORDAN (‡75)		14 Franz CARR	

BEFORE		P	W	D	L	F	A	pts	AFTER		P	W	D	L	F	A	pts
1	Newcastle	18	15	1	2	38	14	46	1	Newcastle	19	16	1	2	40	14	49
22	County	19	3	6	10	21	39	15	23	County	20	3	6	11	21	41	15

100 years ago this week since Newcastle United formed... fourth match in succession in which a player sent off - this time it's Chris Short of County... Sheedy returns from ban to open scoring... United lead at the top now 12 points.

Centenary week marked with win

ONE HUNDRED years ago to the week, Newcastle United was formed out of the rival West End and East End clubs, and this comprehensive victory over the Football League's other Magpies was as good a way as any to celebrate the centenary.

Rather more recently, in April 1991, United had gone to Meadow Lane at virtually the lowest ebb in those 100 years.

On that chastening day, with Jim Smith having quit as manager and Ossie Ardiles bringing a young and nervous side to Nottingham, United offered no resistance to a County side powering its way to promotion.

Only Kevin Scott and Gavin Peacock of the side which surrendered meekly that day were in Kevin Keegan's starting line-up 20 months later; Lee Clark, a substitute then, made three.

The difference between those two Newcastle sides was vast and symbolic - symbolic because of the immense progress made in the ten months since Keegan had replaced Ardiles at St James' Park. County, as if to embellish the contrast, were now in the relegation zone after slipping out of the top division in 1991-92. How the pendulum swings.

The class gap between United and County was there for all to see, and even if it did take the Tyneside Magpies until the second-half to turn their superiority into goals, there was never any way they were not going to win this game.

After an accomplished but frustrating first-half, United needed just two minutes of the second period to edge in front.

Lee Clark, once again an inspiration, found time and space to power a shot at goal and when Notts keeper Steve Cherry could only palm the ball across goal, Kevin Sheedy was on hand to net easily from six yards.

Only rarely did County threaten United after that, and the closest they came to an equaliser was a Robbie Turner header splendidly tipped around the upright by the diving Pavel Srnicek.

Amazingly, for the fourth successive match, a player was sent off - and this time the misfortune belonged to County defender Chris Short. Seventeen minutes from time, Short, already booked for his first-half clash with Gavin Peacock, attempted to inflict grievous bodily harm on Liam O'Brien with a tackle that resembled an Exocet, and took the long and lonely walk.

As a contest, the match was over, and it took only a further 13 minutes for United to confirm it. On 86 minutes, Robert Lee supplied Lee Clark whose low right-wing cross was brushed gently into the net by Gavin Peacock - his 13th goal of the campaign.

Once again Clark was the architect of many of United's best moves and the goal he so rightly deserved would have been his but for a rare moment of inaccuracy. From ten yards Clark blazed wide in injury time, and his run of matches since scoring extended to 20.

But Clark's miss scarcely mattered in the wider scheme of United's march towards the Premier League: now 12 points clear of second-placed Tranmere with 16 victories from 19 League games.

Notts County manager Neil Warnock, in his programme notes, had written: "To spend too long studying the Newcastle team will give you a nervous twitch."

With easily half of the 14,840 crowd from Tyneside, the nervous twitching was restricted to the other half of the crowd. This was almost like a home match for United and the quality gap was evident from first to last.

Twenty months before, United, stuck in a siding, had been passed by the Notts County Express; now, the two trains were travelling in opposite directions. And it was the Newcastle United Intercity that was getting there...

Tuesday 8th December 1992 • San Nicola • 2.00pm

BARI 3 NEWCASTLE UNITED 0

Half-time 2-0 • *Attendance* 1,229

Referee Roger MILFORD (Bristol)
Linesmen LENTI, SCARCELLI

Red Shirts, Red Shorts		Goals
1	TAGLIALATELA	
2	CALCATERRA	
3	RIZZARDI	
4	TERRACENERE †	
5	LOSETO	
6	MONTANARI	
7	LAURERI ‡	
8	CUCCHI	
9	CAPOCCHIANO	5, 27
10	ALESSIO	
11	TOVALIERI	88
Substitutes		
15	BARONE (†60)	
16	CAGGIANELLI (‡66)	

Black and White Striped Shirts, Black Shorts		Goals
1	Pavel SRNICEK	
2	Matty APPLEBY	
3	Mark STIMSON	
4	Steve WATSON	
5	Brian KILCLINE	
6	Steve HOWEY	
7	Franz CARR	
8	Richie APPLEBY	
9	Andy HUNT †	
10	Alan THOMPSON	
11	Kevin SHEEDY ‡	
Substitutes		
12	John WATSON (†45)	
14	David ROCHE (‡60)	

BEFORE	P	W	D	L	F	A	pts
ENGLISH GROUP A							
4 Newcastle	2	0	1	1	1	2	1

AFTER	P	W	D	L	F	A	pts
ENGLISH GROUP A							
4 Newcastle	3	0	1	2	1	5	1

FACTFILE

Heaviest defeat of the season… first time United concede three goals in a game… Appleby brothers Matty and Richie play together in first team for first time… Keegan fields eight reserves… United eliminated from Anglo-Italian Cup.

Goodbye and good riddance

WHEN Newcastle finally made their exit from the Anglo-Italian Cup, they at least had the consolation of doing so in one of Europe's finest soccer arenas.

The Stadia San Nicola was developed especially for the 1990 World Cup and became acknowledged as an architectural gem.

But the 60,000 capacity was scarcely tested by the Anglo-Italian Cup, and certainly not the 1,229 congregation which stirred itself to watch Bari and Newcastle United do battle.

Kevin Keegan opted to field a side made up mostly of reserve team players who would have been accustomed to the ghostly atmosphere.

But they could put up little resistance to a skilful Bari side which generated the sort of passion a 60,000 gathering would have welcomed with firecrackers and horns.

Bari went ahead after only five minutes and coasted thereafter to a comfortable win which duly eliminated United even before the final group match against Cesena. The weather was hardly Italian either: high winds, thunder and lightning and driving rain more suited to the Monsoon Season in the Amazon jungle.

Bari, relegated from Serie A the previous season, had nonetheless been the last side to defeat mighty AC Milan before the Milanese embarked on their phenomenal unbeaten run.

And having beaten Portsmouth 3-0 earlier in the tournament, Bari set about dishing out the same treatment to Newcastle Reserves. The early goal came when full-back Rizzardi overlapped on the left and crossed beyond Brian Kilcline for Capocchiano to score from 12 yards.

United's response caused one or two mild flutters in the Italian defence, with Steve Howey bringing a fine save from Tagliatela, and Alan Thompson shooting into the side netting.

However, the second goal, when it arrived, fell also to Bari. This time Allessio's 27th-minute overlapping run allied to Kilcline's slip left Capocchiano unmarked to thump an unstoppable header past Pavel Srnicek.

By now the result was a foregone conclusion and Alessio should have made it even more certain, but shot wide after rounding Srnicek.

Keegan took the opportunity to experiment, having a look at substitutes John Watson and David Roche in the second half, and pushing Steve Howey into midfield.

Surprisingly United found the net when Kilcline headed in from a corner.

But referee Roger Milford refused to play the patriot and disallowed the goal, apparently for a push which few others spotted.

That left Bari to claim the third goal two minutes from time, two-goal Capocchiano setting up Tovalieri to measure a lob over Srnicek.

In the end, the match became more of a platform for United's fringe players than any meaningful attempt at making progress. Few did themselves any justice on a difficult day, in difficult conditions, and against a difficult team.

United would not bemoan their exit from the Anglo-Italian Cup, and even for the small band of United fans in Italy, the trip was more about seeing how the other half lives than sustaining interest in an empty competition.

Empty grounds, too. The jury had delivered its own verdict.

United enjoy the open spaces

Sunday 13th December 1992 • Oakwell • 3.05pm

BARNSLEY 1 NEWCASTLE UNITED 0

Half-time 0-0 • *Attendance* 13,263

Referee Paul VANES (Warley)

Linesmen O. DYCE, J. RICHARDSON

Red Shirts, White Shorts		Goals	Black and White Striped Shirts, Black Shorts		Goals
1	Lee BUTLER		1	Pavel SRNICEK	
2	Mark ROBINSON		2	Barry VENISON	
3	Gary FLEMING		3	John BERESFORD	
4	Charlie BISHOP		4	Liam O'BRIEN	
5	Gerry TAGGART		5	Kevin SCOTT	
6	Brendan O'CONNELL	49	6	Steve HOWEY	
7	Wayne BIGGINS		7	Robert LEE	
8	Andy RAMMELL		8	Gavin PEACOCK	
9	John PEARSON †		9	David KELLY	
10	Neil REDFEARN		10	Lee CLARK	
11	Owen ARCHDEACON		11	Kevin SHEEDY	
Substitutes			*Substitutes*		
12	Andy LIDDELL (†45)		12	Brian KILCLINE	
14	David CURRIE		14	Paul BRACEWELL	

BEFORE		P	W	D	L	F	A	pts	AFTER		P	W	D	L	F	A	pts
1	Newcastle	19	16	1	2	40	14	49	1	Newcastle	20	16	1	3	40	15	49
16	Barnsley	19	7	3	9	23	19	24	14	Barnsley	20	8	3	9	24	19	27

Tykes end United record run of 19 scoring away league games dating back to January 1... lead stays at 12 points... Archdeacon and Bishop of Barnsley are Sunday winners... only United's second away league defeat of the season.

Tykes triumph in aerial battle

FEW TEAMS had caused United serious problems in the league so far, but Barnsley proved a formidable obstacle in the third live TV match of the season.

The Yorkshire side's rigid five-man defence stifled United's creativity, and their height and strength also cut out the aerial route. It wasn't pretty, but it was effective. The stream of openings which had been created so often and so well by United in previous games dried up as this match became a war of attrition.

The war was won by Brendan O'Connell's 49th-minute header from a Wayne Biggins cross which caught the United defence off-guard at the far post.

Perhaps it was significant that the winning goal, and all the game's best chances, came from headers. Kevin Scott went closest for United, striking the crossbar with a power header in the seventh minute. If that had gone in, there might have been a different story.

Steve Howey also got to the ball in the air seconds before half-time to guide a superb header down towards the bottom corner. But Lee Butler, an inspiration in the Barnsley goal, miraculously got down to save.

The fact that centre-backs Scott and Howey got those chances demonstrates the lack of success of the more skilled Kelly and Peacock up front.

Barnsley's robust forwards, by contrast, had more going for them and Biggins brought a save from Pavel Srnicek in the 17th minute.

On one of the few occasions the Barnsley defence was breached on the ground, Lee Clark wasted all his good work with a weak shot following an incisive one-two with David Kelly.

Before the Barnsley goal, United had looked the better bet for the three points.

But afterwards it was always an uphill struggle as Barnsley grew in confidence and United grew increasingly anxious.

It was only the fourth time in the season that United had found themselves trailing in a League game: and the third in which they were unable to recover the deficit.

And despite heavy United pressure in the final 20 minutes the truth was that Barnsley rarely looked like relinquishing their lead.

Kevin Sheedy will forever regret his failure to guide a simple six-yard header beyond the reach of Butler after great work by David Kelly.

And John Beresford, pitting his wits against his former team, burrowed deep into the area only to shoot into the side-netting.

It was perhaps ironic that United should draw a blank so soon after releasing that ace scorer Micky Quinn to Coventry City, but Keegan was surely justified in his decision.

Many questions were later to be asked of Quinn's departure, but the fact remains that Quinn's wait-for-it-to-come style was alien to the total football concept and pattern developed by United.

Criticism of united's scoring record was invalidated by the simple statistic so often advanced by Keegan in reply. "Top scorers," he would say, without further explanation being needed.

Barnsley were only the third team to keep United's forwards at bay in 20 league games to this stage.

And perhaps it was decreed in the Good Book that any side with a Bishop and an Archdeacon in its ranks would prosper on the Sabbath.

Steve Howey - denied by a great save

Wednesday 16th December 1992 • St James' Park • 7.45pm

NEWCASTLE UNITED 2 CESENA 2

Half-time 1-1 • *Attendance* 4,609
Referee Virginio QUARTUCCIO (Naples)
Linesmen T. Lynch, D. Oliver

Black and White Striped Shirts, Black Shorts		Goals	Red Shirts, Red Shorts		Goals
1	Tommy WRIGHT		1	Stefano DADINA	
2	Matty APPLEBY ❑		2	Flavio DESTRO	
3	Alan NEILSON		3	Luigi PIANGERELLI	
4	Liam O'BRIEN		4	Gianluca LEONI †	
5	Paul BRACEWELL		5	Battista SCUGUGIA	
6	Steve HOWEY †		6	Filippo MEDRI	
7	Franz CARR		7	Alessandro TEODORANI	
8	Gavin PEACOCK	38, 64	8	Filippo MASOLINI	
9	David KELLY		9	Luca PAZZAGLIA	71
10	Lee CLARK		10	Christian LANTIGNOTTI	
11	Richie APPLEBY ‡		11	Dario HUBNER	2
	Substitutes			*Substitutes*	
12	Bjorn KRISTENSEN (†63)		13	CECCARELLI (†63)	
14	Steve WATSON (‡72)				

BEFORE	P	W	D	L	F	A	pts	AFTER	P	W	D	L	F	A	pts
ENGLISH GROUP A								ENGLISH GROUP A							
4 Newcastle	3	0	1	2	1	5	1	4 Newcastle	4	0	2	2	3	7	2

FACTFILE

United wave goodbye to Anglo-Italian Cup... Peacock denied hat-trick by last-minute penalty miss... 4,609 the lowest crowd for a Newcastle competitive home match since World War Two... United finish bottom of Group A with two points from four games.

Peacock brace – but no treble

IT WAS ironic that the most meaningless of all the Anglo-Italian Cup games should produce the most exciting and stylish tie of all.

The paltry 4,609 crowd who turned out on a freezing December night were genuinely entertained by two sides determined to play sufficient good football to more than make up for all that had gone before.

The irony was heaviest, though, for Gavin Peacock, who missed a last-minute penalty and with it the chance of a hat-trick.

Just 18 days earlier, Peacock had handed over a late penalty to David Kelly who completed United's only hat-trick of the season in the defeat of Cambridge United.

This time, when Peacock won a penalty of his own, he failed to emulate Kelly. It's a funny old game, as a certain old goalscorer says.

The spills may have ended with Peacock's penalty, but the thrills had started as early as the second minute when Cesena went ahead with a goal of consummate skill.

The Italians had emerged wearing gloves as protection against the icy conditions, but Pazzaglia had warmed up sufficiently to gallop down the right in the 134th second and cross perfectly for Hubner to dive and head in.

Kevin Keegan, fielding a stronger side than against Bari, also experimented with a three-man defence of Matty Appleby, Alan Neilson and Steve Howey.

Hubner's early goal was scarcely a great start to the experiment,

Captain Peacock - denied a hat-trick

but United's 3-4-3 formation lent itself perfectly to the intriguing contest which followed.

Only two minutes later, Liam O'Brien bulleted a header against Dadina's crossbar from a Peacock centre. Then Paul Bracewell, getting forward frequently, shot just wide after more excellent work from the effervescent Peacock.

Peacock's industry deserved greater reward and it arrived seven minutes from the interval when he grabbed the equaliser.

When Franz Carr's corner was flicked on by Steve Howey, Peacock ghosted in to beat Dadina with the subtlest of touches.

Had the Cesena keeper not superbly saved Peacock's next shot four minutes later, the hat-trick might have come about.

But Peacock did claim his, and United's, second goal in the 64th minute with a move which deserved a far bigger audience.

Bracewell was again the source, penetrating the Italians' defence with a glorious ball for Alan Neilson. Neilson picked out David Kelly with his cross, and Kelly's downward header left Peacock with the simple task of bulging the net from all of two yards.

Cesena, never afraid to attack in the early stages, had been pinned back by United's attacking domination. But they, like Newcastle, were already eliminated from the Anglo-Italian Cup and threw caution to the wind when faced with the need to seek out an equaliser.

They got it, too, in the 71st minute when Hubner escaped on the left flank to set up Pazzaglia for a close-range goal.

Both sides went in search of the winner, and it seemed United had pinched it when, in the closing seconds, Peacock's shot in a goalmouth scramble was kept out by an Italian glove.

Peacock failed to beat Dadina from the spot, and his chance of a little slice of glory was gone.

There would be far greater glory in the months ahead, of course, but at least the Anglo-Italian Cup had, for all its failings, gone out on a high note.

Sunday 20th December 1992 • St James' Park • 3.00pm

NEWCASTLE UNITED 1 MILLWALL 1

Half-time 0-1 • Attendance 26,089

Referee Stephen BELL (Huddersfield)

Linesmen J. JONES, M. ROBINSON

Black and White Striped Shirts, Black Shorts		Goals	Blue and White Shirts, Blue Shorts		Goals
1	Pavel SRNICEK		1	Kasey KELLER	
2	Barry VENISON		2	Ken CUNNINGHAM ❏	
3	John BERESFORD †		3	Ian DAWES	
4	Liam O'BRIEN		4	Andy MAY ❏	
5	Kevin SCOTT ❏		5	Colin COOPER	
6	Steve HOWEY		6	Keith STEVENS	
7	Robert LEE		7	Andy ROBERTS	
8	Paul BRACEWELL		8	Jamie MORALEE †	20
9	David KELLY	75p	9	Ian BOGIE ‡	
10	Lee CLARK		10	Jon GOODMAN	
11	Kevin SHEEDY ‡		11	Phil BARBER	
	Substitutes			*Substitutes*	
12	Brian KILCLINE (†15)		12	Malcolm ALLEN (†61)	
14	Franz CARR (‡71)		14	Alex RAE (‡60)	

BEFORE		P	W	D	L	F	A	pts	AFTER		P	W	D	L	F	A	pts
1	Newcastle	20	16	1	3	40	15	49	1	Newcastle	21	16	2	3	41	16	50
4	Millwall	20	9	7	4	31	18	34	4	Millwall	21	9	8	4	32	19	35

FACTFILE

Kelly's lucky penalty gives United ten-point lead over Tranmere... Bracewell comes in for injured top scorer Peacock... first home score-draw of the season... TV jinx catches United again.

All square after battle of nerves

THERE'S an old saying in football that you earn your own luck, but the decision which brought United to a fortunate point against Millwall stretched even that adage.

United were struggling badly at 0-1 down to a strong and disciplined Millwall side when, with 15 minutes remaining, Robert Lee was challenged from a throw-in inches inside the left edge of the penalty area. Suddenly, a linesman flagged and the referee awarded a penalty. It was a barely conceivable lifeline, and David Kelly gratefully accepted the early Christmas gift with a shot high into the net.

There was little evidence of an offence then, and little via the TV cameras which replayed the incident ad infinitum without clarifying the muddle. The linesman later said he had signalled for a push and a handball by a Millwall defender. "It's a wonder he didn't say a trip, too, just to cover himself," moaned Lions boss Mick McCarthy.

Fortune had indeed come to United's rescue in this pre-Christmas Sunday TV match, and it was impossible not to have sympathy with McCarthy and Millwall.

So a point was salvaged; but the wider implications of this nervous, anxious draw were that

It's a free-for-all in the Millwall goalmouth

United, after considerable success, were now finding it difficult to score goals. Barnsley's massed defence had stopped them a week before, and but for the unwarranted penalty, Millwall would surely have done so again.

Kasey Keller, Millwall's unorthodox American goalkeeper, was as much responsible for denying United as anyone with a series of resourceful saves. But there was no denying that both the quantity and quality of United's chances were now being seriously reduced.

Were teams now getting wise to the Newcastle United style? Millwall certainly appeared to be, though they were aided by the premature departure of John Beresford after only 15 minutes: his confidence that he could play through a flu bug sadly not borne out.

Steve Howey switched to emergency left-back, with Brian Kilcline coming on to partner Kevin Scott at the centre of defence.

United's bright opening quickly faded, and the outlook became positively gloomy when a Kevin Scott error on the edge of the box let in Jamie Moralee to score low to Srnicek's right. Even if Kevin Sheedy hit a post soon after, United's attempts to equalise bore few of the trademarks of quality of previous games.

The Lions, one of the chasing pack and 15 points behind Newcastle, probably deserved victory but so nearly went under in the wake of Kelly's penalty goal. Lee Clark, also below par on the day, produced a 20-yard drive which deserved a goal but instead brought a magnificent save from Keller, contact lenses et al.

If fortune had been so cruel on Millwall as to add a second United goal, it would have been a serious miscarriage of justice.

But Kevin Keegan was undaunted after the match, deflecting questions on the absence of a traditional centre-forward - Quinn had, by now, joined Coventry permanently - with a stock answer: "Top scorers in the first division," Keegan said, pointedly. But for that penalty, he couldn't have said those words.

Saturday 26th December 1992 • St James' Park • 3.00pm

NEWCASTLE UNITED 2 WOLVES 1

Half-time 1-1 • *Attendance* 30,137

Referee Ken LUPTON (Stockton)

Linesmen R. PEARSON, K. THOMPSON

Black and White Striped Shirts, Black Shorts		Goals	Old Gold Shirts, Old Gold Shorts		Goals
1	Pavel SRNICEK		1	Paul JONES	
2	Barry VENISON		2	Kevin ASHLEY ❑	
3	Alan NEILSON		3	Paul EDWARDS	
4	Liam O'BRIEN		4	Mark BURKE	
5	Kevin SCOTT		5	Derek MOUNTFIELD †	
6	Steve HOWEY		6	Lawrie MADDEN ❑	
7	Robert LEE		7	Mark RANKINE	
8	Gavin PEACOCK		8	Paul COOK	33
9	David KELLY	43, 66	9	Steve BULL	
10	Lee CLARK		10	Keith DOWNING	
11	Kevin SHEEDY		11	Mark VENUS	
Substitutes			*Substitutes*		
12	Franz CARR		12	Paul BLADES (†45) ❑ ‡	
14	Paul BRACEWELL		14	Andy MUTCH (‡77)	

BEFORE		P	W	D	L	F	A	pts	AFTER		P	W	D	L	F	A	pts
1	Newcastle	21	16	2	3	41	16	50	1	Newcastle	22	17	2	3	43	17	53
8	Wolves	22	8	9	5	33	26	33	9	Wolves	23	8	9	6	34	28	33

FACTFILE

Capacity 30,137 crowd exactly matches Tranmere game in October... United pass 1991-92 points total of 52 before half-way stage of 1992-93...Neilson in for injured Beresford... Kelly takes tally to 14 with two more... United lead up to 12 points again.

Santa Kelly's Festive Special

ADVERSITY, they say, brings out the best in you. But only once all season had United been able to turn a deficit into victory.

That was at Bristol Rovers in September, when Kevin Sheedy and Liam O'Brien countered John Taylor's opener for Rovers.

In the four pre-Christmas games, United had fallen behind on each occasion; in all four, they failed to win.

So when Wolves' Paul Cook placed a ferocious angled drive behind Pavel Srnicek in the 33rd minute at St James' Park on Boxing Day, the Newcastle fans in the 30,137 capacity crowd feared the worst.

The nerves which had beset United in the draw with Millwall and the defeat at Barnsley were there again in an uncertain opening.

There was little from which to glean encouragement with Wanderers effectively crowding the midfield and squeezing the life out of strikers Gavin Peacock and David Kelly.

It was a severe test of both character and resilience which Kevin Keegan's side looked like failing until a crucial and significant 43rd minute.

Liam O'Brien chanced his arm with a typical long-range volley which brought a fine diving save from Wolves keeper Paul Jones plunging to his right.

Jones, however, diverted the ball only to the byline beyond the left post, and Peacock contorted himself to turn the loose ball back into the six-yard box where David Kelly nudged it over the line.

A defender hooked the ball out and Lee Clark hooked it back in, but the goal had already been given.

The match immediately took on a different aspect, with United, boosted by Kelly's equalis-

er and roared on by the full house crowd, pushing forward for the winner after the interval.

But Wolves, with Steve Bull up front, were to be no pushovers and, indeed, Pavel Srnicek had to come out to save at Bull's feet to prevent his side falling behind again.

Three Wolves men were cautioned as the temperature rose, but early in the second half it was still anyone's game.

Happily, the scales were tipped United's way thanks to a piece of David Kelly magic in the 66th minute.

When a long ball caught out the Wanderers defence and left him in space 18 yards from goal, Kelly had two options.

One was to go in on Jones and risk a one-on-one battle of wits; the other to first-time the bouncing ball before the keeper could gain position.

Within a split-second, the ball was rattling around in the roof of the net. Option Two had clearly proved the best.

A moment of inspiration from Kelly: but still there was an unconvincing air about it all, and the final 24 minutes passed slowly as Wolves in their turn pushed for an equaliser.

It didn't come, and United stretched their lead at the top to 12 points, from Tranmere in second place and West Ham a further three points adrift in third spot.

Kevin Keegan was satisfied enough to describe the defeat of Wolves as "one of the better performances" of his 11 months in charge.

Given the first-goal setback and the quality of the opposition, it probably was. But the class gap which had set United apart in the first three or four months of the season was, for the moment, strangely absent.

Kevin Keegan - "better performance"

Monday 28th December 1992 • The Manor Ground • 3.00pm

OXFORD UNITED 4 NEWCASTLE UNITED 2

Half-time 3-2 • *Attendance* 9,293

Referee David FRAMPTON (Poole)

Linesmen R. KIRK, L. WATSON

Gold Shirts, Blue Shorts		Goals	Black and White Striped Shirts, White Shorts		Goals
1	Paul REECE		1	Pavel SRNICEK	
2	Gary SMART		2	Barry VENISON	
3	Ceri EVANS		3	John BERESFORD	
4	Andy MELVILLE		4	Liam O'BRIEN	9
5	Les ROBINSON		5	Kevin SCOTT ❑	
6	Jim MAGILTON	34p, 81	6	Steve HOWEY	
7	Joey BEAUCHAMP		7	Robert LEE	
8	Mickey LEWIS		8	Gavin PEACOCK †	
9	Chris ALLEN		9	David KELLY	
10	Nick CUSACK	8	10	Lee CLARK	38
11	John DURNIN	4	11	Kevin SHEEDY	
	Substitutes			*Substitutes*	
12	David PENNEY		12	Brian KILCLINE (†77)	
14	Paul WANLESS		14	Paul BRACEWELL	

BEFORE	P	W	D	L	F	A	pts	AFTER	P	W	D	L	F	A	pts
1 Newcastle	22	17	2	3	43	17	53	1 Newcastle	23	17	2	4	45	21	53
16 Oxford	21	5	11	5	30	25	26	16 Oxford	22	6	11	5	34	27	29

FACTFILE

Four goals conceded for only time in season... Lee Clark ends 23-match scoring drought... Oxford's early blitz destroys Newcastle... first two-goal margin of defeat... Tranmere also lose to leave United 12 points ahead.

Horror show at the Manor

CONTROVERSIAL refereeing decisions are reckoned to even themselves out over the course of a season, but Newcastle used up a sizeable slice of the debit column in their heavy defeat at the Manor Ground.

United had benefited from the late penalty against Millwall, but at Oxford eight days later they suffered in triplicate.

Three highly questionable decisions from David Frampton set Newcastle an uphill task then prevented them achieving an improbable comeback.

Ultimately, the hill was just too steep to climb but no United player or supporter will ever be convinced that referee Frampton was anything but an Oxford secret agent.

As early as the fourth minute, the dangerous John Durnin was allowed to break from an apparently offside position and beat Pavel Srnicek one-on-one. For the sixth successive game, United had fallen behind. When former Darlington star Nick Cusack added Oxford's second four minutes later - a header from a Joey Beauchamp cross - the writing was on the wall in letters six feet high.

But almost immediately, Liam O'Brien thundered in an Exocet from 20 yards to bring United back into contention.

The momentum built up by three goals in nine minutes ensured the match sparked and fizzed for the remaining 81.

Cusack could and should have made it 3-1 in the 11th minute but sent a header wide; Lee Clark and Liam O'Brien, dominant in midfield, probed for an opening which Kelly

and Peacock frequently looked ready to exploit. Newcastle were looking more and more likely when, in the 34th minute, the carpet was whipped from under their feet by Mr Frampton.

No-one doubted that Steve Howey's tackle on Chris Allen inside the area was anything but perfectly timed and perfectly legal.

Except Mr Frampton, that is, who, to the stunned disbelief of the entire United contingent, pointed to the penalty spot. Jim Magilton scored easily, and the hill was Everest again.

It was 24 games since Lee Clark had scored, but perhaps the anger and frustration of events so far were behind his extraordinary goal on 38 minutes. A free-kick dropped to the edge of the area for Clark to pivot on one foot and sweep a mighty volley past Reece in the Oxford goal.

Reece was beaten then, but he did superbly to deny David Kelly an equaliser before the frenetic first-half was brought to a close.

At 2-3, United had every chance of taking some reward back to Tyneside, and for much of the second period United buzzed around the home goal. Liam O'Brien, Gavin Peacock and Kevin Scott were all close to an equalising goal which was destined never to arrive.

Instead, in the 81st minute, a third hugely questionable refereeing decision finally destroyed hopes of at least a point. Durnin,

Lee Clark -superb goal

challenged by Scott, fell innocuously, but was granted a free-kick which Scott disputed vociferously enough to be cautioned. Magilton, an outstanding influence on the match, waited for the arguments to settle then lashed a beauty past Srnicek.

For the first time this season, Newcastle had conceded four goals. But a simmering sense of injustice clouded clear judgement on the standard of the performance.

Saturday 2nd January 1993 • St James' Park • 3.00pm

NEWCASTLE UNITED 4 PORT VALE 0

Half-time 0-0 • Attendance 29,873

Referee Allan FLOOD (Stockport)
Linesmen W. NATTRASS, S. GRAHAM

Black and White Striped Shirts, Black Shorts	Goals	Yellow Shirts, Yellow Shorts	Goals
1 Pavel SRNICEK		1 Paul MUSSELWHITE	
2 Barry VENISON		2 Bradley SANDEMAN	
3 John BERESFORD		3 Chris SULLEY	
4 Liam O'BRIEN		4 Ray WALKER	
5 Kevin SCOTT †		5 Peter SWAN	
6 Steve HOWEY		6 Dean GLOVER	
7 Robert LEE	66	7 John JEFFERS	
8 Gavin PEACOCK	49, 62	8 Neil ASPIN	
9 David KELLY ‡		9 Nicky CROSS †	
10 Lee CLARK		10 Martin FOYLE	
11 Kevin SHEEDY	80	11 Ian TAYLOR	
Substitutes		*Substitutes*	
12 Brian KILCLINE (†83)		12 Robin VAN DER LAAN (†74)	
14 Paul BRACEWELL (‡52)		14 Paul KERR	

Another lock-out crowd... Peacock double takes him up to 17... first-ever FA Cup meeting of United and Vale... United's four-goal second half is best 45 minutes of season so far... United's biggest third-round FA Cup victory since 1974... Kelly's carried off with a twisted ankle - but he's okay.

David Kelly fires in at goal

Vale swept aside by touch of grit

AFTER playing, in Kevin Keegan's own words, "Premier League football" for much of the latter part of 1992, 1993 dawned with a different type of examination.

Port Vale, second division promotion battlers following relegation the previous season, arrived on Tyneside determined to prove that more than the FA Cup is a great leveller. And for 45 minutes Vale did just that, silencing the near-30,000 Cup-tie crowd and indisputably enjoying the better of the first-half exchanges.

The rare sound of booing greeted the interval whistle with the scoreline still goalless; a mercy for which United were grateful, having been baffled by Vale's tactical game-plan.

Crowding the midfield and tackling tigerishly at the back, the second division promotion chasers more than matched the first division runaway leaders.

But it was no mere defensive strategy. Vale made excellent chances, too, and Pavel Srnicek needed to be at his best more than once.

Srnicek never needed to be sharper than when Nicky Cross broke clear; happily, the Czech keeper came out on top in the battle of wits. Then, with Srnicek beaten, Kevin Scott scraped a Peter Swan header off the goalline.

Kevin Keegan admitted later that he had given his players a rare earbashing at half-time. "I reminded them we haven't achieved things by just going through the motions," he said.

Something was put right, for sure. The Newcastle side which emerged for the second half could have been 11 completely different players from the group which had trudged disconsolately off at the end of the first.

Such was the difference: Vale, who had scented glory, were contemptuously swept aside by a devastating United.

Within four minutes, the barriers were breached as Robert Lee cut in from the right to try an angled drive which keeper Paul Musselwhite could only parry and, as Neil Aspin dithered, Gavin Peacock muscled in ahead of him to score.

There could have been problems when David Kelly limped off soon after with a twisted ankle, but Robert Lee moved into a central attacking role and looked twice the force he had been when out wide.

It was Lee who robbed Swan to send in Liam O'Brien to create Peacock's second goal in the 62nd minute.

It was Lee who veered in from the left touchline to rattle a superb third on 66 minutes.

And it was Lee who began the move which sent Peacock clean through and on for a hat-trick; Musselwhite nudged the ball away from Peacock's toes, but Kevin Sheedy followed up to score.

If ever a match was won by a one-half performance, this was it.

And while there was massive encouragement in the way United responded to the manager's critical words, there was some concern that Keegan had had to resort to them at all.

Keegan described that first half as "lethargic", though he and Terry McDermott no doubt used stronger words in the privacy of the dressing-room.

Port Vale would go on to prove themselves a side of quality at their own level, sustaining as they did a second division promotion challenge.

But for Newcastle it was a clear warning that nothing would ever be achieved without a touch of true grit to go with the silky skills.

Robert Lee - thrived in a central role

Saturday 9th January 1993 • Ashton Gate • 3.00pm

BRISTOL CITY 1 NEWCASTLE UNITED 2

Half-time 1-2 • *Attendance* 15,446

Referee Keith BURGE (Tonypandy)

Linesmen D. BRAMMER, M. HOLOHAN

Red Shirts, White Shorts		Goals	Black and White Striped Shirts, Black Shorts		Goals
1	Keith WELCH		1	Pavel SRNICEK	
2	Gerry HARRISON †		2	Barry VENISON	
3	Martin SCOTT		3	John BERESFORD	
4	Andy LLEWELLYN		4	Liam O'BRIEN	
5	Matt BRYANT		5	Kevin SCOTT	31
6	Russell OSMAN		6	Steve HOWEY	
7	Gary SHELTON		7	Robert LEE	
8	Junior BENT ‡		8	Gavin PEACOCK	
9	Wayne ALLISON	19	9	David KELLY	22
10	Andy COLE		10	Lee CLARK	
11	Mark GAVIN		11	Kevin SHEEDY †	
Substitutes			*Substitutes*		
12	Mark AIZLEWOOD (†85)		12	Brian KILCLINE	
14	Micky MELLON (‡69)		14	Paul BRACEWELL (†83)	

BEFORE		P	W	D	L	F	A	pts	AFTER		P	W	D	L	F	A	pts
1	Newcastle	23	17	2	4	45	21	53	1	Newcastle	24	18	2	4	47	22	56
18	Bristol City	23	7	6	10	28	44	27	18	Bristol City	24	7	6	11	29	46	27

FACTFILE

*United complete first league double of season. Now 14 points clear at the top...
great fight back after early City goal... City's eighth game without a win...
Keegan notes star performance of Robins striker Andy Cole... first win at Ashton
Gate since 1910.*

Robins denied by thieving Magpies

KEVIN Keegan himself drew the crucial distinction between the Newcastle side he took over in February 1992 and the Newcastle side 14 points clear at the top of division one after victory at Ashton Gate.

"A year ago, we would have lost this game," he said. "On days like today, though, we roll up our sleeves and do battle."

A year ago, the Ossie Ardiles School of Culture was regularly beaten by teams like Bristol City, when brawn all too often outdid brain.

In January 1993, the culture was still there. But the added ingredient of steel had given United an extra edge: a cutting edge which had turned them from soft touch to steamroller.

"It's a blend of skill and steel," Keegan said, "and we will achieve things because of it."

That skill and steel was needed in abundance after Wayne Allison outjumped Pavel Srnicek to full-back Martin Scott's towering centre to open the scoring in the 19th minute.

Within three more minutes, Kevin Sheedy clipped in a free-kick from the right, David Kelly got a tickle, and City full-back Gerry Harrison met it full on to inadvertently head the ball high past his own goalkeeper, Keith Welch.

"My goal. It was going into the other corner from my header," insisted Kelly. No-one - least of all Harrison - was prepared to argue and Kelly had his 15th goal of the season.

The sleeves were still rolled up nine minutes later when the tireless Kelly headed Liam O'Brien's pass into the path of Kevin Scott for a simple goal from 10 yards. The tables had been instantly turned on City, but they were nothing if not determined and forced United back for much of the remaining hour.

It was a significant statistic of this match that City had exactly twice as many shots on target

as United - 14 to seven. And leading the Bristol City line to great effect was a tall and powerful 21-year-old, formerly with Arsenal and currently City's record buy at £500,000.

Andy Cole's pace and power was a major problem for United, and Kevin Scott and Steve Howey were almost at their wit's end in trying to deal with him.

Cole made enough of an impression on United - and Keegan - to remain in the forefront of the manager's mind for another two months before he finally joined United for a club record of £1.75m.

In January, Cole had already hit 13 goals for struggling City, and it was to prove unlucky as, for all his best efforts, the one-goal deficit stayed as it was through to full-time.

City manager Denis Smith, a wise old campaigner who recognised strength of character from afar, gave an intriguing assessment of Newcastle.

"They are a team at peace with themselves," he said.

The confidence borne of 18 wins in 24 League games no doubt had something to do with it, but that does not tell the whole story of resurrection.

Kevin Keegan, in 11 months in the hot seat, had transformed United into a team of real pedigree through the simple expedient of buying genuine class.

But there was added significance in the figure who sat, unused, on the substitutes bench at Ashton Gate this day.

Brian Kilcline had added the steel to the class as Keegan built his team, injecting the side with a will-to-win that wasn't always there before.

"Brian Kilcline did so much for this club when he came here that it breaks my heart not to have room for him in the team," Keegan said on another occasion. "He brought something which lifted the team."

It was called steel.

Saturday 16th January 1993 • St James' Park • 3.00pm

NEWCASTLE UNITED 3 PETERBORO' UNITED 0

Half-time 1-0 • *Attendance* 29,155
Referee Joe WORRALL (Warrington)
Linesmen C. BASSINDALE, G. GRANDIDGE

Black and White Striped Shirts, Black Shorts		Goals	Blue Shirts, White Shorts		Goals
1	Pavel SRNICEK		1	Ian BENNETT	
2	Barry VENISON		2	Noel LUKE	
3	John BERESFORD		3	Ronnie ROBINSON	
4	Liam O'BRIEN		4	Mick HALSALL	
5	Kevin SCOTT		5	Darren BRADSHAW	
6	Steve HOWEY		6	Steve WELSH	
7	Robert LEE	30, 70	7	Worrell STERLING	
8	Gavin PEACOCK		8	Bobby BARNES ‡	
9	David KELLY	88	9	Tony ADCOCK	
10	Lee CLARK		10	Tony PHILLISKIRK	
11	Kevin SHEEDY †		11	David ROCHE †	

Substitutes			*Substitutes*		
12	Brian KILCLINE		12	Graham RETALLICK (†86)	
14	Paul BRACEWELL (†45)		14	Dominic IORFA (‡68)	

BEFORE		P	W	D	L	F	A	pts	AFTER		P	W	D	L	F	A	pts
1	Newcastle	24	18	2	4	47	22	56	1	Newcastle	25	19	2	4	50	22	59
14	Peterboro'	21	8	8	5	32	27	32	15	Peterboro'	22	8	8	6	32	30	32

FACTFILE

60mph gales almost force a postponement… Robert Lee scores his first United double… United man David Roche plays on loan for Peterborough and Posh boss Fuccillo accuses Roche of being unfit… Peterborough's first-ever league visit to St James' Park.

Peterborough are blown away

FEW TEAMS could have played football of a consistently high quality in the gales which swept St James' Park when Peterborough brought the first division's best away record to St James' Park.

Only just short of the 67mph postponement level before the game, the winds threatened to do what Peterborough had little chance of doing on their own: even the game.

We should have known better. Newcastle's football on this impossible day could have belonged to the midsummer Mediterranean rather than midwinter Tyneside.

"Given the conditions," said Kevin Keegan, "this was our best performance of the season." And it was.

Peterborough had nothing to offer in reply as Newcastle systematically outplayed them in midfield and clinically dismembered them at the back.

If there was no comparison to be made between the Posh attack and the Newcastle defence, it was because by and large the action never reached that section of the pitch.

Take away substitute Dominic Iorfa's near-miss and Tony Philliskirk's long-range shot punched out by Pavel Srnicek, and the Czech keeper might as well have brought his 'Learn Yourself English' manual and a chair.

Other than that, it was one-way traffic, and in the fast lane, too.

Leading the charge from first to last was Robert Lee, by now finding the form which had persuaded Keegan to part with £700,000 back in September.

Lee, nothing less than magnificent, helped himself to two excellent goals and left Peterborough with a king-sized headache by which to remember him.

Peterborough manager Lil Fuccillo directed his frustration, unjustly, at his team, branding them "gutless" and picking an argument with Keegan over the fitness - or otherwise - of on-loan David Roche.

But Roche's assessment of the match was more pertinent. "Newcastle tore us apart," he said.

The first goal was somehow delayed until the 30th minute, when Lee struck a remarkable side-on volley to deposit Gavin Peacock's cross over and behind Ian Bennett.

There was to be no repeat of the former Newcastle youngster's goalkeeping heroics of London Road in September, when Bennett played Newcastle single-handed.

Not that Bennett played badly. Had he been on piece-rate, he would have been a wealthy man. More that even he was ultimately overwhelmed by Newcastle's Force 12 attacks.

The second goal arrived, overdue but inevitable, on 70 minutes and again showed Robert Lee at his best.

David Kelly gambled on Lee's pace and strength when he guided a through ball into a 50-50 race between Lee and defender Steve Welsh.

Lee took the knock, resisted, and in full stride stroked a venomous drive across Bennett which was still rising as it hit the far corner of the net.

End of Peterborough. Start of victory celebrations. And Kelly's 88th-minute header from a Gavin Peacock cross was the icing on the cake.

"People who came to watch the game may not have realised there was a 50mph wind blowing," said Keegan. "That's how good our football was."

And so Newcastle ploughed on. Now 14 points clear of Tranmere, West Ham and Millwall, all jostling humbly for second place.

It was almost too good to be true.

Wednesday 20th January 1993 • Roots Hall • 7.45pm

SOUTHEND UNITED 1 NEWCASTLE UNITED 1

Half-time 1-1 • *Attendance* 8,246

Referee Roger WISEMAN (Borehamwood)

Linesmen M. BULLIVANT, R. SAUNDERS

Blue Shirts, Blue Shorts		Goals	Black and White Striped Shirts, Black Shorts		Goals
1	Paul SANSOME		1	Pavel SRNICEK	
2	Andy EDWARDS		2	Barry VENISON	
3	Chris POWELL		3	John BERESFORD	
4	John CORNWELL		4	Liam O'BRIEN	
5	Pat SCULLY		5	Kevin SCOTT	
6	Spencer PRIOR		6	Steve HOWEY ❏	
7	Adam LOCKE		7	Robert LEE	
8	Andy SUSSEX	39p	8	Gavin PEACOCK	28
9	David MARTIN		9	David KELLY	
10	Stan COLLYMORE		10	Lee CLARK	
11	Keith JONES		11	Kevin BROCK	
	Substitutes			*Substitutes*	
12	Steve TILSON		12	Brian KILCLINE	
14	Christian HYSLOP		14	Bjorn KRISTENSEN	

BEFORE		P	W	D	L	F	A	pts	AFTER		P	W	D	L	F	A	pts
1	Newcastle	25	19	2	4	50	22	59	1	Newcastle	26	19	3	4	51	23	60
23	Southend	25	5	7	13	24	35	22	22	Southend	26	5	8	13	25	36	23

FACTFILE

Match brought forward due to Young Conservatives' February conference in Southend... United's second league visit to Roots Hall... point opens up season's biggest lead at the top, 15 points... only the third draw in 26 league games... first away draw in league.

Fifteen points ahead at the top

AT 9.30pm on January 20th, Newcastle United had proudly opened up a 15-point lead at the head of the First Division. But that lead would never be as wide again.

The irony was that the record margin followed one of United's least impressive performances against a Southend side battling desperately to escape the relegation zone.

Even though Gavin Peacock gave his side a 28th-minute lead, Newcastle never looked comfortable.

And after Southend's undisputed penalty equaliser, Kevin Keegan's side had to hang on to the point by their fingertips.

A little-known centre-forward called Stan Collymore, who would later almost attract a near-£2m deal with Nottingham Forest, led the Southend assaults with vigour, courage and no little skill.

It was Collymore who earned Southend their 39th-minute penalty, leaving Kevin Scott in his wake with a sharp turn, and forcing the Scott trip which brought the spot-kick award.

Once Andy Sussex had sent Pavel Srnicek the wrong way to score, the whole nature of the game changed.

Early on, Newcastle had looked good value, with David Kelly curling one shot narrowly over and Barry Venison and Liam O'Brien going similarly close.

And when the early supremacy brought a 28th-minute lead, few would have bet against Newcastle opening up a 17-point lead at the top of the first division table.

The goal came, slightly untidily, from a Lee Clark corner: Liam O'Brien shot into a crowd of players and when the ball span off Steve Howey, Gavin Peacock reacted instantly to fire high into the roof of the net.

Had Barry Venison not been thwarted by Paul Sansome's diving save minutes later, the match might have been out of the home side's reach.

But the Blues deserved huge credit for their refusal to accept Newcastle's dominance; and their battling qualities, if not skills, were enough to knock the league leaders out of their cultured stride.

Sussex's penalty set up an intriguing second half, with Southend now able to enjoy a territorial advantage. Newcastle threatened only in breaks, Sansome saving from Kelly and Robert Lee shooting past Sansome and the far post after fine work by Venison.

But Newcastle's usual smooth-passing game was hustled out of existence as Southend, led by the outstanding Collymore, went for the jugular.

That Newcastle survived was down to the more basic qualities of grit and determination rather than the silky football which had destroyed many sides.

Kevin Keegan had always preached the need to roll up sleeves and battle it out, and he was ready to praise Southend for forcing United into such an approach.

"Teams tend to raise their games against us, and if Southend could produce that type of display every game, they wouldn't be where they are," he said.

"Overall, I thought a draw was a fair result. We dominated the first half and I thought we were unlucky to go in level at half-time.

"However, in the second half Southend came at us and they deserved some reward for their performance."

Barry Venison - came close to scoring

Saturday 23rd January 1993 • Millmoor • 3.00pm

ROTHERHAM UNITED 1 NEWCASTLE UNITED 1

Half-time 0-1 • *Attendance* 13,405

Referee David AXCELL (Southend)

Linesmen J. BARLOW, G. HAMBLIN

Red Shirts, White Shorts		Goals	Black and White Striped Shirts, Black Shorts		Goals
1	Billy MERCER		1	Pavel SRNICEK	
2	Ally PICKERING		2	Barry VENISON	
3	Chris HUTCHINGS		3	John BERESFORD	
4	Ian BANKS		4	Liam O'BRIEN	
5	Nigel JOHNSON ❏	63	5	Kevin SCOTT	
6	Nicky LAW ❏		6	Steve HOWEY ❏	
7	Des HAZEL †		7	Robert LEE	28
8	Shaun GOODWIN		8	Gavin PEACOCK	
9	Tony CUNNINGHAM		9	David KELLY	
10	Shaun GOATER		10	Lee CLARK	
11	Dean BARRICK		11	Paul BRACEWELL	
	Substitutes			*Substitutes*	
12	Chris WILDER (†60)		12	Brian KILCLINE	
14	Jonathan HOWARD		14	Kevin BROCK	

FACTFILE

Newcastle cut Rotherham's visitors' ticket price from £10 to £7.50 and report them to FA... Peacock's disallowed goal allows second division underdogs to fight back... Millers equalise from freak indirect free-kick... Millmoor's first capacity gate for 22 years.

Pressure mounts in the Magpies defence

Goliath survives to fight again

THE LEAGUE was the priority, but the FA Cup was a splendid diversion, and with 15 points spare, Newcastle could afford to expend a little time and energy on the Wembley trail.

The luck of the draw had been kind: an away trip to Rotherham of the Second Division - surely the sort of tie a rampant side like Newcastle would relish.

On paper, perhaps. But football matches aren't played on paper, and Rotherham relished their own role as potential giantkillers.

The Millmoor capacity of 13,405 could have been filled by Geordies alone, such was the interest generated by the tie, and by Newcastle's superb run.

But the travelling fans were limited to 4,000, though the receipts Rotherham might have planned for were reduced somewhat by Sir John Hall's insistence on fair prices for all.

On the field, there were uncanny similarities to the Southend game just past. United took the lead in exactly the same minute - the 28th - but were later forced to scrap for survival in the face of the home side's fierce onslaught.

However, the whole game hinged once again on a controversial refereeing decision which robbed Newcastle of a 2-0 half-time lead.

United were already 1-0 up when, seconds before the interval whistle, John Beresford floated in a cross for which David Kelly challenged and was beaten.

Kelly's attempt carried him out of play over the goalline, and he chose to stay there while the attack went on, Lee Clark set up Gavin Peacock, and Peacock scooped a clever shot over Billy Mercer in the Rotherham goal.

The linesman flagged Kelly offside, the goal was disallowed, and the arguments rumbled on for days after.

"If that had counted, we would have sailed through by three or four goals," claimed Kevin Keegan, though he was far from unhappy at having secured a draw and a replay.

Robert Lee had produced an exquisite finish for the goal that was, even if the row over the goal that wasn't largely eclipsed it.

Lee Clark delivered a low cross to the 18-yard line after a run down the left flank, and Lee, though leaning back, kept the shot low and accurate enough to sweep past Mercer into the bottom left corner. A picture goal.

If Rotherham had been largely overrun in the first period, then perhaps encouraged by the disallowing of Peacock's goal, they emerged for the second fired up for the big push.

Newcastle, apparently content to defend their lead, found the initiative snatched by the underdogs, and the warnings were already evident when Steve Howey had to find a magnificent last-ditch tackle to stop former Magpie Tony Cunningham firing in from close range.

The Rotherham goal, when it did come, was blessed with huge dollops of good fortune.

When referee David Axcell penalised John Beresford for obstruction just outside the area, Rotherham striker Dean Barrick failed to notice the referee's raised arm signifying indirect, and struck a tremendous drive beyond the wall and plumb against the post.

Had the ball gone inside or outside the post, Newcastle would have had a goal-kick. But, by a miracle, it rebounded against the knee of Millers defender Nigel Johnson and into the net from four yards.

Referee Axcell confirmed later that he would have disallowed the goal had it gone in. But on the day, Lady Luck smiled upon Rotherham and frowned heavily upon Newcastle.

The most important consideration of all, though, was that Newcastle were still in the Cup. And the £200,000-plus from the replay would not come amiss at a club still £6m in debt.

Wednesday 27th January 1993 • Kenilworth Road • 7.45pm

LUTON TOWN 0 NEWCASTLE UNITED 0

Half-time 0-0 • Attendance 10,237

Referee Alf BUKSH (London)

Linesmen C. HENDERSON, C. PROUD

White and Blue Shirts, Blue Shorts	Goals	Black and White Striped Shirts, Black Shorts	Goals
1 Alec CHAMBERLAIN		1 Pavel SRNICEK	
2 John DREYER		2 Barry VENISON ❑	
3 Julian JAMES		3 John BERESFORD	
4 Marvin JOHNSON		4 Liam O'BRIEN	
5 Ceri HUGHES		5 Kevin SCOTT	
6 Trevor PEAKE		6 Steve HOWEY	
7 Paul TELFER		7 Robert LEE	
8 Martin WILLIAMS ‡		8 Gavin PEACOCK	
9 Jason REES †		9 David KELLY	
10 Phil GRAY		10 Lee CLARK	
11 David PREECE		11 Paul BRACEWELL	
Substitutes		*Substitutes*	
12 Scott OAKES (†74)		12 Brian KILCLINE	
14 Ian BENJAMIN (‡81)		14 Kevin SHEEDY	

BEFORE		P	W	D	L	F	A	pts	AFTER		P	W	D	L	F	A	pts
1	Newcastle	26	19	3	4	51	23	60	1	Newcastle	27	19	4	4	51	23	61
24	Luton	24	4	10	10	26	45	22	23	Luton	25	4	11	10	26	45	23

FACTFILE

Third away draw in succession cuts United lead to 12 points... bottom v top clash ends even... Hatters recover from 1-5 home Cup defeat in previous game... goalkeepers the stars in tense battle.

Magpies held by hectic Hatters

WHEN IT set the season in August, the Football League fixture computer must have programmed a little midwinter grudge against Newcastle United and their supporters.

In quick succession, United were faced with difficult midweek trips to Southend, Luton and Portsmouth: not exactly local derbies and home for last orders.

Even if the computer wasn't responsible for the Southend game going midweek - Essex police were - United's task clearly wasn't going to be made easy at source.

Luton may have been bottom of the table on January 27th, but there was no bottom-against-top feel about the game, as the Hatters fought with passion and pride.

The upshot was a taut and nervous encounter which balanced on a knife-edge throughout and always stood to be won and lost by one moment of inspiration.

Largely due to the inspiration of both goalkeepers, Alec Chamberlain and Pavel Srnicek, the winning goal never came, and the side with the worst home record in the league shared the honours with the side holding the best away record.

If the better chances fell to United, the most fell to Luton who started strongly and never let up.

In that hectic opening, Martin Williams headed wide with Srnicek out of position, and David Preece, set up by Williams, saw his close-in shot blocked.

Then Northumberland-born defender John Dreyer broke through in the 17th minute but Srnicek timed his dive to perfection.

By the time Phil Gray missed Luton's fourth good chance, United had still to make an impression on the Town defence.

But when they did carve out their first opportunity, it was the best of the match and should have divided the teams.

Gavin Peacock took up Lee Clark's great ball to shoot beyond Chamberlain only for Martin Johnson, racing back, to scoop the ball off the line.

Even then, Robert Lee, following up, looked a certain scorer, but Chamberlain threw himself in the way of the shot to complete a remarkable double escape.

As the pendulum swung ever more rapidly, Gray headed over for Luton and Kelly's header from a Bracewell cross brought another fine save from the agile Chamberlain.

The heavy, muddy pitch sapped the stamina of both sides, but the players drew on their reserves of energy to continue slugging it out.

Kelly, on 59 minutes, made a brave run to work a position from which he shot inches past the far post.

United at last began to assert some degree of superiority in the later stages and Gavin Peacock might have done better than chip a shot straight to Chamberlain when a hard, low shot might have paid better dividends.

Not that Luton were prepared to sit back, and Srnicek again had to be supremely alert to thwart Ian Benjamin as he weaved through the defence nine minutes from time.

As the goalless draw loomed, United went for the kill and in a dramatic final minute might twice have stolen victory.

First, Steve Howey, forging a set-piece up front, squeezed through at inside-left to measure a left-foot shot at the space inside the near post.

Chamberlain leaped to fist the ball behind.

Then, from an impossible position wide on the right touchline, the irrepressible Robert Lee dipped a fearsome volley which looked set to traverse Chamberlain until the keeper arched his back to pull off the last, and best, save of the match.

Sunday 31st January 1993 • St James' Park • 2.55pm

NEWCASTLE UNITED 1 DERBY COUNTY 1

Half-time 0-1 • Attendance 27,285

Referee David ALLISON (Lancaster)
Linesmen I. BILLINGHAM, M.RILEY

Black and White Striped Shirts, Black Shorts	Goals	Yellow and Blue Shirts, Blue Shorts	Goals
1 Pavel SRNICEK		1 Steve SUTTON	
2 Barry VENISON		2 Jason KAVANAGH	
3 John BERESFORD		3 Michael FORSYTH	
4 Liam O'BRIEN	90	4 Craig SHORT ❏	
5 Kevin SCOTT		5 Darren WASSALL †	
6 Steve HOWEY		6 Mark PEMBRIDGE	
7 Robert LEE		7 Tommy JOHNSON ❏	2
8 Gavin PEACOCK		8 Martin KUHL	
9 David KELLY †		9 Paul KITSON	
10 Lee CLARK		10 Marco GABBIADINI	
11 Kevin SHEEDY ‡		11 Mark PATTERSON	
Substitutes		*Substitutes*	
12 Brian KILCLINE (†77)		12 Paul SIMPSON	
14 Paul BRACEWELL (‡63)		14 Ted McMINN (†64)	

BEFORE	P	W	D	L	F	A	pts	AFTER	P	W	D	L	F	A	pts
1 Newcastle	27	19	4	4	51	23	61	1 Newcastle	28	19	5	4	52	24	62
12 Derby	25	10	4	11	40	35	34	12 Derby	26	10	5	11	41	36	35

FACTFILE

United's fourth draw in succession... O'Brien's injury-time goal saves a point as TV jinx strikes again... lead down to 11 points... ex-United boss Arthur Cox says Magpies were lucky... no home league victory over Rams for nine years.

Liam's late show beats TV jinx

PERHAPS it was something to do with the live TV jinx, but once again United struggled to capture their Sunday Best form for the cameras.

Geordie Tommy Johnson's second-minute goal for Derby dictated the course of the next 88 minutes, with United repeatedly pressing forward but County ever dangerous on the break.

And if 88 minutes of nailbiting scarcely helped the physical well-being of the home support, the explosion of relief and joy which greeted Liam O'Brien's injury time equaliser was almost worth waiting for. Almost . . .

Arthur Cox, now Derby manager but formerly at Newcastle, dearly wanted to put one over on his old club and had County's twin strikers Marco Gabbiadini and Johnson been as sharp as they were in the second minute, Cox's wishes might have been granted.

The latecomers in the 27,285 crowd were still wedging themselves into position when Gabbiadini took advantage of a slip by Kevin Scott to create the opening goal.

The former Sunderland star stroked a perfect ground cross along the six-yard line and with Pavel Srnicek unable to stretch far enough, Johnson also stretched and scored.

After the disappointments of three consecutive away draws, such an early reverse was exactly what United didn't need.

Nerves set in and the fluency and style so often seen before was strangely absent.

Even though David Kelly pinballed a reflex shot against the left post, United rarely looked like scoring in the first half.

Lee Clark twice went close: keeper Sutton blocked one shot then, with the keeper beaten for once, Darren Wassall blocked the other.

However, the greater danger came on the counter-attack from a Derby side which had honed the art of the breakaway into a devastating tactic.

An away record of seven wins in 14 League outings before the visit to Newcastle was ample evidence of the effectiveness of the ploy.

And it would surely have been eight from 15 had Gabbiadini not been guilty of an amazing miss in the 70th minute when his strength took him through one challenge then round Srnicek 15 yards from goal, but as the Derby striker turned and the crowd held its collective breath, the man they called Marco Goalo inexplicably scooped his final shot over the bar.

The roar of delight which greeted the miss had its roots in the infamous 1990 promotion play-off semi-final, when Gabbiadini, never to be forgiven, scored Sunderland's second goal in a 2-0 win at St James' Park.

Seven minutes after that let-off, Kevin Keegan sent on the giant Brian Kilcline for David Kelly. "Panic," he explained later when asked about his tactical thinking.

Panic or not, Kilcline it was who distracted the Derby defence in the first minute of injury time as Robert Lee's cross from the right fell for Liam O'Brien at the left post. A chest down, a right-foot thump, and United were level.

Arthur Cox, suitably peeved, was less than gracious afterwards: "That goal should have been academic," he moaned. "We had chances to kill United off." Kevin disagreed, and said so. "Arthur must have been to a different game to me. We had 60 to 70 percent of the possession and I believe we deserved three points."

One point or three, the United manager would be gratified that after chasing a game for 88 minutes, his side had enough left at the end to catch it.

Gavin Peacock in aerial action

Wednesday 3rd February 1993 • St James' Park • 7.45pm

NEWCASTLE UNITED 2 ROTHERHAM UNITED 0

Half-time 0-0 • *Attendance* 29,005
Referee David AXCELL (Southend)
Linesmen R. PEARSON, W. NATTRASS

Black and White Striped Shirts, Black Shorts	Goals	Red Shirts, White Shorts	Goals
1 Pavel SRNICEK		1 Billy MERCER	
2 Barry VENISON		2 Ally PICKERING	
3 John BERESFORD		3 Chris HUTCHINGS	
4 Liam O'BRIEN		4 Ian BANKS	
5 Kevin SCOTT		5 Nigel JOHNSON	
6 Steve HOWEY ‡		6 Nicky LAW †	
7 Robert LEE		7 Chris WILDER	
8 Gavin PEACOCK †		8 Shaun GOODWIN	
9 David KELLY	50	9 Jonathan HOWARD	
10 Lee CLARK	89	10 Shaun GOATER	
11 Paul BRACEWELL		11 Dean BARRICK	
Substitutes		*Substitutes*	
12 Kevin SHEEDY (†87)		12 Des HAZEL	
14 Brian KILCLINE (‡44)		14 Neil RICHARDSON (†84)	

Kevin Keegan completes first year in charge with replay win... second half goals clinch fifth-round tie at Blackburn... Rotherham axe ex-Magpie Tony Cunningham... Bracewell takes over from Sheedy in Newcastle midfield... United fly to Marbella for short break hours after final whistle.

David Kelly opens the scoring

United through in the Lee-way

THE FICKLE fates of the Velvet Bag had by now laid on a tasty little prospect... if United could finally dump Rotherham out of the FA Cup.

Blackburn v Newcastle in the fifth round had, in the eyes of Fleet Street, become Dalglish v Keegan even before Rotherham were edged off the Wembley trail in this fourth round replay.

But the way in which Newcastle earned the Ewood Park tie was less than convincing: without doubt, the two-goal margin flattered Kevin Keegan's side.

Workaday Rotherham comfortably matched their off-colour opponents in the first half, and more than once might have stolen a lead.

Had Shaun Goater and Dean Barrick shown a little more composure in front of goal, another giantkilling might have gone onto the already disconcertingly long Newcastle United list.

With the exception of a Gavin Peacock shot well saved by Billy Mercer, Newcastle looked uncomfortably like the struggling team of 12 months earlier: just before the advent of Mr Keegan as manager.

Whatever Keegan said at half-time, the transformation in the second half was remarkable: here, at last, was something of the slick style which had taken United to the top of Division One.

The watching Dalglish must have wondered which Newcastle side to believe, though Rotherham displayed enough spirit to keep the Blackburn manager watching them too, even after David Kelly's 51st-minute goal.

The opener, when it came, was classically simple and made the observer wonder what all the previous fuss had been about.

A John Beresford cross from the left, a defender's miss, and Kelly turned smoothly in

the box to shoot in off the diving Mercer.

With Liam O'Brien and Paul Bracewell at last dominating midfield, the supply line to the Rotherham strikers was stifled.

But the second goal which would kill the contest remained elusive, with Kelly twice more failing from good positions. Lee Clark, too, galloped through but could not find the necessary power and accuracy to beat Mercer.

No-one would have fancied Newcastle's chances had Rotherham pinched the equaliser their late rally perhaps deserved.

Never were the Yorkshiremen closer to a goal than in the 77th minute, when Ally Pickering, from an impossible position on the right corner of the area, produced a shot of awesome power.

It looked for all the world a goal until Pavel Srnicek launched himself across goal to make a backbreaking save of supreme quality: the best moment of a largely mundane match.

With Srnicek's save went Rotherham's last realistic chance, and it was left to Lee Clark to apply the coup de grace in the 89th minute.

Barry Venison advanced down the right to thread a long ball through Rotherham's depleted ranks which set Clark free on the right touchline. Clark, who had already missed from a similar position, angled in on Mercer's goal and this time shot low across the keeper into the bottom left corner.

Newcastle, after a struggle, were finally through. And the two old Liverpool heroes would meet in opposition at Blackburn ten days hence.

But Fleet Street had not got its prize easily.

Defenders turn suppliers - Barry Venison and John Beresford laid on United's goals

Tuesday 9th February 1993 • Fratton Park • 7.45pm

PORTSMOUTH 2 NEWCASTLE UNITED 0

Half-time 2-0 • *Attendance* 21,028

Referee Dermot GALLAGHER (Banbury)
Linesmen E. GREEN, B.INGRAM

Blue Shirts, White Shorts		Goals		Black and White Striped Shirts, Black Shorts		Goals
1	Alan KNIGHT		1	Pavel SRNICEK ❏	
2	Andy AWFORD		2	Barry VENISON	
3	Ray DANIEL		3	John BERESFORD	
4	Alan McLOUGHLIN		4	Liam O'BRIEN	
5	Kit SYMONS ❏	40	5	Kevin SCOTT	
6	Chris BURNS		6	Brian KILCLINE	
7	Chris PRICE		7	Robert LEE	
8	Mark CHAMBERLAIN †		8	Gavin PEACOCK	
9	Paul WALSH		9	David KELLY	
10	Guy WHITTINGHAM	13	10	Lee CLARK	
11	Warren ASPINALL ‡		11	Paul BRACEWELL †	

Substitutes		*Substitutes*	
12	Darryl POWELL (†87)	12	Kevin SHEEDY (†63)
14	Gavin MAGUIRE (‡31)	14	Alan NEILSON

BEFORE		P	W	D	L	F	A	pts	AFTER		P	W	D	L	F	A	pts
1	Newcastle	28	19	5	4	52	24	62	1	Newcastle	29	19	5	5	52	26	62
5	Portsmouth	28	12	8	8	48	34	44	5	Portsmouth	29	13	8	8	50	34	47

FACTFILE

Goal-guy Whittingham nets his 33rd of the season... David Kelly misses late penalty for United... Pompey's top home gate of the season to date... United lead now down to just seven points... Kilcline in for injured Howey.

Kit-Guy combo sinks Magpies

WITH UNITED'S batteries in need of recharging, Kevin Keegan had taken his players to the sunshine of Marbella within hours of the Cup replay against Rotherham.

Keegan knew a thing or two about relaxing in the millionaire's playground - after all, he had lived there for several years after retiring as a player. And it was a rejuvenated squad which flew straight in to Heathrow for the short journey to the south coast and Fratton Park.

Portsmouth, in February, had still to launch the late promotion run which brought such an anxious finale to the first division season.

But there was clear evidence on this night that Pompey were becoming a genuine force under the leadership of former Newcastle manager Jim Smith.

United didn't play badly: in fact, Keegan was quick to praise the standard of football from both sides on a hugely entertaining evening.

But it was Portsmouth who had the cutting edge known as Guy Whittingham which brought them full points.

Whittingham already had 32 goals to his name, and added No 33 as early as the 13th minute to give his side the crucial advantage.

Pompey full-back Ian Daniel might have beaten Whittingham to the first goal in the 12th minute but for a wasteful finish, but Whittingham showed how it should be dome 60 seconds later. The United defence opened up to the direct run

David Kelly - suffered a penalty miss

and Whittingham went clear to coolly round Pavel Srnicek and roll the ball into the empty net.

Newcastle needed to hit back quickly, but for all their fine approach play they were finding it hard to breach Portsmouth's well-drilled defence.

When Gavin Peacock and Lee Clark finally did so in the 25th minute, David Kelly fired wide. Then Clark beat the offside trap but was thwarted by the advancing Alan Knight; from the rebound, Liam O'Brien shot past the post.

Pompey, encouraged by a season's-best gate, had not won a corner until the 40th minute, but when it did arrive it brought with it the second goal.

Defender Kit Symons moved up for the set-piece and when the ball came to him Symons connected perfectly to leave Srnicek with no chance and United with a vast mountain to climb.

In a second half of great commitment, chances were few, even if quality was high.

But no better chance was there than the penalty awarded to United five minutes from the end, just as desperation was reaching an advanced stage.

John Beresford, playing against his former team, dribbled deep into the penalty area before being brought heavily to earth: a clear penalty, and a glorious chance for Kelly to revive United hopes.

Disastrously, Kelly's driven spot-kick struck the upper edge of the bar and disappeared into the packed crowd, taking with it United's last hope of a dividend.

"Football was the winner," said Keegan. "But they just about edged it and deserved to win."

Jim Smith had words of comfort for United and Keegan after the fourth league game without a victory.

"I still think they will go up," he said. and many good judges shared that view. But the doubts were beginning to creep in.

Saturday 13th February 1993 • Ewood Park • 3.00pm

BLACKBURN ROVERS 1 NEWCASTLE UNITED 0

Half-time 0-0 • *Attendance* 19,972

Referee Keith COOPER (Pontypridd)

Linesmen D. OLIVER, P. NEWTON

Blue and White Halved Shirts, White Shorts	Goals	Yellow Shirts, Green Shorts	Goals
1 Bobby MIMMS		1 Pavel SRNICEK	
2 David MAY		2 Barry VENISON	
3 Alan WRIGHT		3 John BERESFORD	
4 Tim SHERWOOD		4 Liam O'BRIEN	
5 Colin HENDRY		5 Kevin SCOTT	
6 Kevin MORAN		6 Brian KILCLINE	
7 Mark ATKINS ❑		7 Robert LEE	
8 Gordon COWANS		8 Gavin PEACOCK	
9 Roy WEGERLE	89	9 David KELLY	
10 Mike NEWELL		10 Lee CLARK	
11 Jason WILCOX		11 Kevin SHEEDY †	
Substitutes		*Substitutes*	
12 Tony DOBSON		12 Alan NEILSON	
14 Steve LIVINGSTONE		14 Paul BRACEWELL (†68)	

Roy Wegerle's last-minute goal shatters United's dreams... still no FA Cup quarter-final since 1976... first time this season United have two successive blank sheets... Rovers' first win in five games... Keegan misses game with heavy dose of 'flu.

FACTFILE

Pavel Srnicek - beaten in the last minute after a solid performance

Wiggly Wegerle's wonder winner

FOOTBALL can be a cruel game, but rarely can any defeat in Newcastle's long Cup history have been so harsh and heartbreaking as this.

For 90 minutes United had been the equals of Blackburn - Jack Walker's millions et al - but in the 91st, a Roy of the Rovers ending tipped the scales. Roy of the Rovers (fictional version) came to an end during 1992-93, and Roy of the Blackburn Rovers was to leave Ewood Park shortly after this tie.

How United must have wished Wegerle and Blackburn Rovers had never come together at all as this man of unpredictable genius jockeyed his way past Barry Venison and round Brian Kilcline before screwing a surprise shot across Pavel Srnicek and first bounce into the far corner of the net.

Kevin Keegan wasn't there to suffer it. A bad dose of the 'flu had deprived the press of their Dalglish-Keegan face-to-face, and Keegan of a trip to Lancashire. But listening to the radio in his sick bed back at Wynyard, Keegan must have risked a serious relapse as Wegerle drove a stake into United hearts.

Blackburn, without that formidable Geordie Alan Shearer up front, were but a shadow of the side which with him surged to the top of the Premier League early in the season.

And while United appeared content to soak up what little pressure Blackburn could bring to bear, it seemed Rovers had not the class or guile to pierce the Newcastle back four.

Pavel Srnicek had been a veritable rock in dealing with the stream of high balls and crosses as well as the occasional long-range shot.

But this was a tie fought out largely on the tactical middle ground, with United's unusually cautious approach choking the life out of Rovers.

If it all gave rise to a less-than-thrilling tie, it also seemed sure to bring the desired result and a replay at St James' Park 11 days hence.

United, in truth, created next to nothing in the way of goal chances: an early Kevin Scott header easily saved by Bobby Mimms, and a reflex shot from David Kelly which brought an academic save from Mimms - the offside flag was up.

The strength of United's performance was in its controlled resistance to Rovers, and the way in which they so frequently kept the ball away from the danger zones.

The Blackburn supporters were resigned to a replay after Jason Wilcox committed the miss of the match midway through the second half.

Wegerle was behind that, too, his cross-shot being parried by Srnicek and, after Barry Venison had blocked Wilcox's first shot at point-blank range, Wilcox put his follow-up shot impossibly wide of the gaping target.

The Newcastle fans who had queued through the night to buy tickets to the uncovered Darwen End filled Ewood Park with a wall of sound as the replay drew ever closer.

Only Wegerle silenced them and deprived Tyneside of a momentous Cup night.

Back in October, another Premier League side, Chelsea, had knocked United out of the League Cup with a late, late goal at Stamford Bridge.

That one hurt. But it was 'only' the League Cup and didn't hurt half as badly as the FA Cup.

For all United's failures in the FA Cup over the years, its power still runs deep in Geordie hearts.

Terry McDermott - took temporary charge

Sunday 21st February 1993 • Upton Park • 2.55pm

WEST HAM UNITED 0 NEWCASTLE UNITED 0

Half-time 0-0 • *Attendance 24,159*
Referee Keith COOPER (Pontypridd)
Linesmen D. CRICK, P. HARDIE

Claret Shirts, White Shorts	Goals	Black and White Striped Shirts, Black Shorts	Goals
1 Ludek MIKLOSKO		1 Pavel SRNICEK	
2 Kenny BROWN		2 Barry VENISON	
3 Julian DICKS ❏		3 John BERESFORD	
4 Steve POTTS		4 Liam O'BRIEN	
5 Tony GALE		5 Kevin SCOTT ❏	
6 Martin ALLEN ❏		6 Steve HOWEY	
7 Mark ROBSON		7 Robert LEE	
8 Peter BUTLER		8 Gavin PEACOCK	
9 Tony MORLEY		9 David KELLY	
10 Ian BISHOP		10 Lee CLARK	
11 Kevin KEEN †		11 Kevin SHEEDY	
Substitutes		*Substitutes*	
12 Matt HOLMES		12 Brian KILCLINE	
14 Steve JONES (†60)		14 Paul BRACEWELL	

BEFORE		P	W	D	L	F	A	pts	AFTER		P	W	D	L	F	A	pts
1	Newcastle	29	19	5	5	52	26	62	1	Newcastle	30	19	6	5	52	26	63
2	West Ham	30	17	7	6	56	29	58	2	West Ham	31	17	8	6	56	29	59

Newcastle retain four-point lead over Hammers in first v second clash... Howey the injured hero in superb defensive show... two booked in first five minutes... Keith Cooper is same ref for second game running... United's third successive blank... both keepers Czech mates.

Defence sets up a crucial point

STEVE Howey's transition from aspiring young centre-forward to accomplished central defender is one of the great Newcastle United success stories of recent times.

The teenage Howey's promise as a tall, goalscoring striker may or may not have come to fruition. But it's a fair bet that he would never have been as superb up front as he is at the back today.

When he became a defensive experiment in the United reserve side in the latter part of 1991-92, Howey looked instantly as if he was born to the part.

For much of 1992-93 the Wearside youngster, now 21, became an instant star alongside Kevin Scott: his few absences, such as at Blackburn, were keenly felt.

So when he appeared despite a groin strain for the most important league match of the season on this mid-February Sunday at West Ham, his selection was a calculated gamble by Kevin Keegan and Terry McDermott.

The gamble paid off magnificently. For Steve Howey had one of the best games of his short career, striding the Upton Park pitch as if he owned it and forming the central focus of a tremendous defensive display by United.

And if Barry Venison, John Beresford and Kevin Scott deserve their share of the credit for this priceless draw, no-one at Upton Park would take away anything from the 'babe' of the defence.

Others played their part in an absorbing encounter which always seemed likely to be settled, if at all, by a single goal.

Though chances were few and far between, Newcastle could easily have taken full points away from E13.

Before the match, West Ham had moved to within a mere four points of Newcastle at the top; another wrong result would have cut that to a single point.

On that basis, avoiding defeat was just as important as risking everything in pursuit of victory, and United's tactics were adapted accordingly.

The early exchanges were violent, Martin Allen cutting Howey in half with an appalling two-footed tackle which earned a second-minute booking. If Allen's intention was to upset Howey, he failed miserably.

Kevin Scott quickly followed Allen into the book for a bad late challenge on Trevor Morley, but after the early dishonours were shared, the game settled down to a contest of skill.

Lee Clark was close in the seventh minute, but Pavel Srnicek had to use his legs to block Allen's 12-yard drive after a dreadful mix-up between the keeper and Barry Venison.

Srnicek's flying save to divert a curling shot from Allen was of the highest quality and enabled Newcastle to turn around still level.

And early in the second half it looked as though Kevin Keegan's side had enough about them to take all three points.

Robert Lee's 20-yard special warmed the hands of Ludek Miklosko, and Kevin Sheedy only just failed to find the correct but tight angle for an open goal after Miklosko had missed Gavin Peacock's lob.

Clark's long-range shot and Julian Dicks' 30-yard free-kick almost broke the deadlock but the defences closed up the game in the final 20 minutes and the eventual draw became ever more probable.

"It was a fair result," said Keegan. "We are the best two sides in the division, but we tended to cancel each other out."

Future events would bear out the manager's words, but for now he was more than happy to have preserved that four-point lead at the top.

Wednesday 24th February 1993 • St James' Park • 7.45pm

NEWCASTLE UNITED 0 BRISTOL ROVERS 0

Half-time 0-0 • *Attendance* 29,372

Referee Ian CRUIKSHANKS (Hartlepool)
Linesmen J. DEVINE, D. MORRALL

Black and White Striped Shirts, Black Shorts		Goals		Blue and White Quartered Shirts, White Shorts		Goals
1	Pavel SRNICEK		1	Gavin KELLY		
2	Barry VENISON		2	Ian ALEXANDER		
3	John BERESFORD		3	Andy TILLSON		
4	Liam O'BRIEN		4	Steve YATES		
5	Kevin SCOTT		5	Paul HARDYMAN		
6	Brian KILCLINE		6	Andy REECE		
7	Robert LEE		7	Marcus BROWNING		
8	Gavin PEACOCK		8	Justin CHANNING ‡		
9	David KELLY		9	Marcus STEWART		
10	Lee CLARK		10	Carl SAUNDERS †		
11	Kevin SHEEDY †		11	Gary WADDOCK		

Substitutes			*Substitutes*		
12	Paul BRACEWELL		12	John TAYLOR (†70)	
14	Steve WATSON (†45)		14	Billy CLARK (‡47)	

BEFORE		P	W	D	L	F	A	pts
1	Newcastle	30	19	6	5	52	26	63
23	Rovers	30	8	5	17	38	60	29

AFTER		P	W	D	L	F	A	pts
1	Newcastle	31	19	7	5	52	26	64
22	Rovers	31	8	6	17	38	60	30

FACTFILE

Goals drought stretches to four games... minute's silence held for Bobby Moore... fans boo United off at full-time... Steve Watson plays first game in six months - and sets off for World Youth Cup in Australia.

United nerves begin to show

THE HARD bit over, United could now come home and collect three comfortable points off poor, struggling Bristol Rovers.

At least, that was the theory, The practice turned out to be considerably different.

Poor Bristol Rovers were anything but, and rather than a relegation side, they looked every inch United's equals; even if, on the night, that was not a difficult task. United were shocking.

Perhaps it was the Malcolm Allison influence, that ebullient old warhorse breathing new life into Rovers since his surprise appointment as manager.

Perhaps, too, it was a slight case of over-confidence in United, this game sandwiched as it was between trips to Portsmouth, Blackburn, West Ham and Tranmere.

Whatever it was, Newcastle had a collective off-day and by the end of an unhappy evening, the stark truth was that United had now clocked up four successive blank sheets.

For a team which failed to score in only four of the previous 28 league games, this was a major reversal in form, and a massive concern.

There were chances against Rovers: but rarely convincing, and rarely likely to break the deadlock.

Gavin Peacock and David Kelly laboured long and hard up front, but the touch just wasn't there, and a man who took half of each of those names made sure their drought continued.

Gavin Kelly in the Rovers goal was a beacon of quality on a mundane night and dealt splendidly with the few things which got through to him.

A first-half double save from Lee Clark was the pick, though the keeper was grateful to see Brian Kilcline's early header drift wide.

United needed an injection of new ideas and teenager Steve Watson provided exactly that when he came on as a half-time substitute for the out-of-touch Kevin Sheedy.

Watson, completely out of the first-team picture since the season's opener against Southend six months or more before, made an instant impact with his willingness to run at the Bristol defence.

Not that Watson's arrival woke up the rest of the side, and all his best endeavours came to nought.

Indeed Rovers, always willing to counter-attack, might twice have become only the second side to take full points from St James' Park.

In the 64th minute, Paul Hardyman crossed and Marcus Browning, in a good position, headed weakly wide of Pavel Srnicek's goal.

Then Browning beat the United offside trap on the right flank and closed in on goal. 29,372 people held their breath.

Browning inexplicably spurned the option of Marcus Stewart unmarked in front of goal and blazed his angled shot wide. Marcus MkII raged at Marcus MkI, and 29,372 people breathed a vast sigh of relief.

The restlessness of the crowd would have been checked had Gavin Kelly not pulled off a superb save from Gavin Peacock's volley in the 70th minute.

But the nerves jangled on, and the final whistle eventually sounded to a crescendo of booing: a sound rarely heard this season.

Kevin Keegan took exception to the booing, saying: "I don't think these players deserved to be booed off. It's not for me to tell the fans what to do, but it is very important they stick by us."

However, the fans pay their money and take their choice. They booed because Newcastle United had slipped far below the standards they were accustomed to.

And they booed because they were worried...

Sunday 28th February 1993 • Prenton Park • 3.00pm

TRANMERE ROVERS 0 NEWCASTLE UNITED 3

Half-time 0-2 • *Attendance* 13,082

Referee Michael PECK (Kendal)
Linesmen A. BUTLER, S. GRIFFITHS

White Shirts, White Shorts	Goals	Black and White Striped Shirts, Black Shorts	Goals
1 Eric NIXON		1 Pavel SRNICEK	
2 Dave HIGGINS		2 Barry VENISON	
3 Ged BRANNAN		3 John BERESFORD ❑	
4 Dave MARTINDALE		4 Liam O'BRIEN ❑	
5 Steve MUNGALL		5 Kevin SCOTT †	
6 Steve VICKERS		6 Steve HOWEY	
7 John MORRISSEY ❑		7 Robert LEE	26, 87
8 Neil McNAB †		8 Gavin PEACOCK	
9 Chris MALKIN		9 David KELLY	42
10 Ian MUIR ‡		10 Lee CLARK	
11 Pat NEVIN		11 Kevin SHEEDY	
Substitutes		*Substitutes*	
12 Mark HUGHES (†76)		12 Brian KILCLINE (†45) ‡	
14 Kenny IRONS (‡65)		14 Paul BRACEWELL (‡70)	

BEFORE		P	W	D	L	F	A	pts	AFTER		P	W	D	L	F	A	pts
1	Newcastle	31	19	7	5	52	26	64	1	Newcastle	32	20	7	5	55	26	67
6	Tranmere	29	14	6	9	50	38	48	6	Tranmere	30	14	6	10	50	41	48

United end the TV jinx - and the goals drought... tenth away league win of the season... first league win in seven games... Lee hits his seventh and eighth of the campaign... Aldridge-less Rovers destroyed by United... Rovers' fourth game without a goal.

Promotion rivals crushed in rout

AFTER four games without a goal, Newcastle could have wished for a less exacting match than one against a side beaten only once at home in the league all season.

Tranmere had a formidable reputation at Prenton Park: ten wins and four draws from the 15 league games, and 35 goals scored.

But most of those goals had been struck by Republic of Ireland striker John Aldridge, and in Aldridge's absence through injury, the goals had dried up and the home record vanished. Only two goals in five games, a home defeat against Luton, and three matches without a goal before meeting Newcastle. If United had worries about this fixture, then so did Tranmere.

Companions in distress, perhaps, but Rovers' distress was the more acute as United strolled to an unexpectedly comfortable victory on a cold and blustery Sunday afternoon.

The shortage of confidence in both sides was evident in an untidy opening, but it was United who shook the cobwebs away to take a 26th-minute lead which whipped the carpet from under Rovers' feet.

Lee Clark had already given notice of his intentions with a long run and pass which David Kelly put narrowly wide.

Then Clark set off again on the left, weaving inwards past two men to open up the space for a clear sight of goal from 18 yards. He connected weakly, but Rovers keeper Eric Nixon fumbled the ball and stood statuesque as Robert Lee stepped in to roll it back past him and into the right corner of the empty net.

In such narrow margins as a goalkeeping error are the stories of success and recovery written, and United built upon the gift as Tranmere fell nervously apart.

If Newcastle expected a strong Tranmere response, they were pleasantly surprised. Rovers were without inspiration - could Aldridge's absence really have made such a difference? - and their opponents dictated matters at will.

For once, the live TV jinx didn't trouble United; Kevin Sheedy almost rounded off a four-man move, but this time Nixon held his shot.

Then the second goal which put United out of reach arrived three minutes before the interval. Lee Clark planted a left-wing corner on Kevin Scott's head at the near post and David Kelly at the far leaned back to volley under Nixon's leaden body.

The Tranmere goalkeeper may have chosen this vital match to have one of his worst games, but there was no denying United's right to the two-goal half-time lead.

Tranmere did make a token effort at a fightback immediately after the interval, but Pavel Srnicek could have been watching the game in the warmth of the TV lounge for all he was called into action.

Normal service was resumed as United exerted an unshakeable grip, and Lee Clark could have won a penalty from Nevin's challenge but referee Peck saw no offence.

Brian Kilcline, a half-time substitute for the unwell Kevin Scott, was helped off with a back injury on 70 minutes and Paul Bracewell came on. But fears that the lanky Malkin would take advantage of the lack of height at the back (Howey was also sidelined) proved groundless. United simply defended in the Tranmere half.

Nixon blocked a Robert Lee shot and Kevin Sheedy put the rebound wide, then Kelly and Clark created a glorious three-on-one chance, but Sheedy misplaced the crucial final ball.

With Rovers committed to ineffective attack, United found the third and clinching goal in the 87th minute.

Clark was again the creator, drawing the Rovers defence to him and coolly releasing Robert Lee to advance and slide a left-foot shot low past the hapless Nixon.

Saturday 6th March 1993 • St James' Park • 3.00pm

NEWCASTLE UNITED 5 BRENTFORD 1

Half-time 1-0 • *Attendance* 30,006

Referee Ian HENDRICK (Preston)

Linesmen D. OLIVER, P. OXLEY

Black and White Striped Shirts, Black Shorts	Goals	Red and White Striped Shirts, Red Shorts	Goals
1 Pavel SRNICEK		1 Graham BENSTEAD	
2 Barry VENISON		2 Brian STATHAM	
3 John BERESFORD		3 Simon RATCLIFFE †	
4 Liam O'BRIEN		4 Keith MILLEN	
5 Kevin SCOTT	o.g.58	5 Jamie BATES	
6 Steve HOWEY †		6 Billy MANUEL	
7 Robert LEE	72	7 Joe ALLON	
8 Paul BRACEWELL	49	8 Micky BENNETT	
9 David KELLY	24	9 Shane WESTLEY	
10 Lee CLARK	55, 83	10 Gary BLISSETT	
11 Mark STIMSON		11 Paul STEPHENSON	
Substitutes		*Substitutes*	
12 Alan NEILSON (†73)		12 Murray JONES	
14 Kevin BROCK		14 Alan DICKENS (†69)	

BEFORE		P	W	D	L	F	A	pts	AFTER		P	W	D	L	F	A	pts
1	Newcastle	32	20	7	5	55	26	67	1	Newcastle	33	21	7	5	60	27	70
17	Brentford	32	10	7	15	39	46	37	17	Brentford	33	10	7	16	40	51	37

FACTFILE

Lee Clark double leads the way... United open the gap at top to seven points... Robert Lee's 65-yard miracle goal ruled out for offside against Brentford... Mark Stimson a revelation in midfield... 60-goal United England's top scorers again... Kelly takes over as United top marksman.

Bees have their wings clipped

MARK Stimson's contribution to the League season thus far had been to sit on the subs' bench for 90 minutes in the home victory against Tranmere on October 10th. But now, with Kevin Sheedy injured, the former Spurs reserve was drafted into the left side of midfield.

Stimson had played in this position four times for United reserves, and back in his White Hart Lane days had occasionally filled the midfield role with some style. But to most of the 30,006 fans who filled St James' Park this day, this was a whole new version of the Mark Stimson they thought they knew.

Stimmo was superb in the dismantling of a Brentford side to whom football of the Newcastle United variety was quite simply something from another planet. Kevin Keegan reserved special mention for Stimson afterwards. "Terrific," he said. "John Beresford enjoyed playing down the left side with him, and the shirt is Mark's at the moment."

Ironically, within days, Keegan signed Scott Sellars for £700,000 from Leeds and Stimson was consigned to the reserves again.

On the wider scale, this was destruction of a Brentford side which had to be - and was - swept contemptuously aside. Once David Kelly had scrambled the first goal in the 24th minute following an error by keeper Graham Benstead, there was only to be one winner.

With Lee Clark pushing up alongside Kelly, chances came in a torrent: Lee, Clark and Bracewell all went close, and Kelly headed narrowly wide from the best of them.

Somehow it was only 1-0 at half-time. But four minutes after the restart, Paul Bracewell drove in the second after great work from Clark, Stimson and Lee.

The Londoners, with former Newcastle strikers Joe Allon and Paul Stephenson, making his debut, up front, had been expected to give United a run for their money. But Allon and Stephenson were distant spectators as United concentrated the bulk of the action in and around Benstead's area, and inevitably the third goal arrived in the 55th minute.

This time a defensive mix-up was punished by Lee Clark, who moved in to crash a beauty behind Benstead from an angle on the right.

Even when Brentford did score, United did it for them, Kevin Scott diving to head Billy Manuel's left-wing cross in off the far post, to the accompaniment of a few Czech expletives from Pavel Srnicek. Any prospect of a Brentford comeback lasted but 14 minutes: the time it took for Robert Lee to power a header into the bottom corner for the finest goal of the game.

The finest goal that counted, that is. For, three minutes after David Kelly had also had a goal controversially disallowed, Robert Lee 'scored' what should and would have been the goal of a lifetime.

Alan Neilson chased a long ball into the Brentford half only to be beaten to the punch by Benstead, who raced 35 yards from his line to fly-kick the ball back into the Newcastle half.

Robert Lee instantly chested the ball down and, from 65 yards, left-footed an amazing shot back over the retreating keeper's shoulder and merrily on into the unguarded net.

Pandemonium on the terraces. But amongst it all, referee Hendrick had awarded a free-kick for offside, the linesman flagging against a Brentford forward caught napping by Benstead's clearance. Perhaps the only example of a goal disallowed for offside against the team which CONCEDED it?

Nonetheless, Lee Clark added the fifth seven minutes from time, striding through Brentford's defence to shoot between the keeper's legs.

Wonderful entertainment. But the supreme irony was that, in a game of six goals, the biggest talking point should be a goal that wasn't.

Wednesday 10th March 1993 • St James' Park • 7.45pm

NEWCASTLE UNITED 2 CHARLTON ATHLETIC 2

Half-time 2-1 • *Attendance* 29,582

Referee Richard POULAIN (Huddersfield)
Linesmen T. HEILBRON, M. ROBINSON

Black and White Striped Shirts, Black Shorts		Goals	Red Shirts, White Shorts		Goals
1	Pavel SRNICEK		1	Mike SALMON	
2	Mark ROBINSON		2	Darren PITCHER	
3	John BERESFORD		3	Steve GATTING	
4	Liam O'BRIEN		4	Paul BACON	
5	Kevin SCOTT		5	Simon WEBSTER	
6	Steve HOWEY		6	Stuart BALMER	
7	Robert LEE	1	7	Scott HOUGHTON †	
8	Paul BRACEWELL		8	Scott MINTO ❏	
9	David KELLY	45	9	Carl LEABURN	48
10	Lee CLARK		10	Garry NELSON	9
11	Scott SELLARS †		11	Colin WALSH	
	Substitutes			*Substitutes*	
12	Alan NEILSON		12	Alex DYER (†86)	
14	Mark STIMSON (†74)		14	Shaun NEWTON	

BEFORE		P	W	D	L	F	A	pts	AFTER		P	W	D	L	F	A	pts
1	Newcastle	33	21	7	5	60	27	70	1	Newcastle	34	21	8	5	62	29	71
9	Charlton	33	12	11	10	39	32	47	9	Charlton	34	12	12	10	41	34	48

FACTFILE

Robert Lee scores against old team in 48 SECONDS... Srnicek's 25th-birthday blunder lets in Leaburn for second equaliser... Scott Sellars and Mark Robinson make their Newcastle debuts... Stimson replaces Sellars in second half.

Blunders let the points slip away

UNITED'S defence was the tightest in the first division and the rock upon which the midfield and strikers were so often able to build their assaults upon the opposition.

But two of the season's very best performers, Steve Howey and Pavel Srnicek, committed the errors which allowed Charlton to steal a point and deny United the chance to put yet more daylight between themselves and the pursuing pack.

Twice United led; twice Charlton were gifted equalisers.

And despite non-stop pressure in the late second half, the lead refused to come back to United for a third and decisive time.

It looked plain sailing when United surged into the lead after just 48 seconds, Robert Lee taking on Kevin Scott's through ball to drill a rising left-foot shot past the leaping Salmon.

The fans sat back in anticipation, and were in the mood to forgive David Kelly the lapse of shooting straight at the Charlton keeper after a fine ball from Lee Clark.

But they weren't in such a benevolent mood in the ninth minute when Steve Howey, in a rare moment of panic, handed Charlton their first equaliser.

Howey dwelt too long on a simple interception on the edge of the box, lost the ball between tangled feet, and touched it into the path of Garry Nelson who beat Pavel Srnicek low to the keeper's right.

United's response was to lay siege to the Athletic goal, but somehow the conviction which immediately followed Lee's early goal was no longer there.

Though undeniably on top, United could have been caught out again when Carl Leaburn,

unmarked 18 yards from goal, produced a ragged finish, shooting horribly wide of the left post.

Scott Sellars, the new signing in ahead of one-game revivalist Mark Stimson, had been a largely anonymous figure on his debut until first-half injury time.

But when United won a dubious free-kick on the right edge of the 18-yard line, Sellars picked out David Kelly's run, and Kelly's header was perfectly measured into the right corner.

Surely, this time, Charlton could find no way back. But there was a way back, courtesy of Pavel Srnicek.

Three minutes into the second half, Srnicek came for Stuart Balmer's high and hopeful ball but utterly failed to gauge Carl Leaburn's arrival on the scene.

Srnicek flapped at air: Leaburn's head connected first, and the ball bounced almost apologetically into the open net.

The anxiety engendered by two such goals spread through the players and the crowd, and the subsequent attempts at a third goal smacked increasingly of desperation.

For a moment, on the hour, it seemed David Kelly had done it, but he had used an outstretched fist to divert John Beresford's cross into the net.

Then Liam O'Brien, showing great invention, worked a one-two with Clark on the edge of the box to go through one-on-one with Salmon.

Instead of shooting, O'Brien cleverly lifted the ball over the keeper, followed in towards the empty net, and slid mortified into the back of it as Gatting appeared from nowhere to head out from under the bar.

It was, as they say, one of those games, and while the point kept United well ahead of third place, a chance to bring promotion a giant step closer was wasted and lost.

There was still a lot to do and another unnerving home draw didn't help.

Saturday 13th March 1993 • County Ground • 3.00pm

SWINDON TOWN 2 NEWCASTLE UNITED 1

Half-time 0-1 • *Attendance* 17,574

Referee Graham POLL (Berkhamsted)

Linesmen R. THOMAS, A. HOWELLS

Red Shirts, Red Shorts		Goals	Black and White Striped Shirts, Black Shorts		Goals
1	Fraser DIGBY		1	Pavel SRNICEK	
2	Nicky SUMMERBEE		2	Barry VENISON	
3	Paul BODIN	51p	3	John BERESFORD	
4	Adrian VIVEASH ❏		4	Liam O'BRIEN †	
5	Colin CALDERWOOD	55	5	Kevin SCOTT	
6	Shaun TAYLOR		6	Steve HOWEY ❏	
7	Paul HUNT †		7	Robert LEE	
8	Ross MacLAREN		8	Paul BRACEWELL	
9	David MITCHELL ·		9	David KELLY	43
10	Martin LING ❏		10	Lee CLARK	
11	Steve WHITE ❏		11	Scott SELLARS ❏	
	Substitutes			*Substitutes*	
12	Shaun CLOSE		12	Mark ROBINSON	
14	Brian MARWOOD (†78)		14	Andy COLE (†63)	

BEFORE		P	W	D	L	F	A	pts	AFTER		P	W	D	L	F	A	pts
1	Newcastle	34	21	8	5	62	29	71	1	Newcastle	35	21	8	6	63	31	71
4	Swindon	33	16	9	8	57	42	57	3	Swindon	34	17	9	8	59	43	60

FACTFILE

'Handball' goal gives Swindon the points on day of controversy... five booked in bitter battle... £1.75m record signing Andy Cole makes his United debut as 63rd-minute substitute... Swindon move up to third place, 11 points behind United.

White takes hand as United slump

UNDER the leadership of first Ossie Ardiles, then Glenn Hoddle, Swindon Town had earned a reputation for cultured, classy football.

Two marvellously entertaining games between United and Swindon at St James' Park in recent times lived on in the memory.

But on this dark day of violence, intimidation and bitterness, Swindon tore their own reputation to shreds, resorting to unpleasant lengths to get the result they craved.

Portsmouth's former Newcastle manager, Jim Smith, had warned United of Swindon's "over-physical approach" after Pompey's 1-0 defeat at the County Ground two weeks before.

Smith, as United found to their cost, was right. And the feebleness of referee Graham Poll conspired against them.

Kevin Keegan was an angry man after the match as he left Wiltshire empty-handed through Swindon's two-goal second-half fight-back. But it had looked good for United when, between late tackles and furious exchanges, David Kelly had grabbed the lead in the 42nd minute.

Barry Venison picked up a clearance from a corner and Scott Sellars joined in to return the ball into the area, where Kelly chested down and struck a finely-judged shot past Fraser Digby from 15 yards.

Swindon, who had beaten play-off rivals Millwall, Tranmere and Portsmouth in their three previous home games, were committed to claiming their fourth prized scalp.

But only the tomahawks were missing as the County Ground became the Wild West in a fraught second half.

Only six minutes had passed when Liam O'Brien challenged Steve White in the United box in an innocuous position. White went down and Mr Poll pointed, controversially, to the penalty spot. Paul Bodin, once on loan at Newcastle, scored easily from the penalty kick.

White, one of three Swindon players booked for fouls, was to be a central figure, though even he must have laughed up his sleeve at Town's second goal three minutes later.

Everyone in the ground saw White use his hand to control a bouncing ball as he ran on to win a corner. Everyone, that is, except the referee and his two linesmen. But no evil was seen, heard or spoken and when Paul Bodin played in the disputed corner, Colin Calderwood cracked a thunderous shot past Pavel Srnicek.

In the most unjust of circumstances, United, for the first time this league season, found themselves behind after leading.

The salvage operation grew increasingly difficult as time slipped by, Kelly striking just over on the run, and Sellars having his free-kick tipped over.

New £1.75m record signing Andy Cole came on for Liam O'Brien with 27 minutes left to partner Kelly up front, but without success.

In injury time - of which there was plenty - Kevin Scott received a boot in the face as he moved in with only Digby to beat.

But neither the penalty nor the indirect free-kick was awarded, and Swindon celebrated their ill-gotten gains with Glenn Hoddle's Manager of the Month champagne.

Andy Cole - United debut

Saturday 20th March 1993 • St James' Park • 3.00pm

NEWCASTLE UNITED 4 NOTTS COUNTY 0

Half-time 1-0 • *Attendance* 30, 029
Referee Terry HOLBROOK (Wightwick)
Linesmen P. KITSON, W. NATTRASS

Black and White Striped Shirts, Black Shorts		Goals	Purple Shirts, White Shorts		Goals
1	Pavel SRNICEK		1	Steve CHERRY	
2	Barry VENISON		2	Chris SHORT	
3	John BERESFORD		3	Michael JOHNSON ‡	
4	Paul BRACEWELL		4	Dean THOMAS	
5	Kevin SCOTT ‡		5	Paul COX	
6	Steve HOWEY		6	Richard WALKER	
7	Robert LEE	32	7	Gary LUND	
8	Andy COLE	70	8	Mark DRAPER	
9	David KELLY	53, 62	9	Kevin WILSON	
10	Lee CLARK †		10	Paul DEVLIN †	
11	Scott SELLARS		11	David SMITH	

Substitutes			*Substitutes*		
12	Gavin PEACOCK (†77)		12	Steve SLAWSON (†69)	
14	Mark ROBINSON (‡72)		14	Andy WILLIAMS (‡72)	

BEFORE		P	W	D	L	F	A	pts	AFTER		P	W	D	L	F	A	pts
1	Newcastle	35	21	8	6	63	31	71	1	Newcastle	36	22	8	6	67	31	74
16	County	35	9	12	14	42	55	39	19	County	36	9	12	15	42	59	39

FACTFILE

Liam O'Brien ruled out long-term. Bracewell comes in... United's first home league win over County for 67 years... Cole scores on his full United debut... Kelly's pair takes his tally to 23.

Goal king Cole rounds it all off

ANDY Cole had been deployed only as substitute at Swindon following a hectic chase around the country in the days prior, but now, after a full week of preparation, United's record signing made his full debut.

The Tyneside public came to judge, and on the basis of a moderate display by Cole, reserved judgement.

But there was in his 70th-minute goal a signpost to the future which would be so dramatically developed in the following weeks.

United, after a 30-minute spell of blinding brilliance, led 3-0 when David Kelly, wide on the right, slipped a simple angled ball to Cole's feet 14 yards out and with his back to goal at the near post.

With a defender at his heels, Cole showed all the value of £1.75m with a devastating turn and right-foot shot between keeper Steve Cherry and the near post.

Those who had come prepared to doubt Cole's goalscoring ability put their doubts aside: but there were still reservations that Cole could integrate with the flowing, one-touch football which was by now United's trademark.

After a stuttering first period, United had switched on to a period of rampant, glittering football which completely overwhelmed struggling County. Had that standard been produced from first to last, this would surely have been the performance of the season, but as it was, United appeared beset by uncertainty in the early stages.

Only when Robert Lee broke the deadlock on 32 minutes was the blue touch paper lit, and if Lee's goal perhaps owed something to fortune, it was no less welcome for that.

Scott Sellars and David Kelly worked the opening, playing in Lee on the right to strike a shot across Cherry and in off the head of the covering Richard Walker.

The shot may or may not have been net-bound but was credited to Lee: his 11th of the season, and fifth in five games.

Suddenly, United were on fire and six minutes later Lee Clark should have doubled the lead but contrived to shoot wide of an open goal from little more than six yards after Cherry patted the ball to him under pressure.

Notts, brave but limited, had depended upon their shaky defence for any dividend and, once forced to come forward, opened up numerous avenues for the hungry Newcastle forwards.

Inevitably, their fragile house of cards collapsed around them, with Kelly adding the belated second after a cross by Lee and a grotesque miskick by Paul Cox.

Two untidy goals so far: but a third goal of majestic quality made up for any shortfall.

This time, Cole won a ball on half-way to release Clark into oceans of space on the right flank. Clark made ground and picked out David Kelly with a cross of such accuracy that the Republic of Ireland never had to break stride as he guided a header into the top left corner.

County eventually discovered the Newcastle penalty area, and Pavel Srnicek was called upon to make an important save, diving at the feet of the clean-through Mark Draper. Then, as County showed what they might have been capable of with some adventure in their hearts, Gary Lund pinged a snapshot against the bar.

As if to punish County for their daring, United produced the fourth and last goal, and the headline writers produced the inevitable Goal King Cole stories.

"It was a real striker's goal," said Kevin Keegan of Cole's 70th-minute strike, adding: "He will get a few more of them."

Reflecting on United's takeover after the first goal, Keegan went on: "We were in third gear but not fourth - then we went into overdrive and gave the crowd a feast."

Tuesday 23rd March 1993 • Vicarage Road• 7.45pm

WATFORD 1 NEWCASTLE UNITED 0

Half-time 0-0 • *Attendance* 11,634

Referee Roger GIFFORD (Llanbradach)
Linesmen C. BREAKSPEAR, M. DEARING

Yellow, Red and Black Shirts, Red Shorts	Goals	Black and White Striped Shirts, White Shorts	Goals
1 Keith WAUGH		1 Pavel SRNICEK	
2 Jason SOLOMAN		2 Barry VENISON	
3 Barry ASHBY		3 John BERESFORD	
4 Keith DUBLIN		4 Paul BRACEWELL	
5 David HOLDSWORTH		5 Kevin SCOTT	
6 Gerard LAVIN		6 Steve HOWEY	
7 Andy HESSENTHALER		7 Robert LEE	
8 Roger WILLIS †		8 Andy COLE	
9 Paul FURLONG	58	9 David KELLY	
10 Ken CHARLERY ❏		10 Lee CLARK	
11 Gary PORTER		11 Scott SELLARS †	
Substitutes		*Substitutes*	
12 Darren BAZELEY (†78)		12 Brian KILCLINE	
14 Bruce DYER		14 Mark ROBINSON (†73)	

BEFORE		P	W	D	L	F	A	pts	AFTER		P	W	D	L	F	A	pts
1	Newcastle	36	22	8	6	67	31	74	1	Newcastle	37	22	8	7	67	32	74
14	Watford	36	11	9	16	51	64	42	14	Watford	37	12	9	16	52	64	45

FACTFILE

Andy Cole's only game in first five without a goal... Hornets snatch first win in five outings... Furlong goal stops the United bandwagon... United lead still five points, but Portsmouth creep closer.

Toil and trouble for unlucky Mags

KEVIN Keegan's whimsical suggestion that United could end the League season as they started - with 11 straight wins - had been turned into something of a crusade by the press.

After Notts County, it was one down and ten to go. But the sort of run that happens once is a century is hardly likely to happen twice in the same season.

And so it proved on a night of frustration as Watford ended the crusade almost before it had begun.

Watford, after four successive defeats, were considered nothing more than another stepping-stone along the Premier League path: by the fans, if not Kevin Keegan, Terry McDermott and the players.

United dominated, perhaps inevitably: but the longer the match went without a goal to the visitors, so a goal for the home side looked ever more likely.

No game is easy, and when the Fates conspire, it can become impossible; such was the case at Vicarage Road.

United played well in all areas except the most vital one - putting the ball in the net. And even if Watford keeper Keith Waugh, playing his first game of the season, was the busiest and best man on view, he ought to have been beaten more than once. Robert Lee might have been the man to do it, but he shot over on the run after a fine Sellars-Clark move.

By and large, though, the first half became bogged down in a ragged midfield war, and even though United looked the likelier bet, the danger of leaking a goal out of the blue was always there.

After Clark set up David Kelly to bring a fine save from Waugh, and Andy Cole's 20-yard effort was brilliantly tipped over, so it proved.

Following another near-miss from Cole, the goal that old Dame Fortune had planned duly arrived.

Barry Venison's challenge on Gary Porter was scarcely worth the description of foul, but referee Gifford construed it as obstruction and awarded an indirect free-kick on the left.

Porter's cross reached David Holdsworth who headed down and across the six-yard area where, amid an almighty scramble, Paul Furlong squeezed the ball past Pavel Srnicek.

Watford had created little in open play but United's fears that a set-piece could prove their undoing had been horribly realised.

With a mountain to climb and just 32 minutes in which to do so, United poured forward. Cole, showing the power which persuaded Keegan to part with £1.75m, looked increasingly United's best hope of an equaliser.

He brought another resourceful save from Waugh with a 20-yard shot; as did Lee Clark moments after.

It seemed implausible that Keegan's side would leave Vicarage Road empty-handed, but Watford were edging their way to the final whistle with a potent combination of desperation and weight of numbers in defence.

Ken Charlery - United's League Cup executioner at Peterborough in 1991-92 - was booked for timewasting as Watford clung onto their lead. And even in the final minute, when Robert Lee beat Waugh with a venomous shot, defender Barry Ashby materialised on the goalline to turn the ball clear.

It was a bad defeat on a forgettable night. And United had failed to score for the first time in six games.

Robert Lee - denied in the final minute

Sunday 28th March 1993 • St James' Park • 3.00pm

NEWCASTLE UNITED 2 BIRMINGHAM CITY 2

Half-time 0-2 • *Attendance 27,087*

Referee Jim PARKER (Preston)

Linesmen R. FURNANDIZ, G. SPOONER

Black and White Striped Shirts, Black Shorts		Goals	Yellow Shirts, Yellow Shorts		Goals
1	Pavel SRNICEK		1	Bob CATLIN	
2	Barry VENISON		2	Scott HILEY	
3	John BERESFORD		3	John FRAIN	
4	Paul BRACEWELL		4	George PARRIS	
5	Kevin SCOTT		5	Richard DRYDEN	
6	Steve HOWEY		6	Trevor MATTHEWSON	
7	Robert LEE ❑	62	7	Paul MOULDEN	
8	Andy COLE	60	8	Ian RODGERSON	38
9	David KELLY		9	Andy SAVILLE	32
10	Lee CLARK		10	Dean PEER	
11	Scott SELLARS		11	David SMITH	
	Substitutes			*Substitutes*	
12	Brian KILCLINE		12	Paul MARDON	
14	Mark ROBINSON		14	Paul TAIT	

BEFORE		P	W	D	L	F	A	pts	AFTER		P	W	D	L	F	A	pts
1	Newcastle	37	22	8	7	67	32	74	1	Newcastle	38	22	9	7	69	34	75
20	City	37	11	8	18	36	56	41	19	City	38	11	9	18	38	58	42

FACTFILE

United two goals behind at home for first time... two goals in two minutes seals great fightback... Hartlepool old boy Saville scores one and makes one for City... Birmingham owner David Sullivan attacked by fan... Cole makes it two goals from three games, but only three wins in 13 games now for United.

Double-strike secures a point

MARCH was not a good time to have to play Birmingham City.

Previously diving headlong into the Second Division, City had been recently revived by the takeover of so-called porn king David Sullivan.

Sullivan's money and Terry Cooper's blitz of the transfer market had brought together a virtual new team which, playing with verve and style, had risen from the lower reaches of the table with three straight victories.

Electric Blues, perhaps. And a trip to play the League leaders was just the sort of acid test they would relish.

One of the men recruited by Cooper was Andy Saville, a tough, bristle-haired centre-forward not afraid to go in where it hurts if it means hurting the other team.

And Saville hurt United badly when he scored one and made a second for Birmingham in a six-minute first-half spell which shook Newcastle and their fans to the core.

It was less the live TV jinx than City's resilience which kept United from scoring in a first half-hour of fluctuating fortunes.

The initial hammer blow came on 32 minutes when David Smith's low ball in from the left caused enough defensive panic for Saville to pounce and prod the ball past Pavel Srnicek from five yards.

Saville's reaction in front of the Gallowgate End may not have qualified him for the Nobel Peace Prize, but there was no denying that he was unsettling a strangely unsure Newcastle defence.

And six minutes later City became the first visiting side to establish a two-goal lead at St James' Park when Saville supplied the bullet and Ian Rodgerson pulled the trigger.

United's defenders were left gaping at each other in despair as Saville's teasing cross bounced gently along the six-yard line, and Rodgerson was allowed to dive in and turn a simple header into the right hand corner.

This was a severe test of United's character: and they came through it in a second half of passion and mounting drama.

It looked bad for United when Cole blazed wildly over the bar from a perfect position 14 yards out.

But Cole was straight back, showing lightning reactions to divert Scott Sellars' poked cross past Bob Catlin and into the net from close range.

The gateway to a comeback had scarcely been marked when United crashed through it two minutes later, Sellars wriggling down the left flank and whipping over a tantalising ball which tempted Catlin from his line and allowed Robert Lee to slide it in at the far post to score.

Bedlam reigned. Birmingham, surely, would buckle under the heat. Rorke's Drift had nothing on this one.

But, to City's eternal credit, they stood their ground superbly, slowly drawing the sting from United and battling their tenacious way to a fully-deserved point.

David Kelly, Robert Lee and Andy Cole all went close to pinching victory; Steve Howey, in the final minute, swept Kelly's cross over the bar when it seemed impossible not to score.

But Birmingham, as if to remind everyone they they too had teeth, almost won it in injury time, Paul Moulden producing a 25-yard dipping shot which might have beaten a lesser keeper than Srnicek.

For the neutral, it had been a thrilling, rivetting encounter. But neither United nor City could be satisfied at the eventual outcome.

And Portsmouth, 18 points behind United at the start of February, were now an ominous six points away, with West Ham five points adrift.

Saturday 3rd April 1993 • Abbey Stadium • 3.00pm

CAMBRIDGE UNITED 0 NEWCASTLE UNITED 3

Half-time 0-1 • *Attendance 7,925*

Referee Gerald ASHBY (Worcester)
Linesmen W. JORDAN, R. KIRK

Amber Shirts, Black Shorts	Goals	Black and White Striped Shirts, White Shorts	Goals
1 John FILAN		1 Pavel SRNICEK	
2 Andy FENSOME		2 Barry VENISON	
3 Alan KIMBLE		3 John BERESFORD	
4 Paul RAYNOR		4 Paul BRACEWELL †	
5 Mike HEATHCOTE		5 Kevin SCOTT	
6 Phil CHAPPLE ‡		6 Steve HOWEY	41
7 Danny O'SHEA ❑		7 Robert LEE	
8 Steve CLARIDGE		8 Andy COLE ❑	53
9 Michael DANZEY †		9 David KELLY	46
10 Gary CLAYTON ❑		10 Lee CLARK	
11 Neil LYNE		11 Scott SELLARS	
Substitutes		*Substitutes*	
12 Kevin BARTLETT (†63)		12 Brian KILCLINE	
14 Matthew RUSH (‡63)		14 Mark ROBINSON (†71)	

BEFORE	P	W	D	L	F	A	pts	AFTER	P	W	D	L	F	A	pts
1 Newcastle	38	22	9	7	69	34	75	1 Newcastle	39	23	9	7	72	34	78
22 Cambridge	38	9	13	16	40	60	40	22 Cambridge	39	9	13	17	40	63	40

FACTFILE

United's second three-goal defeat of Cambridge... Howey's second goal of the season breaks deadlock... Cole does it again, and Kelly hits No 24... 11th away win of the season equals United 1936-37 club record... five points clear with seven games to go.

United display true masterclass

SIX POINTS ahead of third place and with eight games remaining, United needed a convincing victory to repair the damage inflicted by Watford and Birmingham.

And at Cambridge, they delivered it. Kevin Keegan called this "the best performance of the season", and he had good reason as Newcastle dominated, decimated and finally destroyed the struggling home side.

Let no-one doubt that Cambridge were a very poor side indeed. But let no-one doubt, either, that few teams in Britain could have lived with Newcastle United this day.

The only worry was the long wait for the first goal, but once it arrived two more followed in 12 minutes and it was plain sailing from there on.

Cambridge, at their compact and often intimidating little Abbey Stadium, could have been expected to scrap long and hard for much-needed survival points.

But they rarely got within tackling range of a Newcastle side virtually without a weakness.

Andy Cole, by now settling encouragingly into the side, gave United an extra dimension - and it was one which paid off handsomely.

Route One may not have been United's style before now, but when the chance of a long ball beckoned, there was now some genuine mileage in using it.

Cole chased and harried the Cambridge defenders into a nervous mess, scored one and could have had several.

At the other end, meanwhile, Pavel Srnicek may as well have enrolled for a one-day English Language course at the nearby University for all he was needed against Cambridge's feeble strike force.

But, by contrast, Cambridge's Australian debutant goalkeeper John Filan was more Down and Out than Down Under.

The barrage started early: Barry Venison drove a splended long-range shot just over in the first minute.

Then the procession... Filan saved twice from Robert Lee, and twice from David Kelly. Andy Cole shot over from a good position, then promptly did it again.

"I was beginning to get worried when the first goal wouldn't come," admitted Keegan later.

He needn't have worried, for on 41 minutes Scott Sellars regathered the ball after a half-cleared corner and picked out Steve Howey for a point-blank header past Filan.

One minute after the turnaround, Howey became maker with that rarely-seen Newcastle United tactic: the upfield hoof.

When Howey's hoofed clearance dropped from the skies, Cambridge defender Micky Heathcote obligingly slipped and Kelly galloped through the open channel to slide a shot low past Filan.

Heathcote, once of Sunderland, must have burned with embarrassment at that, and his demeanour wasn't helped by the ease with which Cole steamed past him seven minutes later to despatch a shot across Filan which was on its way back out of the far corner before the keeper had begun his dive.

Newcastle switched off a little in the final half-hour, but might yet have had another, referee Ashby interpreting a foul on Clark - apparently inside the area - as a free-kick inches outside.

Sellars and Kelly also deserved a goal for late efforts but there was still immense satisfaction in the manner, margin and style of the victory.

And with Portsmouth ending their winning run with a draw at Millwall, the gap to third place was eight points again; West Ham remained five adrift in second.

The Holy Grail was drawing nearer...

Wednesday 7th April 1993 • St James' Park • 7.45pm

NEWCASTLE UNITED 6 BARNSLEY 0

Half-time 2-0 • *Attendance* 29,460

Referee Philip WRIGHT (Anderton)

Linesmen I. GRANDIDGE, D. OLIVER

Black and White Striped Shirts, Black Shorts		Goals	Red Shirts, White Shorts		Goals
1	Pavel SRNICEK		1	Phil WHITEHEAD	
2	Barry VENISON		2	Ian HENDON	
3	John BERESFORD	67p	3	Gary FLEMING	
4	Paul BRACEWELL ‡		4	Charlie BISHOP	
5	Kevin SCOTT		5	Gerry TAGGART	
6	Steve HOWEY †		6	Brendan O'CONNELL	
7	Robert LEE		7	Wayne BIGGINS	
8	Andy COLE	16, 44, 46	8	Wayne BULLIMORE ‡ ❑	
9	David KELLY		9	David CURRIE	
10	Lee CLARK	65	10	Neil REDFEARN	
11	Scott SELLARS	72	11	Jamie ROBINSON †	
	Substitutes			*Substitutes*	
12	Brian KILCLINE (†68)		12	Deiniol GRAHAM (†45)	
14	Mark ROBINSON (‡60)		14	Chris JACKSON (‡66)	

BEFORE		P	W	D	L	F	A	pts	AFTER		P	W	D	L	F	A	pts
1	Newcastle	39	23	9	7	72	34	78	1	Newcastle	40	24	9	7	78	34	81
10	Barnsley	39	15	9	15	50	45	54	11	Barnsley	40	15	9	15	50	51	54

FACTFILE

United hit six in league for first time since 1964... United pass club record points total of 80 - now on 81... Cole grabs superb hat-trick for first three of game... Beresford and Sellars net their first Newcastle goals... West Ham lose and Portsmouth go into second place, but United eight points clear.

Barnsley hit by six of the best

IN EVERY season there comes a peak: a game where everything comes together, where each player blends perfectly with the others, and where the opposition is gently massacred as a consequence.

If it happens before a full-house crowd and with your side opening up an eight point lead at the top of the table, then it is the stuff of dreams.

United's fans often dream of nights like this, but for too many years dreams were the closest they ever came to the reality. Yet this was the real thing.

Forget the superb 5-0 against Bristol City. Ignore the marvellous 5-1 against Brentford. The 6-0 against Barnsley was a frighteningly brilliant team performance which eclipsed all that had gone before.

Barnsley's manager, Mel Machin, made a joke of it all afterwards, staggering into the St James' Press room and begging for a double Scotch.

But Machin wasn't joking when he admitted: "We got off lightly with six."

Barnsley simply vanished in a welter of glorious attacking football which brought the 29,460 crowd to fever pitch.

And once Andy Cole had launched himself towards a spectacular hat-trick with a 16th-minute shot through the hands of keeper Whitehead, the floodgates were open and the dambusters marched through.

Cole missed from three yards, Kelly, Lee, Clark and Sellars all went close, Barnsley tottered and collapsed, and Cole made it 2-0 as Barnsley sought the sanctuary of half-time.

This was the pick of the bunch, with Cole retrieving the ball from a clutch of defenders, feeding Kelly on the right, and ghosting into position to head Kelly's immaculate curling cross high past Whitehead from four yards.

How the fans loved it, and how they willed the Cole hat-trick which duly arrived two minutes into the second half.

Robert Lee worked wonders to brush off Fleming and cut the ball back from the byline for Cole to control with his first touch and blaze a shot on the turn past Whitehead's left hand and inside the near post.

Once the dazed Whitehead had contrived to let Lee Clark's 20-yarder slip through his arms for the fourth on 65 minutes, the match became a plaything for United.

Barnsley actually had the audacity to produce their first shot at goal in the 61st minute, and even went so far as to win their first corner in the 71st.

But by then John Beresford had scored his first goal for United, a penalty won by Lee from Fleming's push, and handed to the full-back by regular taker David Kelly.

It was obviously a night of firsts: five minutes later Kelly teed up the sixth for Sellars to join Beresford in the First Goal Club.

The greatest irony of a dazzling night was that leading scorer David Kelly had not been able to put his name on the crowded score-sheet.

But he would never be closer than the late, great run and shot palmed away by Whitehead, or the shot inches wide after a slick one-two with Cole.

"The loveliest thing was at 5-0, and watching them play, and watching the fans with smiles on their faces," said a lyrical Kevin Keegan later.

"And then looking at the new stand going up at the Leazes End, and thinking: Perhaps it's the Geordies' turn at last."

The best performance of the season, Kevin? Keegan pondered for a moment. "The Cambridge match set us up for this," he replied.

The question remained open, and a matter of opinion. But on such a night, it didn't really matter.

Saturday 10th April 1993 • Molineux • 3.00pm

WOLVES 1 NEWCASTLE UNITED 0

Half-time 0-0 • Attendance 17,244

Referee Graham POOLEY (Bishop's Stortford)
Linesmen J. BARLOW, E. CROMPTON

Old Gold Shirts, Black Shorts	Goals	Black and White Striped Shirts, White Shorts	Goals
1 Mike STOWELL		1 Pavel SRNICEK	
2 Darren SIMKIN †		2 Barry VENISON	
3 Mark VENUS		3 John BERESFORD	
4 Keith DOWNING		4 Paul BRACEWELL	
5 Derek MOUNTFIELD		5 Kevin SCOTT	
6 Paul BLADES		6 Steve HOWEY	
7 Mark RANKINE		7 Robert LEE	
8 Paul COOK		8 Andy COLE	
9 Andy THOMPSON		9 David KELLY †	
10 Andy MUTCH	54	10 Lee CLARK	
11 Robbie DENNISON		11 Scott SELLARS ‡	
Substitutes		*Substitutes*	
12 Lawrie MADDEN (†69)		12 Brian KILCLINE (†80)	
14 Mark BURKE		14 Mark ROBINSON (‡66)	

BEFORE	P	W	D	L	F	A	pts	AFTER	P	W	D	L	F	A	pts
1 Newcastle	40	24	9	7	78	34	81	1 Newcastle	41	24	9	8	78	35	81
9 Wolves	40	14	13	13	53	48	55	9 Wolves	41	15	13	13	54	48	58

FACTFILE

Handy Andy's goal too Mutch for United… Cole draws a blank for second time in six full games… Portsmouth and West Ham win again. Lead is cut to five points… Oxford Easter Monday postponement sees Pompey cut gap again to just two points, but Hammers lose at Luton.

No escape from the Wolves cage

FROM the sublime to the substandard. After the champagne of the victory over Barnsley, this was the stale bread and water alternative.

The contrast in the two United displays was stark, and Wolves could easily have taken greater advantage of it than the single Andy Mutch goal which ultimately divided the sides.

Looking jaded and uninspired, United completely failed to impose their will upon opponents who on a better day would have been there for the taking.

"We didn't reach the heights we did against Cambridge and Barnsley and I'm as baffled as everyone else as to why," admitted Kevin Keegan afterwards.

Perhaps the looming prospect of the Premier League shredded the players' nerves more than expected, or perhaps Wolves simply responded better to what was, for them, a big occasion.

Whatever the reason, Wanderers fully deserved their victory and their only regret was that the margin was no wider.

Mutch, without his injured striking partner Steve Bull, had enough chances for a double hat-trick, the first of which arrived in the 15th minute and vanished when Pavel Srnicek held his lame 15-yard shot.

Then Srnicek did well to get down to Andy Thompson's long-range shot and turn the ball for a corner.

A less lenient referee than Graham Pooley might have interpreted David Kelly's nudge on Mutch from a corner as a penalty, and more spot-kick appeals followed when Barry Venison blocked Mutch just feet from the line.

Amidst all this, United's attacks were at best weak. Robert Lee's long shot was straight at keeper Stowell, and a Lee Clark effort was deflected for a corner.

If one side looked like scoring, it was Wolves - and the goal which had always been threatened arrived in the 54th minute.

The move built from the back, with Stowell beating Andy Cole to a 50-50 ball ironically after one of United's better moves.

Stowell threw out to Thompson who sent Rankine down the right touchline. Rankine outwitted Kevin Scott on the run for a low cross along the six-yard line which Pavel Srnicek missed and Mutch didn't.

A penalty appeal immediately afterwards might have brought United level, but when Keith Downing brought down Lee in the Wolves area the referee waved all appeals aside.

Mutch missed yet another chance, allowing Srnicek to save when clear, but United responded with Paul Bracewell picking out Cole, whose intelligent chip almost caught out Stowell.

At last, Newcastle were gaining some momentum and the game's crucial moment came in the 78th minute.

Substitute Mark Robinson, on for Scott Sellars since the 66th minute, crossed from the right and Kelly flung himself forward to turn the ball past Stowell.

For a split second it seemed the match had been rescued, but a linesman had spotted the handball and the goal was - correctly - disallowed.

That was Kelly's last contribution, Keegan sending on Brian Kilcline in his place.

But whereas Kilcline had tipped the balance as a late substitute in the home draw with Derby in January, he was to have no such effect this time.

Only when Kilcline sent Lee into the penalty area in injury time did hope beckon, but Lee's shot was poor, and Stowell saved without discomfort.

The defeat was bad enough. But victories for Portsmouth and West Ham once again reduced United's lead to five points.

Saturday 17th April 1993 • The Den • 3.00pm

MILLWALL 1 NEWCASTLE UNITED 2

Half-time 1-0 • *Attendance* 14,262

Referee Vic CALLOW (Solihull)

Linesmen B. FIRMIN, S. SMITH

Blue and White Shirts, Blue Shorts		Goals
1	Kasey KELLER	
2	Ken CUNNINGHAM	
3	Ian DAWES	
4	Andy ROBERTS	
5	Colin COOPER	
6	Gavin MAGUIRE	
7	Alex RAE	
8	Danny WALLACE ‡	
9	Malcolm ALLEN	
10	Jon GOODMAN †	
11	Phil BARBER	18
Substitutes		
12	Tony DOLBY (†59)	
14	Tommy GAYNOR (‡69)	

Black and White Striped Shirts, Black Shorts		Goals
1	Pavel SRNICEK	
2	Barry VENISON	
3	John BERESFORD	
4	Paul BRACEWELL	
5	Kevin SCOTT	
6	Brian KILCLINE	
7	Robert LEE	
8	Andy COLE †	73
9	David KELLY	
10	Lee CLARK	65
11	Scott SELLARS	
Substitutes		
12	Mark ROBINSON (†80)	
14	Kevin BROCK	

BEFORE		P	W	D	L	F	A	pts
1	Newcastle	41	24	9	8	78	35	81
7	Millwall	42	17	16	9	62	45	67

AFTER		P	W	D	L	F	A	pts
1	Newcastle	42	25	9	8	80	36	84
7	Millwall	43	17	16	10	63	47	67

FACTFILE

Goal King Cole gets seventh in seven games to complete second-half fightback... United win from half-time deficit for first time this season... 12th away league win of season a new club record... 25th league victory of season equals 1926-27 club record.

Lions tamed by Cole and Clark

NO GAME in the promotion run-in came as more of a bonus than this: and the manner of the fightback was as inspiring as the victory itself.

Needing seven points to all but guarantee promotion, United fans were prepared to concede that of the five league games remaining, the visit to Millwall was the most likely to yield nothing.

The Lions, after all, had lost but once at home in the league all season, and had come worryingly close to snatching a victory at St James' Park in December.

There was the real prospect, too, that Portsmouth, away to Notts County, could dislodge United from the top for the first time since mid-September.

The postponement of the Easter Monday home match with Oxford United may have helped the players' physical well-being, but it had also allowed Pompey to narrow the gap between first and second position to just two points.

And when United fell quickly behind at The Den, the anxiety was vivid and tangible.

There was a touch of fortune about Phil Barber's 18th-minute goal, his hopeful cross from the right edge of the box dipping and swerving beyond Pavel Srnicek and lodging inside the far angle.

In a fraught first-half, United came as near to being overrun as in any game of the campaign.

Srnicek, two minutes before the Millwall goal, had excelled in diving to push a shot from Rae over the bar. Shortly after, Cooper struck the left post and, in the ensuing scramble, Allen's drive hit precisely the same spot.

Despite the adverse pressure, United were not without chances, but Andy Cole missed two

fine opportunities created by Lee Clark and John Beresford.

Seven minutes from the interval, Cole was there again, fastening onto a long ball and shooting ferociously, but just too high. It seemed this was not to be United's day.

"I told the lads they were fortunate to be only one goal down at half-time," said Kevin Keegan afterwards. "We changed one or two things, and took hold of the game."

The transformation in the second period was remarkable. Within the first 20 seconds, Clark flashed a shot just wide, and that set the tone of the game. As if to emphasise the point that things were going to be different from now on, Clark brought a sharp reflex save from Kasey Keller minutes later.

From being on the receiving end, United were now in almost total control, but the most crucial statistic - the 1-0 scoreline - remained unchanged.

Until the 65th minute, that is, when the goal United so richly deserved at last arrived.

How apt it was that Lee Clark, a veritable colossus in the second half, should claim it, pouncing with a snapshot after Cole turned Gavin Maguire deep inside the area.

Part of Cole's game is that he will miss several to score one, and the one came in the 73rd minute to induce euphoria among the United fans packed into the Ilderton Road End.

It was a classical goal, too, Brian Kilcline rising to a free-kick to head to the feet of Cole who, with his back to goal, dragged the ball back between two defenders, swivelled and shot firmly to Keller's left.

Predictably, Millwall, with their play-off ambitions now fading rapidly, hurled everything into a final assault on the United goal, and there were one or two flutters.

But the prize on this most important of days was too great to yield, and United held firm. Portsmouth's victory at Meadow Lane made it essential.

Sunday 25th April 1993 • St James' Park • 12.00pm

NEWCASTLE UNITED 1 SUNDERLAND 0

Half-time 1-0 • *Attendance* 30,364

Referee Keith HACKETT (Sheffield)

Linesmen B. LOWE, T. LYNCH

Black and White Striped Shirts, Black Shorts		Goals
1	Pavel SRNICEK	
2	Barry VENISON	
3	John BERESFORD	
4	Paul BRACEWELL	
5	Kevin SCOTT	
6	Steve HOWEY	
7	Robert LEE	
8	Andy COLE	
9	David KELLY	
10	Lee CLARK	
11	Scott SELLARS	10

Substitutes

12 Brian KILCLINE

14 Mark ROBINSON

Red and White Striped Shirts, Red Shorts		Goals
1	Tony NORMAN	
2	John KAY ‡	
3	Michael GRAY	
4	John COLQUHOUN †	
5	Terry BUTCHER	
6	Kevin BALL	
7	Shaun CUNNINGTON	
8	Don GOODMAN	
9	Mick HARFORD	
10	Brian ATKINSON	
11	Gordon ARMSTRONG ❑	

Substitutes

12 Peter DAVENPORT (†78)

14 Martin GRAY (‡59)

BEFORE		P	W	D	L	F	A	pts
2	Newcastle	42	25	9	8	80	36	84
21	Sunderland	42	12	11	19	44	57	47

AFTER		P	W	D	L	F	A	pts
1	Newcastle	43	26	9	8	81	36	87
21	Sunderland	43	12	11	20	44	58	47

FACTFILE

Season's best crowd sees derby double... 26th league win is a new club record... Venison becomes one of the few to captain both sides in Tyne-Wear derbies... Third United defeat of Roker in succession... United now two points from promotion.

Super Sellars sings in the rain

WHATEVER Liam O'Brien could do at Roker Park in October, Scott Sellars could do just as well at St James' Park in April.

O'Brien went into the United treasure chest with his brilliant free-kick winner against Sunderland... and Sellars joined him with an equally superb winner as The Magpies completed the double to move to the very brink of promotion.

When United won a free-kick in the tenth minute of this match, many among the best-of-the-season crowd bemoaned the absence of the injured O'Brien. But cometh the hour, cometh the man, and Sellars stepped up to bend a wicked shot over the wall and in off the right post with Tony Norman utterly helpless.

It was a marvellous way for the £700,000 import from Leeds to cap his emergence as a player of genuine quality after a slightly uncertain start to his Newcastle career.

And the goal drew fulsome praise from both managers, Kevin Keegan labelling it "a classic", and Sunderland player-boss Terry Butcher admitting: "It was a marvellous free-kick."

The morning downpour which had taken the match to the very threshold of a postponement offered United no favours, levelling out the sides as it did. But United deserved massive credit for the way they rose above the conditions and, after the early goal, controlled matters in such a tense and nervous atmosphere.

Though the one-goal lead was never enough on which to relax, the bare statistic of only one Sunderland shot on target in the 90 minutes - and that a hopeful 30-yarder straight to Pavel Srnicek from Brian Atkinson - amply demonstrates United's superiority.

What few chances there were came Newcastle's way, David Kelly failing to beat Norman when clear two minutes before the goal, and

hooking inches over at full stretch eight minutes after.

With puddles on the pitch, many moves were a lottery, but Robert Lee - once more an inspiration - was able to test Norman with an 18-yard left-foot volley.

Sunderland's reluctance to abandon their defensive approach kept the game tight and tense, but Don Goodman and Mick Harford got little out of United's excellent defence.

Barry Venison and John Beresford were given the freedom to double as wingers and made light of the canals inside both touchlines.

The second half continued as a near-copy of the first, Robert Lee's 51st-minute header from a Sellars corner scraping the post, and the same player's 20-yard shot taking a crazy bounce only to strike the diving Norman on the head and spin wide.

Then in the space of 60 seconds, Andy Cole was inches away from Clark's teasing cross in front of an open net, and young Wearsider Steve Howey headed Lee's flick millimetres past the right upright.

Roker player-boss Butcher made a belated gesture at attack with Peter Davenport replacing John Colquhoun 12 minutes from time.

But there was little serious threat to United's lead in the time remaining, and after being temporarily displaced from top spot by Portsmouth the day before, Keegan's side were back in what he called "our rightful place".

Keegan admitted he had doubted the game would finish in the waterlogged conditions, but also accepted referee Hackett was right in his decision to play. "The lads worked hard on a difficult pitch and got what they deserved," said the manager.

And so, after a long season of frequent brilliance and occasional setback, the winning line was in view. If West Ham were to fail to win at Swindon a week hence, Newcastle United would be promoted even before their next match at Grimsby.

Tuesday 4th May 1993 • Blundell park • 8.00pm

GRIMSBY TOWN 0 NEWCASTLE UNITED 2

Half-time 0-0 • *Attendance* 14,402

Referee Terry LUNT (Ashton-in-Makerfield)
Linesmen M. HAIR, L. SHORT

Black and White Striped Shirts, Black Shorts	Goals	Yellow Shirts, Green Shorts	Goals
1 Rhys WILMOT		1 Pavel SRNICEK	
2 John McDERMOTT		2 Barry VENISON ❏	
3 Gary CROFT		3 John BERESFORD	
4 Paul FUTCHER ‡		4 Paul BRACEWELL	
5 Graham RODGER		5 Kevin SCOTT	
6 Jim DOBBIN		6 Steve HOWEY	
7 Tony FORD		7 Robert LEE	
8 David GILBERT †		8 Andy COLE	46
9 Paul GROVES		9 David KELLY	90
10 Clive MENDONCA		10 Lee CLARK	
11 Neil WOODS		11 Scott SELLARS	
Substitutes		*Substitutes*	
12 Mark SMITH (†77)		12 Brian KILCLINE	
14 Gary CHILDS (‡85)		14 Gavin PEACOCK	

BEFORE		P	W	D	L	F	A	pts	AFTER		P	W	D	L	F	A	pts
1	Newcastle	43	26	9	8	81	36	87	1	Newcastle	44	27	9	8	83	36	90
8	Grimsby	44	19	7	18	57	53	64	8	Grimsby	45	19	7	19	57	55	64

FACTFILE

United's fifth win in six matches seals promotion and the First Division championship... Thirteenth away win sets new club record... Cole's eighth goal in nine games... Kelly's 25th of season ends four-game drought... revenge on only side to win in league at St James' Park.

Champions clear the final hurdle

THE GREAT day, when it came, had a modest stage but a momentous scale.

Blundell Park is not one of soccer's most glamourous arenas, but it became a palace of dreams for Newcastle United on this magical and momentous evening.

A small corner of Humberside became a large slice of Tyneside as up to 8,000 United supporters made the 160-mile journey to the east coast; and nonsense of the supposed 3,650-ticket allocation.

United fans were everywhere to celebrate a 2-0 victory which meant far more in the effect than the design, and which was a triumph more of organisation than of dazzling brilliance.

Portsmouth, who could have gone ahead of Newcastle three days earlier, had dutifully slipped up, 4-1, at Sunderland to leave United a mere two points from both the championship and promotion. West Ham, 3-1 winners at Swindon, had moved into second spot on goals scored.

Grimsby, who had beaten Newcastle at St James' Park in October to end the 11-match winning league start, were no-one's idea of a soft touch, and no-one would have grumbled at a draw.

For United, with the cushion of two home games to conclude the season, would have been virtually home and dry; and they were not prepared to sacrifice caution for impatient ambition.

But when it became clear that Grimsby had not the armoury to trouble the Newcastle defence, United swiftly realised that the game was theirs for the taking.

Lee Clark, again dictating in midfield, was the first to come close to a goal, rounding off an exquisite three-man move with a half-volley to the top corner which Rhys Wilmot acrobatically flicked over.

Grimsby's opportunities were half-chances at best, Kevin Scott and Steve Howey forming an impassable central barrier and Barry Venison and John Beresford closing up the flanks.

But when United attacked, it was with incisive, snappy raids which ripped huge chasms in the home defence.

One such assault ended with a David Kelly header from an Andy Cole cross: Wilmot moved quickly across to save. But Wilmot was beaten all ends up when Robert Lee moved onto Cole's astute pass on the right to drive a low shot against the inside of the post.

The frustration of that near-miss was exploded 21 seconds into the second half when Andy Cole sent the travelling hordes into ecstasy with the opening goal.

Lee was the creator, ending a forceful run through the middle with a pass measured into the stride of Cole, who shimmied and slid a carefully-placed shot past Wilmot and into the corner.

Amidst the frantic celebrations which greeted the goal, a safety gate in the perimeter fence burst open and United fans came tumbling out. The game was held up for six minutes as the injured were treated.

But the stoppage scarcely upset the rhythm, and United contained the Mariners sufficiently well for Pavel Srnicek's contribution to be limited to two cosy catches and one diving save.

One goal is never a comfortable margin, and Lee Clark's attempt to widen it was denied by Wilmot in the 74th minute. Then Lee brought another fine save from the Grimsby keeper.

But when Cole sent Kelly through in injury time to dribble round the keeper and resist a stumble to squeeze a left-foot shot into the net, the partying could - and did - begin in earnest.

Thursday 6th May 1993 • St James' Park • 7.45pm

NEWCASTLE UNITED 2 OXFORD UNITED 1

Half-time 0-0 • *Attendance* 29,438

Referee Alan FLOOD (Stockport)

Linesmen G. BRADBURY, W. GOWERS

OXFORD UNITED

Black and White 'Striped Shirts, Black Shorts		Goals	Maroon Shirts, Maroon Shorts		Goals
1	Pavel SRNICEK		1	Paul REECE	
2	Barry VENISON		2	Gary SMART	
3	John BERESFORD		3	Mike FORD	
4	Paul BRACEWELL ‡		4	Mickey LEWIS ❑	
5	Kevin SCOTT		5	David COLLINS	
6	Brian KILCLINE		6	Andy MELVILLE	
7	Robert LEE †		7	Jim MAGILTON	
8	Andy COLE	78	8	Joey BEAUCHAMP	
9	David KELLY		9	Paul WANLESS ‡	
10	Lee CLARK	70	10	Matthew MURPHY †	
11	Scott SELLARS		11	Chris ALLEN	
	Substitutes			*Substitutes*	
12	Mark ROBINSON (†45)		12	David PENNEY (†74)	
14	Gavin PEACOCK (‡61)		14	Nick CUSACK (‡74)	79

BEFORE		P	W	D	L	F	A	pts	AFTER		P	W	D	L	F	A	pts
1	Newcastle	44	27	9	8	83	36	90	1	Newcastle	45	28	9	8	85	37	93
15	Oxford	44	13	14	17	51	54	53	15	Oxford	45	13	14	18	52	56	53

FACTFILE

It's nine out of ten for Cole... 28th league win of the season... newly-crowned North-East Player of the Year Lee Clark celebrates with a goal... sixth win in seven puts United eight points clear at the top... Gavin Peacock back after ten-week absence.

After the Lord Mayor's show...

AFTER all the emotion and achievement of the title-clinching night at Grimsby 48 hours earlier, it was difficult to escape the feeling of anti-climax.

The rearranged fixture against Oxford crowded too closely upon Grimsby, and was no more than a prelude to the last-day party against Leicester upon which most minds were focused.

The fans were there in their usual numbers, of course, but the passion which would have been engendered by a chase for promotion points was missing. The upshot was the sort of uninspired game which had been a trademark of the pre-Keegan days, but which in 1992-93 had become a distant memory.

In truth, Oxford almost made nonsense of the bookmakers' 8-1 pre-match odds against an away victory.

Only in the final half-hour did Newcastle look anything like the side which had blown away the First Division ever since August.

And by then, ironically, Kevin Keegan was on his way home to Wynyard, the victim of a persistent stomach bug which could scarcely have been soothed by the tepid nature of his team's performance.

"Kevin was passing Washington when our first goal went in, and Peterlee when the second went in," joked assistant manager Terry McDermott afterwards.

"And when Oxford pulled one back - that was when he crashed."

Newcastle could indeed count themselves fortunate not to have crashed before the late goals burst which ultimately earned their 28th league win of the campaign.

Only a remarkable last-ditch block by Brian Kilcline on Paul Wanless in the 49th minute, and a backsliding save by Pavel Srnicek from debutant Matthew Murphy, had held the fort.

Oxford left-winger Chris Allen, a lithe and pacy speed merchant, gave Barry Venison a difficult night, and Jim Magilton, scorer of two against Newcastle in December, took the paint off the crossbar early in the second half.

In reply, Robert Lee miskicked from ten yards after Paul Reece had blocked Scott Sellars' 20-yard shot, and John Beresford, played into the clear by David Kelly, allowed the keeper to advance and deny him.

The tempo of the match was finally changed on the introduction of Gavin Peacock, a forgotten figure during his 12-match absence, as a 61st minute substitute for Paul Bracewell.

Peacock, with a point to prove, displayed sufficient enthusiasm to rouse his colleagues into something resembling the excellence of earlier months.

Almost immediately, Andy Cole sent Kelly through the middle to shoot narrowly wide; three minutes later, Newcastle were ahead.

Cole was involved again, touching a ball into the path of Lee Clark who, from 22 yards, drove a splendid low shot wide of Reece and into the bottom left corner.

At a stroke, the passion was ignited, Oxford trembled, and Cole twice bit at the cherry from six yards: his first shot blocked, his second sliced horribly wide.

Cole is never afraid to miss, though, and less than 60 seconds later he was back with a quite magnificent turn which left David Collins facedown, then a fulminating strike into the roof of the net.

Oxford, deservedly, reduced the deficit in the very next minute, Nick Cusack diving to head Gary Smart's right-wing cross wide of Srnicek from 12 yards.

But Newcastle were determined that even if the party rehearsal had gone badly, they were going to prove the old adage that the sign of a good team is to win without playing well.

Sunday 9th May 1993 • St James' Park • 3.00pm

NEWCASTLE UNITED 7 LEICESTER CITY 1

Half-time 6-0 • *Attendance 30,129*
Referee Bob NIXON (Wirral)
Linesmen R. HORSWELL, J. JONES

Black and White Striped Shirts, Black Shorts	Goals	Blue Shirts, Blue Shorts	Goals
1 Pavel SRNICEK		1 Kevin POOLE	
2 Barry VENISON		2 Gary MILLS	
3 John BERESFORD ‡		3 Mike WHITLOW	
4 Mark ROBINSON		4 Richard SMITH ❑	
5 Kevin SCOTT		5 Steve WALSH	82
6 Steve HOWEY †		6 Colin HILL	
7 Robert LEE	13	7 David OLDFIELD	
8 Andy COLE	5, 40, 66	8 Steve THOMPSON	
9 David KELLY	28, 34, 45	9 Julian JOACHIM †	
10 Lee CLARK		10 David LOWE	
11 Scott SELLARS		11 Neil LEWIS ‡	
Substitutes		*Substitutes*	
12 Brian KILCLINE (†60)		12 Simon GRAYSON (†45)	
14 Gavin PEACOCK (‡53)		14 Phil GEE (‡45)	

BEFORE		P	W	D	L	F	A	pts	AFTER		P	W	D	L	F	A	pts
1	Newcastle	45	28	9	8	85	37	93	1	Newcastle	46	29	9	8	92	38	96
6	Leicester	45	22	10	13	70	57	76	6	Leicester	46	22	10	14	71	64	76

FACTFILE

Brian Kilcline and Barry Venison receive Championship trophies before the game... First time since 1946 that two United players get three in the same match... first time since 1946 that United get six in one half... Kelly and Cole both grab second hat-tricks of the season... Cole's tally is 12 in 11 games - Kelly reaches 28.

Seventh heaven for King Kevin

NO-ONE could seriously believe, after all that had gone before, that anything more could happen in the Newcastle United Story 1992-93. But on the ceremonial final day, United went one step further than their best.

The last match against Leicester was made in heaven: an uplifting, thrilling, riotous parade of brilliance which wrote a fitting finale and launched United into the Premier League on a wave of emotion.

It spilled over with drama, with poetic, pulsating football, with an atmosphere which sent the senses reeling: a carnival in the sunshine, a piece of theatre with a cast of thousands.

And the Premier League clubs awaiting United's arrival raised a collective eyebrow at the sheer force and ferocity of it all.

Leicester, play-off candidates themselves, did not play badly, but were blown away in a first-half described by Kevin Keegan as "perfection".

And it was a personal triumph for David Kelly, who scored three times in 17 minutes to become only the fifth Newcastle player in history to claim a first-half hat-trick.

Kelly played a leading role in the opening goal on five minutes, chesting down John Beresford's deep cross as it dropped over Steve Walsh and driving in a left-foot shot which Kevin Poole could not hold; Cole thumped in the rebound.

On 13 minutes, perhaps the finest goal of the afternoon, Robert Lee working an exquisite one-two with Cole and curving a right-foot shot away from Poole and inside the far left post.

Cole was involved again in the third goal 15 minutes on, robbing David Oldfield by the right corner flag and supplying Lee Clark whose cross was perfectly measured for Kelly to head his 26th goal of the season.

It was almost unreal, but six minutes later it was 4-0, Kelly this time sweeping a left-foot shot across Poole after Scott Sellars reached the byline and Clark perceptively touched on his cut-back.

Then Cole was back five minutes from the interval, thundering a volley beyond Poole after Kelly had chased and headed down a long punt from Pavel Srnicek.

As Leicester stumbled dizzily on, Kelly headed a carbon-copy of his first in injury time: this time from Mark Robinson's cross.

Had the interval not come, United must surely have reached double figures, but as it was, the break lulled the tempo and City drew second wind.

But there was still Andy Cole's 66th-minute strike, a run and shot which brought his own hat-trick and took his tally to 12 in 11 games since joining United in March.

Who can forget the crowd scenes as the Andy Cole Song rang out from all sides; as grown men who thought they'd seen it all wiped away tears of joy and disbelief?

The pre-match presentation of the First Division championship trophy had whipped up a frenzy, and the cascade of goals turned frenzy into euphoria.

Chairman Sir John Hall could scarcely have had such a match in mind when he produced his plans for a Fun Day Sunday, but it was a perfect way to grace the occasion.

It mattered little that Steve Walsh headed a consoldtion goal over Srnicek eight minutes from time: better the memory of Pavel's exceptional double save from Richard Smith 12 minutes earlier.

By then, the nature of the occasion far outweighed mere technicalities. Newcastle United had announced their arrival in the Premier League in loud, proud style.

And a brave new world lay ahead.

Monday 27th July 1992 • Tynecastle • 7.30pm

HEARTS 1 NEWCASTLE UNITED 0

Half-time 0-0 • *Attendance* 11,105

Referee Joe TIMMONS (Musselburgh)

Linesmen D. PRENTICE, J. MOFFAT

White and Maroon Shirts, White Shorts	Goals	Black and White Striped Shirts, Black Shorts	Goals
1 Henry SMITH		1 Tommy WRIGHT	
2 Alan McLAREN		2 Barry VENISON	
3 Tosh McKINLAY		3 John BERESFORD †	
4 Craig LEVEIN		4 Bjorn KRISTENSEN ‡	
5 Gary MACKAY		5 Brian KILCLINE #	
6 Peter VAN DE VEN		6 Steve HOWEY §	
7 John ROBERTSON †		7 Franz CARR ††	
8 George WRIGHT		8 Gavin PEACOCK	
9 Ian BAIRD ‡	49	9 David KELLY	
10 Ally MAUCHLEN #		10 Kevin KEEGAN ‡‡	
11 Eamonn BANNON §		11 Kevin SHEEDY	
Substitutes		*Substitutes*	
Scott CRABBE †		Kevin BROCK †	
Glynn SNODIN ‡		Kevin SCOTT ‡	
Wayne FOSTER #		Ray RANSON #	
Neil BERRY §		Andy HUNT §	
		Micky QUINN ††	
		Lee CLARK ‡‡	

FACTFILE

Ex-Newcastle centre-forward Ian Baird headed the goal which defeated a United side including manager Kevin Keegan. Keegan used six substitutes as he tested tactical ideas, and United were denied a draw by Hearts Keeper Henry Smith, who pulled off fine saves from Hunt, Clark, Brock and Quinn.

Saturday 1st August 1992 • Bootham Crescent • 3.00pm

YORK CITY 1 NEWCASTLE UNITED 3

Half-time 0-1 • Attendance 3,424

Referee G. Bradbury (York)

Linesmen S. RENNISON, M. COTTINGHAM

Red Shirts, Blue Shorts	Goals	Black and White Striped Shirts, White Shorts	Goals
1 Chris MARPLES †		1 Tommy WRIGHT	
2 Andy McMILLAN		2 Barry VENISON	
3 Tony BARRATT		3 John BERESFORD †	
4 Nigel PEPPER		4 Paul BRACEWELL	
5 Steve TUTILL		5 Brian KILCLINE	
6 Paul ATKIN		6 Kevin SCOTT ‡	
7 Jon McCARTHY		7 Lee CLARK	
8 John BORTHWICK ‡		8 Gavin PEACOCK #	46
9 Paul BARNES #		9 David KELLY	
10 Gary SWANN		10 Steve WATSON §	
11 Ian BLACKSTONE		11 Kevin SHEEDY ††	17

Substitutes		*Substitutes*	
Dean KIELY (†45)		Alan NEILSON (†45)	
Darren TILLEY (‡45)	63	Ray RANSON (‡45)	
Steve BUSHELL (#79)		Micky QUINN (#61)	
		Franz CARR (§61)	79
		Alan THOMPSON (††45)	

FACTFILE

United were always in control against the third division side and after Kevin Sheedy chipped the first goal on 17 minutes, Gavin Peacock added a second in the first minute of the second half. Darren Tilley pulled one back for City, but Franz Carr put the issue beyond any doubt.

Tuesday 4th August 1992 • Belle Vue • 7.30pm

DONCASTER ROVERS 1 NEWCASTLE UNITED 1

Half-time 0-0 • Attendance 3,951

Referee C. BASSINDALE (Doncaster)
Linesmen G. SCOTT, A. GREAVES

Red Shirts, White Shorts	Goals	Black and White Striped Shirts, Black Shorts	Goals
1 Paul CRICHTON		1 Tommy WRIGHT †	
2 Colin DOUGLAS		2 Darron McDONOUGH	
3 Steve PRINDIVILLE		3 John BERESFORD	
4 Mark HINE		4 Paul BRACEWELL	
5 Andy CROSBY		5 Brian KILCLINE	
6 Dave TALLON		6 Kevin SCOTT ‡	
7 Jamie HEWITT		7 Kevin BROCK #	
8 Eddie GORMLEY †		8 Lee CLARK	
9 Peter HERITAGE		9 David KELLY	
10 Mike JEFFREY	83	10 Micky QUINN	
11 Brian ROWE		11 Kevin SHEEDY	
Substitutes		*Substitutes*	
Grant MORROW (†80)		Pavel SRNICEK (†45)	
		Bjorn KRISTENSEN (‡68)	
		Liam O'BRIEN (#68)	75

FACTFILE

Little Doncaster gave United a tough time and refused to accept defeat even when they fell behind to Liam O'Brien's 75th minute goal, created from a Kevin Sheedy cross. Seven minutes from time, Mike Jeffrey beat Kilcline on the right and shot past Tommy Wright.

Saturday 8th August 1992 • St James' Park • 3.30pm

NEWCASTLE UNITED 1 MIDDLESBROUGH 0

Half-time 1-0 • *Attendance* 8,548
Referee Alan DAWSON (Jarrow)
Linesmen T. HEILBRON, W. NATTRASS

Black and White Striped Shirts, Black Shorts		Goals	Red Shirts, White Shorts		Goals
1	Tommy WRIGHT		1	Ian IRONSIDE	
2	Barry VENISON		2	Gary PARKINSON	
3	John BERESFORD		3	Jimmy PHILLIPS	
4	Paul BRACEWELL		4	Alan KERNAGHAN †	
5	Brian KILCLINE		5	Jon GITTENS	
6	Kevin SCOTT		6	Jamie POLLOCK	
7	Lee CLARK		7	Bernie SLAVEN ‡	
8	Gavin PEACOCK	75p	8	Willie FALCONER	
9	David KELLY		9	Paul WILKINSON	
10	Kevin BROCK		10	John HENDRIE	
11	Kevin SHEEDY		11	Tommy WRIGHT	

Substitutes

Pavel SRNICEK
Ray RANSON
Micky QUINN
Mark STIMSON
Steve HOWEY

Substitutes

Nicky MOHAN (†45)
Michael O'NEILL (‡45)
Andy PAYTON
Robbie MUSTOE
Andrew COLLETT

FACTFILE

Gavin Peacock, who had rejected a possible move to Boro in the summer, eliminated the Teessiders from the Exhibition Superchallenge with a 38th minute penalty. Newcastle were always the better team and the penalty came when Ian Ironside dropped the ball and Jon Gittens held back Peacock as he moved in for the kill.

Sunday 9th August 1992 • St James' Park • 3.30pm

NEWCASTLE UNITED 3 SPORTING LISBON 5

Half-time 3-0 • *Attendance 7,764*

Referee Ken REDFERN (Whitley Bay)
Linesmen J. BETTS, C. GORDON

Black and White Striped Shirts, White Shorts	Goals	Green and White Hooped Shirts, Black Shorts	Goals
1 Tommy WRIGHT		1 Tomislav IVKOVIC	
2 Ray RANSON		2 NELSON †	
3 Mark STIMSON		3 Paulo TORRES	
4 Steve HOWEY		4 BARNY	
5 Brian KILCLINE		5 Carlos JORGE	
6 Kevin SCOTT †		6 Emilio PEIXE	
7 Franz CARR		7 Luis FIGO	
8 Gavin PEACOCK	45, 45	8 FILIPE	67, 71
9 Micky QUINN		9 Ivailo YORDANOV	
10 Lee CLARK	21	10 Krasimir BALAKOV	62, 90
11 Kevin SHEEDY		11 Jorge CADETE ‡	80

Substitutes	*Substitutes*
Pavel SRNICEK	MARINHO (†70)
Darron McDONOUGH (†68)	Jose LEAL (‡83)
Bjorn KRISTENSEN	SERGIO
Alan NEILSON	AMARAL
Kevin BROCK	CAPUCHO

FACTFILE

United sacrificed a 3-0 half-time lead to Bobby Robson's Portuguese stars. Lee Clark put the Magpies ahead and Gavin Peacock scored twice just before the interval. But Sporting turned the tables in a dramatic second half to score five times through Cadete, Balakov (2) and Filipe (2).

Kevin KEEGAN

Date of Birth 14.2.51
Birthplace Armthorpe
Position Manager

● In a glittering career, there wasn't much Kevin Keegan hadn't done - but managing a team to the First Division Championship was one of them.

Kevin, who skippered United to promotion in 1984, left football behind for eight years after retiring.

Wealthy enough not to need a job in football, Kevin was still tempted back to the club he loves at a time of crisis, with United near the bottom of the then Second Division in Feb 92.

United survived, but the dream machine was up and running, and 1992-93 turned the dream into reality as the team he built swept to the top.

To the list of credits which includes Football League Championships, the FA Cup, the European Cup, the UEFA Cup, the German Bundesliga title, Footballer of the Year, European Footballer of the Year twice, and given the OBE... add Manager Magnificent.

It's a long way from Peglers Brass Works where Kevin started out, but is there any limit to what this Midas of the soccer world can achieve?

Terry McDERMOTT

Date of Birth 8.12.51
Birthplace Liverpool
Position Assistant Manager

● While Kevin Keegan, inevitably, takes most of the limelight, Terry McDermott plays the support role which doesn't always get the credit it deserves.

Terry Mac is the morale man at St James', never one to remain serious for long, but always ready with expert advice when needed.

He has several things in common with KK: not least the fact he also played for United, in two spells, and for Liverpool between times.

As a right-half, Terry was an integral part of the 1973-74 team which reached Wembley only to lose to Liverpool in the FA Cup Final.When he returned to Newcastle to play alongside Kevin in September 1982, he again formed an essential part of a splendid team.

Terry was growing accustomed to a life of leisure when he received the call from Kevin Keegan to return to life in the pressure cooker.

He accepted, and the rest is history. But Terry McDermott - "my buffer", says Kevin - knows how to handle the pressure.

Derek FAZACKERLEY

Date of Birth 5.11.51
Birthplace Preston
Position First-team Coach

● The unsung hero of the Newcastle United coaching staff, 'Faz' has truly come into his own as a coach able to call on his 15 years experience as a player.

A resolute centre-back in his day, he holds the Blackburn Rovers appearances record and still has a home in the Lancashire town. But his future lies with Newcastle United after brilliantly fulfilling Kevin Keegan's faith in him.

When Kevin arrived at Newcastle in 1992, Faz looked likely to be on the way out until the new manager saw the potential of the coach at work.

Faz remained as reserve team coach - among his tactical triumphs was the switching of Steve Howey from attack to defence - and earned the first-team coaching slot in 1992-93.

Formerly a player-manager with Finnish club, Kumu, Faz also played for Chester, York City and Bury after his days at Blackburn.

After the achievements of 1992-93, he is now one of the most valued members of the St James' Park staff.

John BERESFORD

Date of Birth   4.9.66
Birthplace   Sheffield
Position   Left-back

● An exciting overlapping left-back whose superb form at St James' Park earned a full England substitute's roll in 1992-93.

Signed from Portsmouth for £650,000 in June 1992 only after a proposed move to Liverpool fell through at the last minute, but now rated one of the best left-backs in United's history.

Started out at Manchester City then joined Barnsley before blossoming after his switch to Fratton Park four years ago.

1992/93 United Record

	Played	Gls
League	42	1
F.A. Cup	4	0
League Cup	4	0
A.I. Cup	2	0
Total	**52**	**1**
Full United Record	**52**	**1**

International honours
England Youth
England Schools

Paul BRACEWELL

Date of Birth   19.7.62
Birthplace   Stoke
Position   Midfield

● Former Sunderland captain recruited for £250,000 17 days before John Beresford to become Kevin Keegan's first 1992 close-season signing.

Injury disrupted his early-season hopes, but he recovered to fill Liam O'Brien's shirt in mid-March and played a brave and vital part in the 11-match promotion run-in. Has played and lost in 4 FA Cup Finals.

A skilful schemer who also played for Stoke City and Everton before leading Sunderland to the 1992 FA Cup Final. His move here split Roker Park but proved a huge bonus for United.

1992/93 United Record

	Played	Gls
League	19(6)	2
F.A. Cup	2(2)	0
League Cup	0	0
A.I. Cup	2	0
Total	**23(8)**	**2**
Full United Record	**23(8)**	**2**

International honours
England full   3   0
England U-21   12(1)

Kevin BROCK

Date of Birth   9.9.62
Birthplace   Middleton Stoney
Position   Midfield

● Stylish midfield man whose contribution to the promotion campaign was limited by the arrival of Kevin Sheedy and later Scott Sellars.

The former Oxford and Queens Park Rangers star is nonetheless a valuable player to have in reserve and has played an important part in the Pontins League side.

Will never be forgotten for his courageous performance as cover for injured goalkeeper Tommy Wright in the 3-2 victory at Birmingham City in November.

1992/93 United Record

	Played	Gls
League	4(3)	1
F.A. Cup	0	0
League Cup	2	0
A.I. Cup	2(1)	1
Total	**8(4)**	**2**
Full United Record	**162(11)**	**17**

International honours
England U-21   4
England B   1
England Schools

Franz CARR

Date of Birth	24.9.66
Birthplace	Preston
Position	Right wing

● A speedy, tricky winger ousted by the arrival of Robert Lee and transferred to Sheffield United on an initial three-month loan basis in January.

Bought for £250,000 from Nott'm Forest in May 1991, Franz was capable of sheer brilliance but inconsistency proved a major let-down.

Also played for Sheffield Wednesday and West Ham in earlier loan periods, but often dogged by injury at Newcastle and expected to sign permanently for The Blades after helping them stay in the Premier League.

1992/93 United Record

	Played	Gls
League	8(2)	1
F.A. Cup	0	0
League Cup	1(2)	0
A.I. Cup	3(1)	0
Total	**12(5)**	**1**
Full United Record	**25(8)**	**3**

International honours
England U-21	7(2)	1

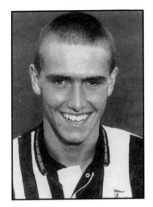

Lee CLARK

Date of Birth	27.10.72
Birthplace	Newcastle
Position	Midfield

● One of United's greatest success stories of recent years, Lee was on the point of leaving after failing to win his place in Jim Smith's and then Kevin Keegan's team which fought off relegation in 1991-92.

Has all the skills and added pace to burst onto the First Division scene in '92-3 to become the only ever-present in the season. Tipped for top international honours and acknowledged as a young star with a magnificent future

Lee is a Geordie and proud of it, and after supporting the team from the terraces, ident- ifies closely with the fans now.

1992/93 United Record

	Played	Gls
League	46	9
F.A. Cup	4	1
League Cup	5	0
A.I. Cup	3	0
Total	**58**	**10**
Full United Record	**112(10)**	**18**

International honours
England U-21	4	0
England Youth		
England Schools		

Andy COLE

Date of Birth	15.10.71
Birthplace	Nottingham
Position	Centre-forward

● United's record signing at £1.75m in March, Andy added pace and strength to the side and bagged 12 goals in 11 games to win the hearts of the fans.

When United's first bid fell short of Bristol City's valuation, it seemed Andy was destined not to play for Newcastle, but the manager's determination finally forced City's hand.

Formerly with Arsenal, Andy was Bristol city's record £500,000 signing and first caught Keegan's eye during United's 2-1 win at Ashton Gate in January.

1992/93 United Record

	Played	Gls
League	11(1)	12
F.A. Cup	0	0
League Cup	0	0
A.I. Cup	0	0
Total	**11(1)**	**12**
Full United Record	**11(1)**	**12**

International honours
England U-21	1(2)	1
England Youth		

Steve HOWEY

Date of Birth	26.10.71
Birthplace	Sunderland
Position	Central defender

● Steve began life as a young centre-forward but when coach Derek Fazackerley tried him at centre-half in the reserve side, a new star was born.

Likened in many quarters to the great Alan Hansen, Steve's strength and composure has won him many admirers and he is now another of United's bright young stars tipped for international honours.

Made his full Newcastle debut in the last First Division game at Old Trafford in May 1989 with United already doomed to relegation.

1992/93 United Record

	Played	Gls
League	41	2
F.A. Cup	3	0
League Cup	5	0
A.I. Cup	4	0
Total	**53**	**2**
Full United Record	**70(16)**	**4**

International honours
None

David KELLY

Date of Birth	25.11.65
Birthplace	Birmingham
Position	Striker

● United's top scorer with 28 goals in the promotion season, and a striker of deadly skill and accuracy. Led the forward line successfully, then combined brilliantly with Andy Cole from March onwards.

After disappointing spells with Leicester and West Ham, David, who began with Walsall, has found his true home and will now hope to prove his ability in the top flight.

A Republic of Ireland international, he had the distinction of scoring a hat-trick on his full Eire debut against Israel.

1992/93 United Record

	Played	Gls
League	45	24
F.A. Cup	4	1
League Cup	4	2
A.I. Cup	4	1
Total	**57**	**28**
Full United Record	**83**	**39**

International honours

Eire full	17	7
Eire U-21	5	

Brian KILCLINE

Date of Birth	7.5.62
Birthplace	Nottingham
Position	Central defender

● Described by Kevin Keegan as one of the most important signings ever made at Newcastle, 'Killer' raised the spirits during difficult times and took on the role of club captain as United surged towards the Premier League.

Always available to cover in defence, Killer is a regular substitute and came on 14 times during the season.

Formerly with Notts County, Coventry and Oldham, he lifted the FA Cup as Coventry skipper in 1987 but made little impression at Oldham before joining Newcastle in February 1992.

1992/93 United Record

	Played	Gls
League	7(12)	0
F.A. Cup	1(2)	0
League Cup	2	0
A.I. Cup	5	0
Total	**15(14)**	**0**
Full United Record	**27(14)**	**0**

International honours

England U-21	2	0

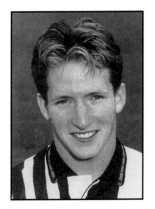

Robert LEE

Date of Birth   1.2.66
Birthplace   London
Position   Striker

● Robert's pure skill and attacking attributes have won him a special following among Tyneside's soccer public.

Since signing from Charlton Athletic for £700,000 in September 1992, he has got over an uncertain start to captivate the fans with his direct and highly-skilled approach.

Joined United after turning down Premier League Middlesbrough, and now has the platform on which to demonstrate his considerable ability.

1992/93 United Record

	Played	Gls
League	36	10
F.A. Cup	4	2
League Cup	3	1
A.I. Cup	0	0
Total	**43**	**13**
Full United Record	43	13

International honours
England U-21   -(2)   0

Alan NEILSON

Date of Birth   26.9.72
Birthplace   Wegburg (GER)
Position   Defender

● A former juniors skipper, Alan's maturity and self-confidence has stood him in good stead since his United first-team debut at Watford in March 1991.

The son of an RAF officer, Alan was stationed in Cyprus when he wrote to four English clubs seeking trials, and was taken on by Newcastle.

An excellent prospect for the future, Alan proved a capable defensive stand-in for both Barry Venison and John Beresford in the championship season.

1992/93 United Record

	Played	Gls
League	2(1)	0
F.A. Cup	0	0
League Cup	1	0
A.I. Cup	3	0
Total	**6(1)**	**0**
Full United Record	26(2)	1

International honours
Wales full   -(1)   0
Wales U-21   3

Liam O'BRIEN

Date of Birth   5.9.64
Birthplace   Dublin
Position   Midfield

● Liam had hit his top form before shin problems ruled him out of the promotion run-in from March onwards.

His forceful midfield play and explosive shooting became a major weapon in Kevin Keegan's armoury, and Liam will forever be remembered for the goal at Sunderland in October which gave United their first Roker Park win for 36 years.

Signed from Manchester United for £300,000 in November 1988, he was previously with Bohemians and Shamrock Rovers in his native Ireland.

1992/93 United Record

	Played	Gls
League	33	6
F.A. Cup	4	0
League Cup	3	1
A.I. Cup	3	0
Total	**43**	**7**
Full United Record	157(22)	20

International honours
Eire full   10   0
Eire U-23   1

Gavin PEACOCK

Date of Birth 18.11.67
Birthplace Welling
Position Midfield/Striker

● A quality player of balance and skill, Gavin was described as "my best signing" by Kevin Keegan after agreeing to sign a new contract at St James' Park last season.

Varying between midfield and attack, he scored 18 valuable goals in '92-93 before being sidelined by a persistent injury.

Formerly with Queens Park Rangers, Bournemouth and Gillingham, Gavin, a deeply religious man, was brought to Tyneside in a part-exchange deal involving Wayne Fereday in November 1990.

1992/93 United Record

	Played	Gls
League	29(3)	12
F.A. Cup	4	2
League Cup	4	2
A.I. Cup	2	2
Total	**39(3)**	**18**
Full United Record	**117(3)**	**46**

International honours
England U-19
England Youth
England Schools

Micky QUINN

Date of Birth 2.5.62
Birthplace Liverpool
Position Centre-forward

● A goalscoring hero in his time, but displaced early in the 92-93 season and sold to Coventry in December after an initial loan period.

Many doubted the wisdom in selling such a proven scorer when United were trying to strengthen the forward line, but Keegan felt Quinn's penalty-area style was not suited to his total football concept.

At Wigan, Stockport, Oldham and Pompey before coming to United in June '89 for £600,000, Quinn has always proved his goals touch, and did so again with a remarkable scoring burst for Coventry in the top flight.

1992/93 United Record

	Played	Gls
League	4(1)	2
F.A. Cup	0	0
League Cup	2(2)	0
A.I. Cup	2(1)	3
Total	**8(4)**	**5**
Full United Record	**131(8)**	**68**

International honours
None

Ray RANSON

Date of Birth 12.6.60
Birthplace St Helens
Position Right-back

● A reliable full-back whose place went to Barry Venison, Ray joined his old club Manchester City on a free transfer in January.

Previously with City and Birmingham, Ray captained the England U-21 side but was dropped into the Manchester City 'A' team under Billy McNeill.

Finished on just over 100 appearances for Newcastle, and was a great stabilising influence on a young defence in the days of Smith and Ardiles. Still in the Premier League Manchester City side at the end of the 92-93 season.

1992/93 United Record

	Played	Gls
League	3	0
F.A. Cup	0	0
League Cup	1	0
A.I. Cup	-(1)	0
Total	**4(1)**	**0**
Full United Record	**95(6)**	**1**

International honours

England U-21	8(2)	0
England 'B'	1	0
England Youth & Schools		

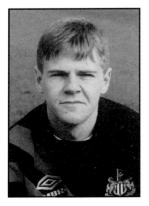

Mark ROBINSON

Date of Birth 21.11.68
Birthplace Manchester
Position Defender/midfield

● Signed from Barnsley for £450,000 on the same March day as Scott Sellars, Mark, now valuable squad cover, has shown his ability with a number of solid displays as substitute.

Joined Barnsley on a free transfer from West Bromwich Albion in 1987 and made his debut against Albion in the 1987-88 season.

A near ever-present in the Barnsley second division side in 1991-92, he caught the eye in particular in the Oakwell side's 1-0 defeat of United in December.

1992/93 United Record

	Played	Gls
League	2(7)	0
F.A. Cup	0	0
League Cup	0	0
A.I. Cup	0	0
Total	**2(7)**	**0**
Full United Record	**2(7)**	**0**

International honours
None

Kevin SCOTT

Date of Birth 17.12.66
Birthplace Easington
Position Centre-half

● United's longest serving player, Kevin came through the juniors, was part of the 1985 FA Youth Cup-winning side, and made his league debut in September 86, scoring against Sheffield Wednesday.

The man who signed him was Jack Charlton, who knew a thing or two about centre-halves and predicted a big future for the six-footer from East Durham.

Formerly team captain, Kevin's strength and height is an invaluable asset in defence and his partnership with Steve Howey was one of the season's highlights.

1992/93 United Record

	Played	Gls
League	45	2
F.A. Cup	4	0
League Cup	5	0
A.I. Cup	2	0
Total	**56**	**2**
Full United Record	**251(3)**	**8**

International honours
None

Scott SELLARS

Date of Birth 27.11.65
Birthplace Sheffield
Position Left midfield

● Signed in March despite a long spell out through injury. After taking a few games to get back into his stride, Scott became a significant figure in the promotion push.

Slightly-built but with deceptive strength, this former England U-21 international has tremendous skill and vision as well as an eye for goal - as witness his free-kick winner against Sunderland in April.

Formerly of Leeds United and Blackburn, Scott has now made the left-midfield spot his own and his experience will be a major asset in the Premier League.

1992/93 United Record

	Played	Gls
League	13	2
F.A. Cup	0	0
League Cup	0	0
A.I. Cup	0	0
Total	**13**	**2**
Full United Record	**13**	**2**

International honours
England U-21 2(1) 0

Kevin SHEEDY

Date of Birth	21.10.59
Birthplace	Builth Wells
Position	Left midfield

● After playing an important part in balancing United's midfield in the opening months of the season, Kevin lost his place to Scott Sellars in March.

Kevin Keegan's first signing in February 1992 on a free transfer from Everton, the Eire international played 13 times in the successful fight against relegation from division two in 1991-92.

Formerly with Hereford and Liverpool, Kevin was a target of United when with Liverpool reserves but eventually arrived on Tyneside in the twilight of his proud career.

1992/93 United Record

	Played	Gls
League	23(1)	3
F.A. Cup	2(1)	1
League Cup	4	0
A.I. Cup	4	1
Total	**33(2)**	**5**
Full United Record	**46(2)**	**6**

International honours
Eire full   44   7
Eire U-21
Eire Youth

Pavel SRNICEK

Date of Birth	10.3.68
Birthplace	Ostrava (CZ)
Position	Goalkeeper

● A former soldier in the Czech army, Pavel came to Newcastle in January 1991 after being spotted by Jim Smith, who paid out £350,000.

His early days were beset by errors in a struggling team, but Pavel bravely overcame the criticism and has now achieved cult status at St James' Park.

Powerfully-built but superbly agile, Pavel replaced the injured Tommy Wright in November and held onto the first-team place for the remainder of the season.

1992/93 United Record

	Played	Gls
League	32	0
F.A. Cup	4	0
League Cup	0	0
A.I. Cup	5	0
Total	**41**	**0**
Full United Record	**64**	**0**

International honours
Czech U-23   3   0

Mark STIMSON

Date of Birth	27.12.67
Birthplace	Plaistow
Position	Left-back/midfield

● Signed from Tottenham Hotspur in 1989 for £150,000, Mark was a first-team regular and had made almost 100 appearances before the 1992-93 season started.

However, the arrival of John Beresford at No3 meant Mark's opportunities were strictly limited, though on being drafted into midfield for the March defeat of Brentford, he earned huge praise for his cultured performance.

Previously with Leyton Orient and Gillingham, he was offered terms with six London clubs before choosing Spurs.

1992/93 United Record

	Played	Gls
League	1(1)	0
F.A. Cup	0	0
League Cup	0	0
A.I. Cup	2	0
Total	**3(1)**	**0**
Full United Record	**100(4)**	**3**

International honours
None

Alan THOMPSON

Date of Birth   22.12.73
Birthplace   Newcastle
Position   Midfield

● One of the brightest young stars at Newcastle, England Youth international Alan has recovered magnificently from a broken neck sustained in a car crash in September 1990.

Forced his way into the first-team in 1991-92, but failed to claim a regular place, though at 19 he has his career ahead of him.

Blessed with a powerful and accurate left foot, Alan was chosen for the World Youth Cup in Australia last season and has attracted interest from major clubs.

1992/93 United Record

	Played	Gls
League	1(1)	0
F.A. Cup	0	0
League Cup	0	0
A.I. Cup	3	0
Total	**4(1)**	**0**
Full United Record	**17(3)**	**0**

International honours
England Youth

Barry VENISON

Date of Birth   16.8.64
Birthplace   Consett
Position   Right-back

● A highly experienced defender who won two championship medals with Liverpool, Barry rejected a new Anfield contract to come home to the north-east

His full-back pairing with John Beresford is rated as one of the best in United's history, and Barry certainly brought all his experience to bear in the 1992-93 promotion campaign.

At 20, he became the youngest player to captain a side at Wembley when he led Sunderland in their 1985 Milk Cup Final defeat against Norwich.

1992/93 United Record

	Played	Gls
League	44	0
F.A. Cup	4	0
League Cup	4	0
A.I. Cup	3	0
Total	**55**	**0**
Full United Record	**55**	**0**

International honours
England U-21   10   0
England Youth

Steve WATSON

Date of Birth   1.1.74
Birthplace   Newcastle
Position   Defender/midfield

● Hailed as a wonderboy when he burst onto the scene at 16, Steve became the club's youngest-ever debutant when he came on as a substitute at Wolves in November 1990.

Still only 19, he has well over 50 first-team appearances to his name, but in 1992, after playing in the first game against Southend, he found himself out of the side for the next six months.

A product of the Wallsend Boys Club, Steve was in the England Youth side alongside Alan Thompson in the recent World Youth Cup in Australia.

1992/93 United Record

	Played	Gls
League	1(1)	0
F.A. Cup	0	0
League Cup	0	0
A.I. Cup	2(1)	0
Total	**3(2)**	**0**
Full United Record	**54(9)**	**1**

International honours
England Youth

Tommy WRIGHT

Date of Birth   29.8.63
Birthplace   Belfast
Position   Goalkeeper

● Kevin Keegan is lucky indeed to have two such fine keepers as Tommy Wright and Pavel Srnicek, though his problem is keeping them both happy when one has to settle for reserve team football.

Northern Ireland international Tommy was the man in the first-team until injured at Birmingham in November, and was thereafter unable to dislodge Srnicek.

That did not stop Billy Bingham calling him up for the Irish national side five times in the season, and this £30,000 signing must now be worth many times that amount.

1992/93 United Record

	Played	Goals
League	14	0
F.A. Cup	0	0
League Cup	5	0
A.I. Cup	1	0
Total	**20**	**0**
Full United Record	**81**	**0**

International honours
N. Ireland full	13	0
N. Ireland U-23	1	0

Appearance statistics do not include friendly matches

The following list of players appeared only in the Anglo-Italian Cup competition:

Matty APPLEBY

Date of Birth   16.4.72
Birthplace   Middlesbrough
Position   Defender
1992/93 United Record

	Played	Goals
A.I. Cup	2(1)	0
Full United Record	**26(1)**	**0**

Richie APPLEBY

Date of Birth   18.9.75
Birthplace   Middlesbrough
Position   Left wing
1992/93 United Record

	Played	Goals
A.I. Cup	2	0
Full United Record	**2**	**0**

Peter GARLAND

Date of Birth   20.1.71
Birthplace   Croydon
Position   Midfield
1992/93 United Record

	Played	Goals
A.I. Cup	-(1)	0
Full United Record	**2(1)**	**0**

Andy HUNT

Date of Birth   9.6.70
Birthplace   Thurrock
Position   Striker
1992/93 United Record

	Played	Goals
A.I. Cup	2	0
Full United Record	**50**	**13**

Bjorn KRISTENSEN

Date of Birth   10.10.63
Birthplace   Malling (DEN)
Position   Defender
1992/93 United Record

	Played	Goals
A.I. Cup	3(1)	1
Full United Record	**91(1)**	**5**

David ROCHE

Date of Birth   13.12.70
Birthplace   Wallsend
Position   Defender/midfield
1992/93 United Record

	Played	Goals
A.I. Cup	-(1)	0
Full United Record	**39(1)**	**0**

John WATSON

Date of Birth   14.4.74
Birthplace   South Shields
Position   Forward
1992/93 United Record

	Played	Goals
A.I. Cup	-(1)	0
Full United Record	**-(2)**	**0**

BARCLAYS LEAGUE DIVISION ONE

	HOME					AWAY					TOTAL					
	P	W	D	L	F	A	W	D	L	F	A	W	D	L	F	A	Pts
Newcastle United	46	16	6	1	58	15	13	3	7	34	23	29	9	8	92	38	96
West Ham United	46	16	5	2	50	17	10	5	8	31	24	26	10	10	81	41	88
Portsmouth	46	19	2	2	48	9	7	8	8	32	37	26	10	10	80	46	88
Tranmere Rovers	46	15	4	4	48	24	8	6	9	24	32	23	10	13	72	56	79
Swindon Town	46	15	5	3	41	23	6	8	9	33	36	21	13	12	74	59	76
Leicester City	46	14	5	4	43	24	8	5	10	28	40	22	10	14	71	64	76
Millwall	46	14	6	3	46	21	4	10	9	19	32	18	16	12	65	53	70
Derby County	46	11	2	10	40	33	8	7	8	28	24	19	9	18	68	57	66
Grimsby Town	46	12	6	5	33	25	7	1	15	25	32	19	7	20	58	57	64
Peterborough	46	7	11	5	30	26	9	3	11	25	37	16	14	16	55	63	62
Wolves	46	11	6	6	37	26	5	7	11	20	30	16	13	17	57	56	61
Charlton Athletic	46	10	8	5	28	19	6	5	12	21	27	16	13	17	49	46	61
Barnsley	46	12	4	7	29	19	5	5	13	27	41	17	9	20	56	60	60
Oxford United	46	8	7	8	29	21	6	7	10	24	35	14	14	18	53	56	56
Bristol City	46	10	7	6	29	25	4	7	12	20	42	14	14	18	49	67	56
Watford	46	8	7	8	27	30	6	6	11	30	41	14	13	19	57	71	55
Notts County	46	10	7	6	33	21	2	9	12	22	49	12	16	18	55	70	52
Southend	46	9	8	6	33	22	4	5	14	21	42	13	13	20	53	64	52
Birmingham City	46	10	4	9	30	32	3	8	12	20	40	13	12	21	50	72	51
Luton Town	46	6	13	4	26	26	4	8	11	22	36	10	21	15	48	62	51
Sunderland	46	9	6	8	34	28	4	5	14	16	36	13	11	22	50	64	50
Brentford	46	7	6	10	28	30	6	4	13	24	41	13	10	23	52	71	49
Cambridge United	46	8	6	9	29	32	3	10	10	19	37	11	16	19	48	69	49
Bristol Rovers	46	6	6	11	30	42	4	5	14	25	45	10	11	25	55	86	41

PONTINS LEAGUE DIVISION ONE

	P	W	D	L	F	A	Pts
Aston Villa	34	21	8	5	64	32	71
Nottingham Forest	34	20	8	6	77	46	68
Blackburn Rovers	34	18	10	6	60	37	64
Leeds United	34	15	8	11	59	44	53
Bolton Wanderers	34	15	8	11	48	49	53
Manchester United	34	13	13	8	58	50	52
Liverpool	34	13	10	11	47	43	49
Sheffield Wednesday	34	13	10	11	51	48	49
Leicester City	34	12	12	10	42	38	48
Wolverhampton W.	34	13	6	15	46	55	45
Notts County	34	12	8	14	56	52	44
Newcastle United	34	12	7	15	36	43	43
Sheffield United	34	10	10	14	54	59	40
Sunderland	34	11	6	17	57	57	39
Barnsley	34	9	11	14	48	58	38
Stoke City	34	8	8	18	38	56	32
Manchester City	34	7	9	18	34	68	30
Rotherham United	34	5	6	23	29	69	21

NORTHERN INTERMEDIATE LEAGUE

	P	W	D	L	F	A	Pts
Barnsley	32	21	6	5	62	36	69
Huddersfield Town	32	20	3	9	70	45	63
Leeds United	32	18	7	7	85	41	61
Newcastle United	32	19	2	11	68	31	59
Middlesbrough	32	14	9	9	55	38	51
Bradford City	32	15	5	12	62	48	50
Sunderland	32	14	7	11	75	56	49
Darlington	32	14	7	11	40	38	49
Sheffield Wednesday	32	11	10	11	36	36	43
York City	32	13	4	15	49	55	43
Sheffield United	32	10	9	13	64	72	39
Scarborough	32	11	4	17	56	83	37
Rotherham United	32	9	8	15	46	57	35
Hull City	32	9	8	15	51	66	35
Scunthorpe United	32	7	13	12	41	62	34
Doncaster Rovers	32	3	13	16	34	73	22
Hartlepool	32	4	5	23	29	86	17

STATISTICAL ROUND-UP

FIRST TEAM APPEARANCES 1992/93

Player	Lge	Gls	LC	Gls	AIC	Gls	FAC	Gls	Total	Gls
Matty APPLEBY	-	-	-	-	2(1)	-	-	-	2(1)	-
Richie APPLEBY	-	-	-	-	2	-	-	-	2	-
John BERESFORD	42	1	4	-	2	-	4	-	52	1
Paul BRACEWELL	19(6)	2	-	-	2	-	2(2)	-	23(8)	2
Kevin BROCK	4(3)	1	2	-	2(1)	1	-	-	8(4)	2
Franz CARR	8(2)	1	1(2)	-	3(1)	-	-	-	12(5)	1
Lee CLARK	46	9	5	-	3	-	4	1	58	10
Andy COLE	11(1)	12	-	-	-	-	-	-	11(1)	12
Peter GARLAND	-	-	-	-	(1)	-	-	-	(1)	-
Steve HOWEY	41	2	5	-	4	-	3	-	53	2
Andy HUNT	-	-	-	-	2	-	-	-	2	-
David KELLY	45	24	4	2	4	1	4	1	57	28
Brian KILCLINE	7(12)	-	2	-	5	-	1(2)	-	15(14)	-
Bjorn KRISTENSEN	-	-	-	-	3(1)	1	-	-	3(1)	1
Robert LEE	36	10	3	1	-	-	4	2	43	13
Alan NEILSON	2(1)	-	1	-	3	-	-	-	6(1)	-
Liam O'BRIEN	33	6	3	1	3	-	4	-	43	7
Gavin PEACOCK	29(3)	12	4	2	2	2	4	2	39(3)	18
Mick QUINN	4(1)	2	2(2)	-	2(1)	3	-	-	8(4)	5
Ray RANSON	3	-	1	-	(1)	-	-	-	4(1)	-
Mark ROBINSON	2(7)	-	-	-	-	-	-	-	2(7)	-
David ROCHE	-	-	-	-	(1)	-	-	-	(1)	-
Kevin SCOTT	45	2	5	-	2	-	4	-	56	2
Scott SELLARS	13	2	-	-	-	-	-	-	13	2
Kevin SHEEDY	23(1)	3	4	-	4	1	2(1)	1	33(2)	5
Pavel SRNICEK	32	-	-	-	5	-	4	-	41	-
Mark STIMSON	1(1)	-	-	-	2	-	-	-	3(1)	-
Alan THOMPSON	1(1)	-	-	-	3	-	-	-	4(1)	-
Barry VENISON	44	-	4	-	3	-	4	-	55	-
John WATSON	-	-	-	-	(1)	-	-	-	(1)	-
Steve WATSON	1(1)	-	-	-	2(1)	-	-	-	3(2)	-
Tommy WRIGHT	14	-	5	-	1	-	-	-	20	-
Own Goals	-	3	-	-	-	-	-	-	-	3

Largest Attendance   30,364 v Sunderland (H) 25.4.93

Lowest Attendance*   6,725 v Mansfield (CCLC) (A) 26.8.92

Biggest Victories   6-0 v Barnsley (H) 7.4.93
7-1 v Leicester City (H) 9.5.93

Biggest Defeats*   2-4 v Oxford Utd (A) 28.12.92
0-2 v Portsmouth (A) 9.2.93

Most Goals in a Game   3: David Kelly v Cambridge Utd (H) 28.11.92
v Leicester City (H) 9.5.93
Andy Cole v Barnsley (H) 7.4.93
v Leicester City (H) 9.5.93

(not including Anglo-Italian Cup)

FIRST TEAM GOALSCORERS

28	Kelly	18	Peacock
13	Lee	12	Cole
10	Clark	7	O'Brien
5	Sheedy, Quinn		
2	Bracewell, Brock, Howey, Scott, Sellars		
1	Beresford, Carr, Kristensen		
3	Own Goals (for)		

PONTINS LEAGUE APPEARANCES

	A	G		A	G
Alderson	2	0	Mtawali	2	0
Andersson	1	0	Murray	4(2)	0
Appleby M	24(2)	0	Neilson	26	0
Appleby R	9(7)	1	O'Brien	1	0
Armstrong A	12(4)	1	Papavassiliou	1	0
Armstrong S	1	0	Peacock	3	1
Bracewell	9	1	Quinn	7	2
Brock	18	1	Ranson	10	0
Carr	6	0	Robinson	5	0
Cormack	6(6)	0	Roche	19(3)	1
Dinning	3(2)	0	Salou	1	2
Elliott R	9(2)	1	Sheedy	3	0
Garland	10	0	Srnicek	10	0
Garner	7	0	Stimson	25	2
Hunt	17	5	Thompson	27	7
Kilcline	11	0	Watson J	18(5)	4
Kirkham	1	0	Watson S	20(1)	2
Kristensen	19	2	Wild	3	0
McDonough	11	1	Wright	12	0
Morton	1	0			

N.I.L. APPEARANCES

	A	G		A	G
Aiston	1(1)	0	Keen	8	0
Alderson	22(5)	3	Kirkham	24(4)	1
Anderson	9(1)	0	McAlindon	2(1)	0
Appleby R	27	4	McGiven	-(1)	0
Armstrong A	27(3)	21	Morton	2	0
Armstrong S	7	0	Murray	22	4
Baldwin	2(5)	0	Pepper	2(1)	0
Christie	4(4)	0	Phillips	1	0
Cormack	25	2	Rushworth	1	0
Degnan	-(2)	0	Stephenson	2	0
Dinning	28(3)	0	Stokoe	5(3)	1
Elliott R	10	2	Thompson	20	8
Elliott S	2	0	Thornton	3	0
Finlay	4(4)	0	Walton	10(3)	1
Greenwood	16(9)	4	Watson J	28	8
Harper	9	0	Watson S	22	7
Hayes	3	1	Wild	4	0

RESERVE TEAM RESULTS & SCORERS 1992-93

PONTINS CENTRAL LEAGUE

Aug	20	H	SUNDERLAND	3-2	McDonough, M. Appleby, Thompson
	27	A	Sheffield Wednesday	2-1	Kristensen, Thompson
Sep	3	H	ROTHERHAM UNITED	2-1	Quinn 2 (1 pen)
	9	A	Wolverhampton W.	0-1	
	16	H	LEICESTER CITY	1-0	J. Watson
	24	A	Nottingham Forest	0-1	
Oct	1	H	NOTTS COUNTY	1-1	R. Appleby
	7	A	Bolton Wanderers	1-2	Stimson
	13	A	Manchester City	3-1	Armstrong, Stimson, Kristensen
	21	H	STOKE CITY	1-0	o.g.
	27	A	Sheffield United	1-2	Thompson
Nov	9	A	Blackburn Rovers	0-3	
	18	H	LEEDS UNITED	1-0	Hunt
	25	H	MANCHESTER UNITED	2-3	J. Watson 2
Dec	9	H	LIVERPOOL	0-4	
	14	A	Barnsley	2-1	S. Watson, Roche
	23	A	Leeds United	0-1	
	30	H	BLACKBURN ROVERS	1-0	S. Watson
Jan	13	H	NOTTINGHAM FOREST	1-1	Hunt
	25	A	Leicester City	0-0	
Feb	4	H	SHEFFIELD WEDNESDAY	1-2	Hunt
	10	A	Sunderland	0-4	
	15	A	Rotherham United	2-1	Hunt, J.Watson
	17	H	WOLVERHAMPTON W.	4-0	Salou 2, Elliott, Hunt
	23	A	Notts County	2-1	Bracewell, Brock
Mar	3	H	BOLTON WANDERERS	0-0	
	17	H	ASTON VILLA	0-0	
	31	A	Manchester United	1-1	Thompson
Apr	14	H	BARNSLEY	0-1	
	20	A	Liverpool	1-1	Thompson
	28	H	SHEFFIELD UNITED	1-2	Thompson
May	3	A	Stoke City	2-3	Thompson, Peacock
	6	A	Aston Villa	0-1	
	12	H	MANCHESTER CITY	0-1	

NORTHUMBERLAND SENIOR CUP

Jan	6	H	ALNWICK TOWN (Rnd 2)	10-0	Thompson 3, McDonough, S. Watson 3, Hunt 2, Belisle (o.g.)
Mar	24	A	Blyth Spartans (SF)	3-1	Roche, Brock, Thompson
May	1	H	BLUE STAR (F)	1-2	J. Watson

NORTHERN INTERMEDIATE LEAGUE FIXTURES 1992-93

Aug	8	H	SCUNTHORPE UNITED	1-2	Murray
	15	A	York City	1-3	Greenwood
	22	H	DARLINGTON	1-2	J. Watson
	29	A	Sunderland	7-0	Thompson 3, Kirkham, Greenwood, R.Appleby, Walton
Sep	12	A	Sheffield Wednesday	2-0	Greenwood, A. Armstrong
	26	A	Hartlepool United	2-1	A. Armstrong, Murray
Oct	3	H	BARNSLEY	1-2	R. Appleby
	10	A	Doncaster Rovers	3-1	Thompson, Alderson, A. Armstrong
	17	H	SCARBOROUGH	3-0	S. Watson, Alderson, A. Armstrong
	24	A	Middlesbrough	0-2	
	31	A	Sheffield United	3-0	A. Armstrong, J. Watson, R. Appleby
Nov	7	H	BRADFORD CITY	2-1	A. Armstrong 2
	14	A	Leeds United	1-3	S. Watson
	21	H	HULL CITY	7-0	S. Watson 3, A. Armstrong, Murray, Cormack, J. Watson
	28	A	Rotherham United	0-2	
Dec	12	H	YORK CITY	3-0	Greenwood, A. Armstrong, Alderson
Jan	9	H	SHEFFIELD WEDNESDAY	1-1	S. Watson
	16	A	Huddersfield Town	0-1	
	22	H	HARTLEPOOL UNITED	1-0	R. Appleby
	27	A	Darlington	3-0	Thompson, A. Armstrong 2
Feb	6	H	DONCASTER ROVERS	5-0	A. Armstrong 3, Stokoe, S. Watson
	13	A	Scarborough	3-1	A. Armstrong, Thompson (p), J. Watson
	20	H	MIDDLESBROUGH	1-0	Thompson
	27	H	SHEFFIELD UNITED	3-0	J. Watson, Hayes, Alderson
Mar	6	A	Bradford City	0-1	
	20	A	Hull City	3-0	Murray, Elliott 2
	27	H	ROTHERHAM UNITED	3-0	Cormack, A. Armstrong, Thompson
Apr	3	H	HUDDERSFIELD TOWN	0-1	
	8	H	LEEDS UNITED	2-2	J. Watson, A. Armstrong
	12	H	SUNDERLAND	2-0	Armstrong, J. Watson
	26	A	Scunthorpe United	3-0	A. Armstrong 2, J. Watson
May	8	A	Barnsley	1-5	A. Armstrong

NORTHERN INTERMEDIATE LEAGUE CUP

Sep	5	A	Leeds United (Rnd 1)	1-1	Thompson
	30	H	Leeds United (Rnd 1 Rep)	*4-2	Thompson, A. Armstrong, Alderson 2
Jan	30	A	Middlesbrough (Rnd 2)	2-1	Thompson, S. Watson
Mar	1	A	Sunderland (SF)	0-1	

FA YOUTH CUP

Dec	5	A	York City (Rnd 2)	0-2	

* *After extra-time*

SUBSCRIBERS' ROLL-CALL

1 David Holbrow	52 Sean Honnor	103 Mr John Kenneth Carry
2 Jeremy Parwani	53 Joe Ridley	104 Stephen Blakey
3 Mr C. D. & Mrs V. J. Taylor	54 Malcolm Colby	105 John Lawlor
4 Mrs A. Taylor	55 Michael Hall	106 Jonathan Buffey
5 Kevin Hunter	56 Sean Belcher	107 Mr P. Davison
6 Gary Sutherland	57 M. L. Roberts	108 John Foley
7 Michael Hogg	58 John Joseph Wilson	109 Mr Mark Edward Hall
8 Paul Graham	59 David Albany Stewart	110 Mark Chow
9 Alistair K. Black	60 Gordon Lundgren	111 Jamie Judd
10 Ross James Gassney	61 Jordan Thomas John Lisle	112 Julie Stanford
11 James Rooney	62 Graeme Albert Charles Lisle	113 Glen Iley
12 Gordon Smith	63 Lance Robson	114 Ernie Woodhall
13 K. S. Gray	64 Thomas Bolton	115 Keith Million
14 A. Gray	65 Lee & Josh Brown	116 Geoffrey Milburn
15 Peter Rae	66 The Gosling Family	117 Mrs Ann Dodd
16 Sean Knighton	67 Ken Smith	118 Robert C. Paylor
17 Christel Tridgel	68 John Turnbull	119 Ian Young
18 Andrew Haley	69 Keith Talbot	120 Ian Wilkinson
19 Alan Dormer	70 J. E. Fleck	121 Mr Jackson Davison
20 Mr R. McMillan Snr.	71 Amy Lena Watson	122 Aidan Braithwaite
21 David Gray	72 Victoria Lynn	123 Colin Robson
22 Stephen Napier	73 Morgan David Cook	124 Peter Johnson
23 Sharon Atkinson	74 Mark Waddell	125 Peter Watson
24 Peter Maxwell	75 Michael J. P. Gaff	126 Paul John Flook
25 Malcolm Thompson	76 Eileen Braley	127 John Flook
26 Mr Michael de Hesellum	77 Tony Pearson	128 Marc Convery
27 Andrew Hush	78 Jeremy Nicoll	129 Keith Hately
28 Callum Robert Terry	79 Tony Toward	130 David J. Shepherd
29 Simon Mark Watson	80 Dean West	131 Paul Clark
30 Barry Richardson	81 Joe & Loren Barclay	132 Olive Sherry
31 Philip Dodds	82 Iain Richardson	133 Richard Law
32 Michael Adam Weddell	83 Kevin Bramley	134 Lloyd Naylor
33 Callum D. Longstaff	84 Malcolm Campbell	135 Michael Ballard
34 Colin Jarvis	85 J. Keith Cheesman	136 Gareth Matthews
35 Dennis Sanderson	86 A. R. Jobson	137 Graeme Proud
36 Daniel Duggan	87 Ron Murray	138 David Kilner
37 Peter J. Gibson	88 Liam Hugh Lavelle	139 Gareth Harrison
38 Joe Carpenter	89 Jon-Paul Allison	140 Lee David Graham
39 Monty	90 Mr E. G. Brown	141 Thomas Pinkney
40 Craig Andrew Forster	91 Stephen Metcalfe	142 Samantha Askew
41 Michael Wilde	92 Ian Hately	143 Craig Consiglio
42 Peter Laverick	93 Robert Jackson Smith	144 Phil Wright
43 Eric William Johnson	94 Philip James Myers	145 Neil Henderson
44 Joy Farms	95 Emma Robson	146 Paul Southern
45 I. P. Coulson	96 David J. Nobbs	147 Ian R. Messenger
46 Mr R. T. Connor	97 Brian Reay	148 Mr David Robson
47 Jane McCartney	98 Jeff King	149 Ian Shanks
48 Allan D. Barnsley	99 Daniel Stout	150 Graeme Boots
49 Michael James Lillico	100 Wayne David Turnbull	151 Michael E. Capstick
50 Ian Straughan	101 Debra Ashworth	152 Joe Anthony Fiddes
51 Sarah Jobling	102 Alan Collins	153 Anthony John Fiddes

154 Daniel Gray	205 Liam Barton	256 Malcolm Scott
155 Barry James Westlake	206 Michael Guard	257 Michael Monk
156 Steven Michael Westlake	207 Ian Riches	258 Geoff Morton
157 Graham Clark	208 Vicki Porter	259 A. E. Williamson
158 Phil Rodgers	209 Jonathan Summers	260 James & John Davison
159 Paul Wigham	210 David Burn	261 Stephen Jones
160 Neil Robert Pringle	211 Nick Duffy	262 Mr Adrian Karl Skelton
161 The Kelters Family	212 John James Shone	263 Mr Jonathan Pyman
162 Neil Rutherford	213 John Bruce	264 Keith James
163 Simon Green	214 Kathryn Buist	265 Paul Dennis Atkinson
164 Des Button	215 D. Hunter	266 Mark Henderson
165 Colin Knott	216 Alan Price	267 John Robinson
166 Alan Knott	217 Joanne Joicey	268 William Woodhouse
167 Thomas & Pamela Laverick	218 Dave Raper	269 Paul Armes
168 Dale Lang	219 Michael Maloney	270 James Michael Overton
169 Derek Luke	220 Tony Aimers	271 Malcolm Tom Gibson
170 Gary Luke	221 Gerald D. Simmons	272 Glen A. W. Robson
171 Alan Hobbs	222 John J. Wigham	273 Neil Swinney
172 John Edminson	223 Eileen Labross	274 David Thompson
173 Bogdan Tomiczek	224 Gary Clay	275 Mrs E. Jones
174 Frank Carver	225 Ross Douglas Bailey	276 Gordon 'Twitch' Mitchell
175 Alan Carrick	226 Mark Farrington	277 John Turnbull
176 Raymond Walton	227 Michael & Marie Crane	278 Dave Ridley
177 Trevor Smith	228 Margaret Hay	279 Peter Edge
178 Ken Arnold	229 Kathryn Busby	280 Mark Moore
179 Mr Paul Toland	230 Mr E. Robson	281 Bill Welsh
180 Michael Whitfield	231 Gordon Young	282 Terry Armstrong
181 Paul O'Pray	232 Andrew Blain	283 Gordon Basford
182 Craig J. Johnston	233 J. C. Barnard	284 Neville Holborn
183 Mr Kevin Bulman	234 Christopher J. Warren	285 Michael Peter Cuthbert
184 David Seeley	235 Richard M. Warren	286 Geoffrey Winnard
185 Mr Andra Maitchell	236 Geoff Dick	287 George William Green
186 John David Jones	237 David John Porwol	288 Darren Usher
187 Toon Armee (H'pool Squad)	238 Karl Tempest	289 John Shelley JP, MIPM
188 Paul Lynch	239 Catherine E. Gray	290 Michael I. Malia
189 John Lynch	240 Brian Gowens	291 Peter G. Coates
190 Nicky Jellema	241 Miss Catherine Ann Mair	292 Colin Ford
191 Stephen Joseph Reed	242 Mark Elliott	293 Paul Bowie
192 Graeme Charlton	243 Steven R. G. Stoker	294 Mark Bowie
193 R. E. Overton	244 R. T. Collinson	295 Paul Kirby
194 Stephen Cross	245 Graham Campbell	296 George Vickers
195 Iain J. Martin	246 Neil Dixon Forster	297 Edward Dean
196 Dennis Martin	247 Mr David Henderson	298 B. W. Kyle
197 Stephen Long	248 George E. Stokes	299 David Walker
198 Michael John Gray	249 Russell Hargreaves	300 Bill Fife
199 Les Gray	250 Gordon Davis	301 Stephen Gibson
200 Leo Taylor-Wilson	251 Peter Todd	302 Sarah Fothergill
201 Mr James T. Handy	252 Tony Stephenson	303 Mr A. V. Ridley
202 Sharron M. O'Malley	253 Dave Stephenson	304 Mr R. M. Pill
203 David Rowe	254 Gary Hogg	305 Mr P. J. Eggleston
204 Philip Elliott	255 Donald Burnett	306 Thelma Dixon

307	Tom Dixon	358	Andrew Sadler	409	Adrian Freemantle
308	John Alder	359	Miss Alison Rudd	410	Robert McLean Jnr.
309	Philip Gledson	360	Brian Fenn	411	Carole Scott
310	Johnny Sharp	361	Michael Hutchings	412	Kevin Fairless
311	Chris Harding	362	Mr Ian Skinner	413	Jon Pickett
312	Bill Dixon	363	Joe & Nikki Shipley	414	David G. Parker
313	Anthony Wilkes	364	Tony Fell	415	Craig & Christopher Brennan
314	Gary Thompson	365	Richard Henderson	416	Jeff Spike
315	Benjamin Evans	366	Philip Cowan	417	Colin Jarrett
316	Philip Riches	367	Steven Robinson	418	Karen F. Stephenson
317	Mr Brian Lythgoe	368	Christopher Conroy	419	James A. Turnbull
318	Andy Wood (Prudhoe)	369	P. Harris	420	Michael Murphy
319	Jack Wood (Totnes)	370	Alistair Mark Reay	421	Kevin Robson
320	Craig Duller (Totnes)	371	Lesley Helen Halkyard	422	James Kidd
321	Philip Wood	372	David Love	423	David Macdonald
322	Robert Hogg	373	Mr Dennis James	424	Chris Alexander
323	Ronald Wood	374	Martyn	425	Ian John Heslop
324	Craig Twist	375	Bill Stainton	426	Gary Dodd
325	Danny Kibbler	376	Chris Curry	427	Chris Nicholson
326	Lee Robert Bainbridge	377	Colin Campbell	428	M. D. Dufton
327	Rob Murray	378	Brian Robson	429	Mr G. Dufton
328	David Peter Lanning	379	Paul Graeme Jude	430	Andy & Joanne Graham
329	Keith Slater	380	Cairoli Cristiano	431	Keith Spooner
330	Jayne Harrison	381	Jane Taylor	432	Justine Rochester
331	Christopher Gillespie	382	Gordon Kelly	433	Andrew Scotney
332	J. W. Foster	383	Mrs E. Brown	434	Richard Steel
333	Paul James Loughlin	384	Colin Jackson	435	Jonathan Cairns
334	Mr Brian Scollick	385	David Winder	436	Robin Prouse
335	Kathleen Bradley	386	Michael Manghan	437	Kevin Arrowsmith
336	Martin Edward Talbot	387	Bill Laube	438	Graham Brown
337	Ethan Rivers	388	Ian Colbert	439	Alan Thompson
338	Mr Robert Berry	389	G. & E. Shenton	440	Oliver Murray
339	Rob Wingate	390	Jane Emmett	441	Ean Belton
340	Adele Caisley	391	J. M. Hindmarsh	442	Richard N. Barron
341	Ian Forster	392	Allen Derek Johnson	443	Neill Davy
342	Allan J. Graham	393	Andrew J. Bennett	444	Debbie Lister
343	Michael Hardy	394	Kenneth Bell	445	Adam Stephen Kelly
344	Steve Power	395	Ged Oxley	446	Forbsey
345	Alan Carr	396	Philip Taylor	447	Peter Bainbridge
346	Ray Steinberg	397	Paul John Smith	448	Kevin F. Hill
347	Paul Michael Moore	398	Stephen Coulson	449	Anthony Turner
348	Mr Ian Steel	399	Michael Irving	450	Jay Graham
349	Paul Kevin Champ	400	Michael J. Pilch	451	Jonathan Baker
350	David Endean	401	Simon Bell	452	Anthony Dolphin
351	Ray McDermott	402	B. S. Carter, Wallsend	453	John Dixon
352	Graeme Paul Bell	403	I. W. Carter, Hull	454	Keith John Thompson
353	Christopher Bell	404	Andrew Paul Taggart	455	Andy Wilson
354	Jerome Borkwood	405	Paul L. Johnson	456	Mr Kevin Enfield
355	Mr J. & Mrs A. Orr	406	Debbie Buck	457	Anthony Crawford
356	Alex Williams	407	David Caisley	458	Roy Peck
357	Denis White	408	Glyn Chambers	459	David Horsfall

SUBSCRIBERS' ROLL-CALL

460 Kevin Grey (8)	511 Raymond Kelly	562 Kenneth J. Tiffin
461 Edward Alfred Mitchell	512 David Emerson	563 Steven George Bell
462 Karan Ann Dunn	513 Siobhan L. D. Palmer	564 Stephen Hern
463 Andrew Milne	514 Ernest Dobson	565 David Graham
464 Nigel Sowerby	515 Paul Sainty	566 Steve 'Freddie' Smith
465 Paul Dixon	516 Allan Deeming	567 James Andrew Burns
466 Philip Thornton	517 Steven J. Slater	568 T. A. Mitchell
467 Craig Wappett	518 Mark John Thompson	569 Graham Donald Roberts
468 Miss Robyn Venables	519 Graham Wallis	570 Lee Gladders
469 Mr David Venables	520 Dave Bone	571 Heather Elizabeth Chadwick
470 Mr J. M. Alexander	521 Michael J. Boaden	572 Gary J. T. Monk
471 Jason Wilkes	522 Keith Topping	573 David Foster Monk
472 Keith A. Glynn	523 Ben Gordon Robert Leslie	574 Bill McCarthy
473 Melvyn Hughes	524 Alan Candlish	575 Peter Harden
474 Richard Hughes	525 Darren Greener	576 Ivan Robson
475 Mark Needham	526 Laura Graham	577 Roy Richardson
476 Karl William Clasper	527 Gillian Halse	578 Peter & Paul Lazenby
477 Edwin Moir	528 Dean Christopher	579 Dave Harrison
478 Stephen Hanson	529 Victoria A. Charlton	580 Leslie Alexander Mould
479 Jacqueline Hanson	530 Deepak Jain	581 Jon & Pam Preston
480 Dennis Rocke	531 Shaune Pearson	582 Keith Douglas
481 Mark Robert Smith	532 George W. Blair	583 Steven Brown
482 Allan Barron	533 Victoria Carroll	584 Mark Barber
483 Leslie Smith	534 Charlotte Potts	585 Kathleen Smith
484 Vicky Hostler	535 Brian Davidson	586 Keith Charlton
485 Victoria Johnson	536 Anthony G. Higgins	587 Graeme Dixon
486 Elaine Richardson	537 Ken Hodcroft	588 Alex Welch
487 David N. Ewles	538 M. Slatford	589 Stephen Sloan
488 Paul Brian Gowans	539 Chris Sadler	590 Lee Sabiston
489 Anthony Taylor	540 Paul Edgar	591 E. J. McCoy
490 Simon Hildrey	541 Nik Joplin	592 Kelly Marie Thompson
491 Michael P. Taylor	542 Malcolm R. Hutchinson	593 Mark Connelly
492 Joanne Louise Burnie	543 Adrian Conway	594 David Burton
493 Ian Wilson	544 Anthony Scott Fisher	595 Mr George Arrowsmith
494 K. D. Scott	545 Ian Smith	596 Iain Ambrosini
495 Andrew Graham	546 Richard J. Stanfield	597 Peter Roy Curry
496 Ian Spark	547 Charles Chrisp	598 Lisa Rutherford
497 Darren Brooks	548 John Branfoot	599 Ian Charlton
498 Daniel Walker	549 Sarah Branfoot	600 Michael-Lee Boyd
499 John Edward Armstrong	550 D. W. V. Branfoot	601 Jane Dalrymple
500 James Williams	551 Steve Little	602 Louise Storey
501 Victor Honeybell	552 Barry A. Hunter	603 Edward Wakenshaw
502 Derek Ian Whitworth	553 Niall Welsh	604 Louise Hudspith
503 J. T. Moody	554 Vicki Wilson	605 Daniel Kennedy
504 David J. Ridley	555 Paul Hemphill	606 Paul Knox
505 Stewart Walton	556 Christopher Suggett	607 Kirk Anthony Bowen
506 Steven Leslie Shaw	557 P. P. St Jacques	608 Mark Noble
507 Craig Steven Walker	558 Ian Embleton	609 Vince Rogers
508 Mr R. Reed	559 Stephen Tansey	610 Robert Reed
509 Stephen Faulkner	560 Brian O'Neill	611 Paul & Alan McPherson
510 Anthony R. Spooner	561 David, James, Robert, Bone	612 Richard Brian Hogg

SUBSCRIBERS' ROLL-CALL

613 Tony Keegan Savage	664 Neville Reed	715 Michael Andrew Craggs
614 Richard Watts	665 Elizabeth S. Henzell	716 Dale Wighton
615 Alan Watts	666 Craig Hopton	717 Ben Wilkie
616 Chris Watts	667 Derrick Wells	718 D. N. Bowman
617 Andrew Scott	668 Lewis Oliver Gray	719 Brian Herdman
618 Anthony Millington	669 Mr Duncan Hindmarsh	720 David Ormsby
619 Garry Hall	670 Miss Judith Hindmarsh	721 Paul Miller
620 Dave McManus	671 Mr J. Bryan Hindmarsh	722 Jonathan Stewart (London)
621 David John Fletcher	672 Mark Alan Peacock	723 Joseph Taylor (Ryton)
622 Jay Eltringham	673 Caren Linda Nicolson	724 Daniel Harry Gray
623 Steven Theobald	674 Alex Brook	725 Andy Dancer
624 Miss E. Bridges	675 Norman Walker	726 Steve Whitehead
625 Barry Barkes	676 Kevin F. Elgar	727 Ian Watson
626 Dick Reed	677 Paul & David Carpenter	728 Anthony E Jackson
627 Christopher Yates	678 David Dalrymple	729 D. M. Pearson
628 Joseph Cosgrove	679 Christopher M. Jenkinson	730 Mick Corneliusson
629 Christopher Lilley	680 Bryan Levey	731 Peter Harris
630 Lee Ash	681 J. Whitehead	732 Michael Allen Gorman
631 Peter Wilkinson	682 Derek Alderson	733 David Mark Edwards
632 Christopher Hall	683 Ian William Hepple	734 Eric Hogg
633 George Caulkin	684 Lynne Williamson	735 Caroline Morgan
634 Graeme Thompson	685 Mr J. Ingram	736 Grahaeme Hesp
635 John T. Colley	686 R. L. Walker	737 Kathleen Lovell
636 Steven L. Liddle	687 Norman Alexander	738 John Short
637 Michael Sewell	688 Matthew Smith	739 Philip Jobson
638 Karen Ferguson	689 Robin Black	740 Mark Robert Moorhead
639 Kenneth Cartman	690 Kenneth M. McManus	741 Claire Hedley
640 Ian Michael Hope	691 Malcolm Imray	742 Edwin Post
641 Andrew Needham	692 Michael John Murray	743 Michael G Post
642 John Frain	693 Trevor Walker	744 Micky Woodcock
643 Caroline J. Barber	694 Shane Michael Cooper	745 Mr P. A. Lee
644 P. M. Hopper	695 Jim Rickleton	746 Douglas Rawlinson
645 Graham N. Walker	696 Michael Grant	747 Stephen John Bland
646 Ross Goldie	697 Ian Nicholson	748 T. Conroy
647 Steve McKenna	698 David Dixon	749 Patrick Humble
648 James McGeary	699 Peter Kenneth Chamley	750 K. G. McQueen
649 Scott Moore	700 Amanda Kearns	751 David Coulson
650 Simon Moore	701 Gary Cumpson	752 Claire Tennet
651 M. E. Hudson	702 Steve Wakefield	753 Mark Wightman
652 John Maltman	703 Tony Clarkson	754 Janis Sterling
653 Gareth Tromans	704 Martin James Ball	755 Philip Crulley
654 Paul Donnelly	705 Stephen A. Cassidy	756 Arthur Swinney
655 Alan Cochrane	706 Dominic Barnes	757 Geoff Bell
656 W. R. Ridden	707 Allan Riddell	758 James Pirie
657 Anthony Ross Millen	708 Andrew Thompson	759 Ian Wilkin
658 Raymond Dixon	709 David Mark Jackson	760 Steven Johnson
659 Alison Forster	710 Mr Derek McKie	761 Louise Ransome
660 Mr Paul Alan White	711 Katherine Lilian Caisley	762 Simon Rathmell
661 C. A. Perry	712 Jonathan Caisley	763 Matthew W. Taylor
662 Billy Hunter	713 Edward Smith	764 Craig Robert Finnigan
663 Liam Bates	714 Matthew Jones	765 David Terence Turner

766	Mr Michael W. Clark	817	Malcolm Taylor	868	Newcastle Central Library
767	Peter Davidson	818	Neil Pattison	869	Newcastle Central Library
768	Karen M. Sibley	819	Angela Simmons	870	Paul Suttill
769	Graeme Preston	820	Keith Angles	871	Christopher Smith
770	David Potts	821	M. & J. Roberts	872	P. J. Davison
771	Peter Dobson	822	Mr Warren Percival	873	Martin Dillon
772	D. D. M. Rankin	823	Keith J. Mason & Family	874	Robert Ian Swan
773	Rod Cockburn	824	Tony D. Naylor	875	Robert Gallon
774	Nick Vince	825	D. W. Barnes	876	J. V. Stanbridge
775	Ms Norma Phillips	826	James Scorfield	877	Jack D. Blackbird
776	Darren Phillips	827	Pete Tate	878	Mr Gary McGregor
777	Ronnie Skinner (Tasmania)	828	Matthew Quinn	879	Norman B. Mackillop
778	Duncan Wraight	829	Dave Greaves	880	Nigel Hudspeth
779	John Collingwood	830	Terence Slattery	881	Stephen Gamsby
780	Mr David Anthony Dodds	831	Mr Tom Heaney	882	John Gilchrist
781	David Potts	832	Michael Hood	883	Fiona J. Robson
782	Emma Watson	833	Stephen Lee Shield	884	Ben Worrall
783	Gordon Reid	834	Susan Weavers	885	George Lowdon
784	Geof Cartwright	835	Alan Dunn	886	Michael Jordan
785	Ernie Staples	836	Phil Greaves	887	Ray Scott
786	Alan Emmerson	837	Brian Craig Toft	888	Simon Fairbairn
787	Christopher A. Emmerson	838	Michael H Reay	889	Mark Thomas Morgan
788	David P. Emmerson	839	Graeme Topping	890	Keith Page
789	Anthony M. Emmerson	840	Norman Hickin	891	Leigh Newton
790	David Gibson	841	Ray Pearson	892	R. M. Falcon
791	Daniel Gibson	842	Peter Driver	893	Neil Carr
792	Charles L. Cain	843	Paul Bullock	894	Richard Jenkins
793	Michael Scurr	844	Gavin Haigh	895	Stephen Mordue
794	Stuart G. Forster	845	Ian "Tiff" Ramsey	896	Graeme Herdman
795	Ian R. Calder	846	Lewis Ashford Wright	897	Mark Jones
796	Wendy J. Calder	847	T. E. Pescod	898	Leslie and David Usher
797	Stuart A. Calder	848	Alan Goldsmith	899	Paul Gilroy
798	Bobby Greenlands	849	Ryan Lewins	900	Tom Murray
799	Steve Bolam	850	Paul Turnbull	901	Anne Hughes
800	Michael Sinclair	851	I. J. Connaghan	902	Alan John Justice
801	W. J. Renwick	852	L. Le Quelenec	903	Glen & Wayne Newton
802	Jeff McKever	853	A. D. Hall	904	Greg Coffell
803	Dianne Nicola Robinson	854	Stuart James Blair	905	Reginald Simpson
804	David Telfer	855	David Carr	906	Paul Kelly
805	Liam Humble	856	Martin Alan Blair	907	Carmel Theresa Morrison
806	Paul Colin Warren	857	Tony Porter	908	Polly Walter
807	David G. Wilkinson	858	James David Bush	909	Colette V. Mullier
808	Chris Rogerson	859	Stephen James Bush	910	James Kelly
809	Ian Humble	860	Simon Andrew Bass	911	Rachel Crabtree
810	Joe Durham	861	Dr. Brian Jones	912	Richard Hogg
811	David Dixon	862	Mr Robin Anthony Ranson	913	Brian Oswald
812	Marc Alderson	863	Hugh Peter Docherty	914	Vernon Taylor
813	David Andrew Robinson	864	Newcastle Central Library	915	Philip Gouldbourne
814	Ken Gray	865	Newcastle Central Library	916	George Armitage
815	Phil Mitchell	866	Newcastle Central Library	917	Mark Worth
816	Christopher Hughes	867	Newcastle Central Library	918	Phil Thompson

919 William Bain	970 W. D. Siddle	1021 Steven James Dawson
920 Christopher Malone	971 Mr C. E. Robson	1022 JM, ON & AW Jackson
921 John Guard	972 William McCall Murray	1023 David R. Palmer
922 Christopher Cooper	973 Kenneth Holland	1024 Thomas R. Palmer
923 Christopher English	974 Martin McKeon	1025 Nigel Prettyjohns
924 Brian Joseph English	975 David and John Lloyd	1026 Roger Talbot
925 Christopher English Snr.	976 Neil McCloud	1027 Neil Arthur
926 Alex Wolens	977 Karyn McCloud	1028 Miss Alex Marshall
927 P. J. Mills	978 David Heron	1029 Michael Snowball
928 Mr Keith Russell	979 Mark Crudace, Stringers FC	1030 Barry Holmes
929 Michael W. Nicklin	980 Jonathan Bruce Dixon	1031 Barry Wallace
930 John Pickering	981 Balwant Pandya	1032 Derek Robert Rowell
931 Steven Burke	982 Miss L. Grimes	1033 Sean Kenneth Storey
932 Iam Alan Burn	983 Sarah Docherty	1034 Peter Howard Brown
933 John Jermyn	984 Brian Laskey	1035 Graham Pyle
934 Gordon Phillips	985 Cameron Price	1036 David Lee
935 Sean Dodds	986 Geoff Gray	1037 Richard Neville Jones
936 Kevin Heslop	987 Simon Elphick	1038 Andrew Garner
937 Stephen David Malthouse	988 Celtic Brian	1039 Neil Morton
938 Graham Robert Malthouse	989 Christopher T. K. Thirlaway	1040 Peter Adamson
939 Robert James Clow	990 Christopher Coan	1041 Andrew Robert Grant
940 Alistair James Clow	991 I. Wilson	1042 Daniel Ramshaw
941 Gary Walton	992 David Coulson	1043 David Robson
942 Mr John Ball	993 Ronald George Myers	1044 Warwick Shepherd
943 Steven Kempster	994 Colin Foster	1045 John Shepherd
944 Ian Beattie	995 Jonathon C. Hawkins	1046 Martin Wannop
945 Ron Brunton	996 Mr A. S. Osborne	1047 Stephen A. Smith
946 Sarah Knighting	997 Dave and Jacqui Joughin	1048 Michael Preston
947 Jimmy Blatt	998 Nic Earl	1049 T. McCallum
948 Mr Allan Sykes	999 Stephen Brennan	1050 Gary Walters
949 Brian Blackett	1000 Liam Grant Patterson	1051 Peter Holgate
950 Paul Curry	1001 Jason Miller	1052 Patrick Hart
951 John Miley	1002 Dale John Binney	1053 Craig Cusack
952 Carl Grant	1003 Steve Wood	1054 Sue Allen
953 D. M. Nichols	1004 Wayne Dobson	1055 Kelly Rutherford
954 Gavin James Hall	1005 Gordon Satterthwaite	1056 Mark A. Rawlinson
955 David Harwood	1006 Julie Grant & David Grant	1057 Stephen David Handy
956 Peter Harwood	1007 Paul Scott Miller	1058 David Rogers
957 Alice & Louise Burn	1008 P. Simpson	1059 Gary O'Neill
958 Chris Wilkie	1009 Mr E. A. P. Nugent	1060 George Lowrey
959 Steven Watson	1010 Gary Coe	1061 Kirk Haddon
960 Jeffrey Bone	1011 Robert Martin	1062 Andrew Haddon
961 Steven Wood	1012 Nigel Weir	1063 Stephen Yan Wong
962 Glenn Todd	1013 George Richard Weir	1064 Mr Chris Scott
963 Benjamin Wright	1014 John Liddell	1065 Robert Young
964 John Welch	1015 John Furness	1066 Fred G. Clark
965 Alexander Huggins Cooper	1016 Roger Siddle	1067 Ian James Smith
966 Darren T. Green	1017 Alan Denham	1068 Ian Scurfield
967 W. R. Maughan	1018 Bryan Hollinshead	1069 Paul Foster
968 Neil Heffernan	1019 Raymond Skipsey	1070 Derek J. Goodburn
969 Jean V. Cressey	1020 Scott Hood	1071 Andrew Robson

1072 Paul Luke	1123 Christopher Muse	1174 Peter Redhead
1973 Catherine Laura Taylor	1124 John James Hall	1175 Steve Edgar
1074 Christopher Taylor	1125 Graham Dawson	1176 Stuart Dunkerley
1075 James McIntyre	1126 Terry Coyle	1177 Michael Holloway
1076 Andrew Roberts	1127 Ally McCarley	1178 Andrew Lawson Gwynne
1077 Mr J. E. Morton	1128 Darren Cranton	1179 Jeremy Hance
1078 Sandra Williams	1129 David Alan Bell	1180 David Verdon Calford
1079 Ian Robert Brown	1130 Nicholas Hoyes	1181 Jack Turner
1080 Alan Robert Brown	1131 George Holden	1182 Alex Byers
1081 Graeme Symonds	1132 Michael Heywood	1183 Michael Emmerson
1082 Chris Gaffney	1133 John Marley	1184 Paul Holbrook
1083 Rev. Neil Passmore	1134 Colin Morgan	1185 Stuart Ford
1084 Jane Cross	1135 Richard Fairbairn	1186 G. T. Collinson
1085 Neil Sidney McQueen	1136 Mr & Mrs G & D. M. Edgar	1187 Garry Payne, H'Pool Mag
1086 Michael Joseph Freeman	1137 Paul Lynch	1188 Simon Steggles
1087 Mark A Coleran	1138 Adam Forsyth	1189 Bob Day
1088 Andrew Veitch	1139 A. J. Robinson	1190 Katy Barrons
1089 David Ramsey	1140 Simon Lamb	1191 David Sørensen
1090 Sean Whelan	1141 Dave Gaiger	1192 Neil Sørensen
1091 Kieran Whelan	1142 Brian Hughes	1193 Nigel Pattinson
1092 Stan Henderson	1143 Carl A. Gracie	1194 Jeff Siddle
1093 Steven Smith	1144 Paul J. Fairweather	1195 Aidan Robertson
1094 Scott Taylor	1145 David Fairweather	1196 Peter Robertson
1095 G. Hedley	1146 Ian T. Jackson	1197 Thomas Carney
1096 Martin Rowntree	1147 Susan Fuller	1198 Ian D. Renwick
1097 Anthony Lang	1148 Mark Allen Fairless	1199 Michael Goldsmith
1098 Robert E. F. Heslop	1149 Gordon Bone	1200 Richard Fitzsimmons
1099 Peter John Longstaff	1150 Richard Hopper	1201 Dominic Fitzsimmons
1100 Shannon Joy Richardson	1151 Michael D. Harper	1202 Amy Victoria Newman
1101 J. L. Blackett	1152 Michael John Ord	1203 Dr. Christopher Palmer
1102 Alan James Nash	1153 Sean Paul Thompson	1204 Matthew Gilbert
1103 Carl Michael Reid	1154 Louis Azzopardi	1205 Michael Gilbert
1104 Rod Gibson	1155 Mr Paul Hoban	1206 Peter Gilbert
1105 Vince Edes	1156 Chris McCourt	1207 Jamie Hayes
1106 Richard Hall	1157 Paul & Bobby McKeown	1208 Keith Coppin
1107 Timothy Duncan	1158 David & Ceri Low	1209 Huw Davies
1108 Stephen Ward	1159 Joe Camilleri	1210 Stephen Hill
1109 Christopher M. Meadows	1160 P. J. Mabon	1211 Ian Skinner
1110 Philip Lisle Meadows	1161 T. F. Mabon	1212 Claire M. Skinner
1111 A. L., E. D. & N. G. Meadows	1162 Nick Iley	1213 Paula E. Tracey
1112 Bruce D. Reid	1163 Ian Cameron	1214 Tony Ormston
1113 David Blackburn	1164 John E. Topham	1215 Steve Winter
1114 Harvey M. Pryor	1165 Craig Peddie	1216 Doreen Nixon
1115 Kevin J. Evans	1166 Philip James Hodgson	1217 Susan Smailes
1116 A. W. Wakefield	1167 Hayley Morrell	1218 Michael Smailes
1117 David Ross Atkinson	1168 John L. Greenwell	1219 Paul Eden
1118 Michael Crass	1169 Derek Pouton	1220 John Philip Bailey
1119 John Ahmed	1170 J. F. Coulthard	1221 Coral Dawn Willins
1120 John Trewick	1171 Paul Luckley	1222 David Hall
1121 Stephen Byrne	1172 Richard E. G. Gardiner	1223 Jim Mulvey
1122 Paul Z Robson	1173 Russell J. Gardiner	1224 Iain Mulvey

SUBSCRIBERS' ROLL-CALL

1225 Craig Hodgson	1276 David Leslie Ross	1327 Richard Ford
1226 David Lowrey	1277 Colin Edwards	1328 Adam James Watkins
1227 J. W. Lowrey	1278 David Dyer	1329 Michelle Hughes
1228 Tom Storrar	1279 Peter S. Black	1330 Steven Huddart
1229 Robert W. Dixon	1280 Matthew James Steven	1331 Geoff Boyle
1230 Darin Fawcett	1281 Jonathan Steven	1332 Richard Edwin Slack
1231 Ian Parkin	1282 Peter Anthony Lumley	1333 Michael Hogan
1232 David Bell	1283 Peter Sewell	1334 Luke Wraith Jones
1233 David Mercer	1284 Brenda M. Wilkinson	1335 Rod Clarke
1234 Geoffrey Tarn	1285 Ian Robinson	1336 Stephen Michael Taylor
1235 Mark Lawson	1286 Sophie Webster	1337 David G. Kitchen
1236 Susan McDougal	1287 Darren Russell Tonks	1338 K. Butler
1237 Mark Eden	1288 Ryan Scott Tonks	1339 Rory Stuart Adamson
1238 Alan Shearer	1289 J. Stephen Shear	1340 Mark Ian Little
1239 Craig Duncan	1290 Neil Foster	1341 Brian Rootham
1240 David Meppem	1291 Gavin English	1342 John Scott
1241 Andrea Meppem	1292 Eddy Hope	1343 Steven Cummings
1242 Terry Meppem	1293 Paul Stephen Hunter	1344 Alan Beresford
1243 David Hewitt	1294 Mark Stobbs	1345 Robert Coulson
1244 Shaun Haney	1295 Keith Leggoe	1346 David J. Bowman
1245 Stephen Powns	1296 Tony Taylor	1347 Neil Brown
1246 William James Lake	1297 Biffa Richardson	1348 Christian Hannah
1247 Jonathan Ord	1298 Alan Armitage	1349 Paul Scott
1248 Michael Campion	1299 Paul English	1350 Colin John Marr
1249 Rowena Jones	1300 Mal Taylor	1351 David Ian Lidster
1250 Andrew John Walker	1301 M. T. Hardman	1352 David Lee
1251 John Joseph Hodgson	1302 John Boynton	1353 Sarah Ann Shannon
1252 Ewan John Barclay	1303 Tom Howe	1354 Mr Gary Nicholson
1253 Daniel Wilkinson	1304 Emma Dowson	1355 I. H. Mudie
1254 Ashley James	1305 David John Rowe	1356 Paul Robert Munro
1255 Andy Gardner	1306 Brian Wilfred Jobling	1357 Pete Bennett
1256 Steven Brown	1307 Steven Ingram	1358 David Clouston
1257 Stuart Kennedy	1308 Richard Pilling	1359 Daniel Carmichael
1258 Mark Henzell Adamson	1309 Alistair & Jen Spears	1360 Alan Brown
1259 Antony Thane	1310 David Robb	1361 Paul David Foster
1260 Mark William Huddart	1311 Peter J. Ruddick	1362 Kevin Crawford
1261 Paul Bandeen	1312 Steve Fairfax	1363 Glyn Wade
1262 David Batey	1313 Peter Stafford	1364 Stuart Peters
1263 Ian Reay	1314 Mike Pigott	1365 Paul Golightly
1264 Stuart Woods	1315 Michael Robinson	1366 Mark Forbes
1265 Alan & Maureen Carter	1316 Kevin Harris	1367 Katherine & Andrew Linkie
1266 Mark Edward Dixon	1317 R. T. Milburn	1368 Mr Stephen Rooney
1267 Ted Whitfield	1318 Neil Patterson	1369 Malcolm Rowland
1268 Adam Bell	1319 David Anthony King	1370 Mark Surtees
1269 Kris Bainbridge	1320 Richard Pearson	1371 Jerry Luck
1270 Christopher B. Lane	1321 Stephen Alan Stones	1372 Fred Tron
1271 Kenneth & Karen Quinn	1322 G. J. Mulholland	1373 P. A. Simpson
1272 Mark Edward Brown	1323 George Bible	1374 Ian Jerrard
1273 Norman Holland	1324 Gary Hewitson	1375 Paul Willis
1274 Lynda Smith	1325 Philip Clarkson	1376 Michael Elgy
1275 Paul Ross	1326 Steven Edgar	1377 Peter R. Langston

SUBSCRIBERS' ROLL-CALL

1378 Steve Atkinson	1429 Daniel Hall	1480 Les Ruffell
1379 Mr Scott Kelly	1430 Gary Freeman	1481 Stephen Masters
1380 Andrew Easton	1431 J. R. Finn	1482 Andrew James Armstrong
1381 Amelia Margaret Knowles	1432 P. B. Douglass	1483 Gavin Joseph Brown
1382 Ken Potts	1433 Colin Mutter	1484 Brian Kevin Pirrie
1383 Aurora Louise Thirlaway	1434 Keith L. Rutherford	1485 John Davison
1384 Alan Johnson	1435 Anne Grealy	1486 Sarah Louise Raine
1385 Michael Hall	1436 Jamie Dalrymple	1487 John L. Gallon
1386 Kenneth Harbottle	1437 Stephanie Outterside	1488 Gordon Nicol
1387 Peter Welsh	1438 Stephen Wafer	1489 Keith Atkinson
1388 Stephen Emery	1439 Mark Hall	1490 Thomas Clare
1389 Natasha Lambert	1440 Lewis Rimington	1491 Mr T. Williamson
1390 W. H. Swann	1441 Paul Dominic Reynolds	1492 Martin H. Roberts
1391 Michael James Cook	1442 Christopher Meighen	1493 Paul Lawson
1392 Jeremy Pells	1443 Gary Smith	1494 Graeme Turner
1393 Karl Furlong	1444 Andrew Usher	1495 K. C. Pugmire
1394 Mr David Wightman	1445 Mr Paul Mark Scott	1496 Jonathan R. Carroll
1395 Mr Bruce Walker	1446 John Robert Nicholas	1497 Craig Barrass
1396 Stephen J. Littlewood	1447 Kieran James Flannery	1498 Anthony 'Goldie' Golding
1397 Bob Murray	1448 Philip Walker	1499 Liz Scott
1398 Grant Slater	1449 Keith McLellan	1500 Eddy Oliver
1399 John Wood	1450 Sheila Cassidy	1501 Glenn Hall
1400 George Thomas Gray	1451 Bob Ashburn	1502 Christine Jones
1401 R. Martyn Plummer	1452 David Paul Shepherd	1503 Ian Callender
1402 Mark Plummer	1453 Gary Block	1504 A. H. Green
1403 Tony Cawson	1454 Scott Wilson	1505 Daniel Pulman
1404 Roger M. Douglass	1455 Simon Smith	1506 David Dumble (Berwick)
1405 Greg Purdie	1456 Michael A. Hughes	1507 Paul Hundrup
1406 Chin Siew Min	1457 R. F. Davidson	1508 Alan McNeil
1407 Mark Ashton	1458 J. Loyd	1509 Tom Hutchinson
1408 Nick Ashton	1459 Kevin Mather	1510 B. Singleton
1409 Paul Marr	1460 Shane Summers	1511 Adrian Gaskill
1410 Alistair Wilson	1461 George H. Farrar	1512 John Morrison
1411 Gavin Buck	1462 Jeff Blades	1513 John A. Kennedy
1412 Louise Waugh	1463 Brian Woollett	1514 Jill Robinson
1413 Richard Lamb	1464 Roy Clark	1515 J. M. K. Smith
1414 Andrew J. Nelson	1465 Mark Bowman	1516 Darren Pearson
1415 Steve Foukes	1466 Jair Franz Vieser	1517 Eric Anderson
1416 J. Alexander Scott	1467 Anne Jenkins	1518 Liam Hedley
1417 George Middleton	1468 Steven Phillips	1519 Anthony Thompson
1418 Jason Sellick	1469 Philip Tennant	1520 Mark Railston
1419 Ron Wilson (Catterick)	1470 Paul T. Forster	1521 Robert Graham Lowes
1420 Stephen McKenna	1471 William Hayward	1522 Simon Hill
1421 Ronald Taylor	1472 Stephen Thompkins	1523 Neil Bullock
1422 Martin Buglass	1473 Chris Preston	1524 Malcolm Hall
1423 Allan Michael Beckwith	1474 Paul Watson	1525 Brian W. Huddart
1424 Peter D. McCarthy	1475 Lawrence Lamb	1526 Andrew Henderson
1425 Peter Briggs	1476 John Robert Gibson	1527 Arthur Temple
1426 Neil Gallagher	1477 Stuart Pringle	1528 Susan Marshall
1427 Alan Wilcock	1478 Shawn Watson	1529 Richard S. Hall
1428 Mstr. Richard J. Southwick	1479 Kenneth Stewart Brown	1530 Kevin Randall

SUBSCRIBERS' ROLL-CALL

1531 Mr A. Ellsbury	1582 Neil J. Davidson	1633 Ian Elliott
1532 Steven Hodgson	1583 Stuart A. Dumbarton	1634 Simon Corbett
1533 Ernest Wears	1584 Andrew Wright	1635 Ian Robinson
1534 M. Beveridge	1585 Jon Andrew Grant	1636 Declan Harrington
1535 Dr. K. Beveridge	1586 Derek Graham	1637 Graham Thompson
1536 Andrea Mason	1587 Dennis Railton	1638 Sarah Scott
1537 Paul Tavendale	1588 Andrew Dennis Railton	1639 Mark Skelton
1538 Robert Watts	1589 Elisa J. Elliott	1640 John Osborn
1539 Darren Watts	1590 Bernard Yellowley	1641 Darren Lawler
1540 Paul Frith	1591 Leslie Sparham	1642 Mark Lawler
1541 Nathan Ducker	1592 Jimmy Beresford	1643 John Nixon
1542 Phillip Thomson (Brampton)	1593 Christopher Ian Haxon	1644 Stephen John Middleton
1543 Andrew Harbottle	1594 Colin Riches	1645 Sean Mulroy
1544 Kev Davies (Rotherham)	1595 Alan Birbeck	1646 Linda Levey
1545 Mr S. D. Redpath	1596 Tim Gleave	1647 David & Samantha Marcus
1546 Mr K. M. Slatter	1597 David John Willoughby	1648 Stephen Levey
1547 Mr A. Amers	1598 Sean Mowbray	1649 Fraser Wilson
1548 Mr D. Amers	1599 Richard Mills	1650 Neil Carr
1549 Jacqueline Younger	1600 Christian Caygill	1651 David Redford
1550 Mark Easton	1601 Christopher P. Brown	1652 Andrew David Burn
1551 Ian and Julia Straker	1602 Neil Cameron Eyes	1653 Jonathan Paul Burn
1552 Patrick F. Brennan	1603 Liam A. Crowe	1654 Michael C. Burn
1553 Mervyn Waring	1604 Angela Crossey	1655 James Stewart Tarbit
1554 John Edmund Lewis	1605 David Taylor	1656 Alan Grace
1555 Martin Edmund Lewis	1606 Ryan Douglas	1657 Ian Newton
1556 Rod May	1607 Jane Mary Trattles	1658 David Wallbanks & Lads
1557 Adam Steven Young	1608 David Conway	1659 Barrie W. Hudson
1558 Iain E. Nicolson	1609 Kevin Bennett	1660 Michael Knott
1559 Malcolm Graham	1610 James Robert Brown	1661 James A. Dewhirst
1560 Richard J. Meehan	1611 Stephen Wilkinson	1662 Stuart Mather
1561 J. Derek Meehan	1612 Jane & Craig Sinclair	1663 Dominic Munroe
1562 Sara Peng	1613 Brian Anderson	1664 Andrew Lambert
1563 Jonathan A. J. Davis	1614 Miss Andrea Glen	1665 Alison C. Potter
1564 W. Neil Middlemass	1615 Mr Ian Glen	1666 Miss Karen Barton
1565 Nick Mitford	1616 Kevin Douglas	1667 Dennis Wade
1566 Allen Sharples	1617 'Audi' Quantrill	1668 David Robert Henderson
1567 Darren Keith McDougal	1618 Michael Kirkham	1669 Paul Metters
1568 Mr W. Bennett	1619 Gordon W. Mullen	1670 Stephen J. Brunt
1569 Victoria Beresford	1620 Mr Dereck Thompson	1671 Andy Newham
1570 Leslie Robson	1621 Neil Armstrong	1672 Glen David Stuart
1571 Mr L. J. Shippen	1622 Michael Armstrong	1673 Mandy Thomson
1572 Craig Littlefair	1623 John Parker	1674 Susan MacKenzie
1573 Julie Vowles	1624 Lisa Ann Hewitt	1675 Reginald D. Bradley
1574 Tony Stephenson	1625 Callum Ruffman	1676 Rob Wilson
1575 Colin & Anne Brown	1626 Bruce Ruffman	1677 Lee (Burt) Reynolds
1576 Ross Alexander Bowman	1627 Mark Narron	1678 Andrew Carr
1577 D. Milburn	1628 Dave Harrison	1679 Kevin and Paul Sutcliffe
1578 David Taylor	1629 Ian Ghirlando	1680 Howard R. Dodsworth
1579 Stuart Urquhart	1630 Lee Evans	1681 Raymond Wallis
1580 James Wilkinson	1631 Tony Reay	1682 Michael Evans
1581 Laura Jayne Baggaley	1632 Paula Mason	1683 David Hogg

SUBSCRIBERS' ROLL-CALL

1684 P. A. Grehan	1735 Jason Shinn	1786 Derek & Lisa Marie Ellison
1685 Sam Joseph Bell	1736 James Josephs	1787 'Woodentop' Bullivant
1686 Ken Davison	1737 David Maughan	1788 Duncan McKay
1687 Gavin Burrell	1738 Mr. Thomas R. Morgan	1789 Alan Rutherford
1688 Michael J. Walker	1739 David Blakey	1790 Brian Rutherford
1689 David Ronald Jackson	1740 Colin Atkinson	1791 Colin Andrew Wafer
1690 David Brewis	1741 David Atkinson	1792 Stephen Gardner
1691 Tracy Huntley	1742 Daniel Stephen Chester	1793 Michael Walsh
1692 Esme Ryder	1743 Peter Charles	1794 Ian Young
1693 Adrian George Barber	1744 George Morgan	1795 Marc & Nicola Flannery
1694 Steve Corrigan	1745 Fiona Bennett	1796 Mr David Joughin
1695 Les Bridge	1746 Jane & David Dean	1797 David J. Errington
1696 Ken Martin	1747 Derek Cooper	1798 Catherine Cole
1697 Phyllis Martin	1748 Iain Hush	1799 Robert Paul Marshall
1698 David Dando	1749 Ken Grenfell	1800 Christopher Davies
1699 Andrew Atkinson	1750 Barry Graham	1801 Dale Brotherton
1700 Graham Wilson	1751 John McCormella	1802 David Kemp
1701 E. & D. Miller	1752 Ian Turnbull	1803 Gary Paul McCartney
1702 Elizabeth Ann Douglas	1753 Geoff Herron	1804 Sam Plant
1703 Mick Robson	1754 Nigel Percival	1805 Gary M. Clark
1704 Liam Anthony Harris	1755 Roger D. M. Walton	1806 Gavin Bolam
1705 David Carl Maughan	1756 Tom E. F. Walton	1807 Gary Ramm
1706 Peter James Johnson	1757 David H. Knowles	1808 Michael Joyce
1707 Christopher Barlow	1758 Malcolm Graham	1809 Alex Cullen
1708 David McElhone	1759 Gordon Raymond Black	1810 J. G. White
1709 Marjorie Whinfield	1760 Paul Moran	1811 J. J. Dover
1710 Fiona Copeland	1761 David C. Graham	1812 A. Dodds
1711 Kevin Thomas	1762 David Neil Twizell	1813 William Swann
1712 Robert Pattinson	1763 David Paul Gorham	1814 Karen Swann
1713 Peter Crozier	1764 Craig Hornsby	1815 Richard Swann
1714 Brian Lowery	1765 Paul 'Yogi' Brewin	1816 Mark Swann
1715 Neill Nugent	1766 Fletcher Sowerby	1817 Anthony Britton
1716 Simon Sherratt	1767 Gregory Codling	1818 Peter Clancy
1717 Ian White	1768 Kevin and Craig Bratt	1819 Keith Ging
1718 David Storey	1769 Doug Robbie	1820 Darrell Hawksworth
1719 Stephen M. Venus	1770 John Mandell	1821 Alexander Lee Hawksworth
1720 Neil Devine	1771 John Hall	1822 Linda Littleton
1721 Colin Simpson	1772 Tim Wakefield	1823 David Armstrong
1722 Mr & Mrs McIver	1773 Andrew Edward Young	1824 Jonathan Elliott
1723 Christopher David Laws	1774 Glenn Hawthorn	1825 Matthew Elliott
1724 Alan Stevenson	1775 Andrew Ormond	1826 James R. Gill
1725 Andrew Fisher	1776 Stuart Green	1827 Thomas Rowden
1726 Thummanoon Kongchumcheun	1777 Jane Tennant	1828 Alec McIntosh
1727 Paul Hateley	1778 C. H. G. Thompson	1829 R. Thompson
1728 James E. M. Brooks	1779 Steve Murray	1830 Anthony Myers
1729 Raymond G. Potter	1780 Tony Smith	1831 Helen Myers
1730 Richard Burton	1781 Miss Sandra Huzzard	1832 D. Moses
1731 Tony Taylor	1782 M. G. Bailey	1833 Ian Michael McElroy
1732 Peter Noble	1783 Declan Harrington	1834 Beverley Harris
1733 Michael Little	1784 Ricky and Daniel Hale	1835 Paul Trainor
1734 G. M. Eastlake	1785 Tony Ellison (Toony)	1836 Rocky Chaddha

1837 Barrie N. Gardner	1888 James G. Beresford	1939 Derek A. Quelleron
1838 Susan Gibbons	1889 Kirk Edward Groundwater	1940 Neil Hindson
1839 Jeff Collin	1890 Dave Arnold	1941 J. C Dixon
1840 Leslie Young	1891 Richard Chipchase	1942 Andrew James Robertson
1841 Mandy Hope	1892 Peter McCarthy	1943 Derek Leighton
1842 Victor Cariglio	1893 G. H. Huddart	1944 Malcolm Avery
1843 Ian Gowland	1894 Paul Foster	1945 Paul Richard Tinlin
1844 Raymond Hodgkins	1895 Bryce Owens	1946 Mr J. Young
1845 Kathleen Armes	1896 Mr Cameron Shiels	1947 Mark Mason
1846 Neil Armes	1897 Sharon Lewis	1948 W. B. Tasker
1847 Richard J. Laing	1898 Sarah Gallagher	1949 Terry Scott
1848 Garry McDowall	1899 Denis Birkett	1950 Scott McBarron
1849 John & Chris Maddox	1900 M. J. Cool	1951 Kai S. Ng
1850 Stephen Brown	1901 Stephen Patrick Jackson	1952 Theresa S. Russell
1851 Ian Alexander	1902 John M. Brown	1953 William Henry Porter
1852 Lol Kindley	1903 David Robert Etherington	1954 Steven Charlton
1853 Mark Dawson	1904 John Kinghorn	1955 Martin Murphy
1854 Bob Wiffen	1905 Alan Lowther	1956 Malcolm Gibson
1855 Jonathan Bell	1906 Graeme Proud	1957 Iain Gray
1856 Ian Carroll	1907 Bill Pearson	1958 Peter Ellis
1857 Steven Wombwell	1908 Graham Elliott	1959 Shaun Patrick Stone
1858 Laura J. Greenwell	1909 Phillip Anthony Osborne	1960 Andrew Shaun Dixon
1859 Stephen Michael Collins	1910 Harold Glendinning	1961 Stephen Tibbs
1860 John Morris	1911 Philip Robinson	1962 Peter D. O'Neill
1861 Colin Fretwell	1912 Ian Wright	1963 Nick Laughton
1862 Les Pearson	1913 Roger Wright	1964 Glen Gardiner
1863 Alan Goodfield	1914 Keith Taylor	1965 Neil Clark
1864 Steven Lawson	1915 Peter Nicholson	1966 Andy Hately
1865 Michael Harle	1916 Charles Smith	1967 Mark Moffitt
1866 Peter Dolton	1917 Drew Hardy	1968 David Chapman
1867 Jeff Rowe	1918 Derek Clark	1969 Fraser John Wilcock
1868 Dennis Oliver	1919 Davey Aird	1970 Stewart James Watlen
1869 Alan Oliver	1920 Colin Walker	1971 Neil McCarthy
1870 Richard Spowart	1921 Ben Ould	1972 M. Tazey
1871 Dominic Bloomfield	1922 Steven Sweeting	1973 Graham, David & D. Fletcher
1872 Richard S. Wells	1923 John Jennings	1974 Jim McGuiggan
1873 A. J. Robson	1924 Anthony Wilson	1975 Andrew V. Glaister
1874 J. A. Lamb	1925 Stephen Grenfell	1976 Paul Moulding
1875 Adam Warren	1926 Daniel Morrell	1977 Keith John Laidler
1876 Antony Warren	1927 R. N. Dickson	1978 Martin R. Davies
1877 Peter Todd	1928 Douglas Bidgood	1979 Douglas Murray
1878 David Lough	1929 Lee M. Petty	1980 Robert William Smith
1879 Alex Fothergill	1930 Alan Hamilton	1981 Ian Morgan
1880 Laurie Deimel	1931 Simon Purvis	1982 Ian Richard Lowdon
1881 Algernon Sidney	1932 George Eastland	1983 David Anthony Cave
1882 Martin Heley	1933 Dale Kirk	1984 Chris Donachie
1883 Gary and Andrew Pringle	1934 Stephen Drew	1985 Eleanor Smith
1884 Mr Alan Patrick	1935 John Faulkner	1986 Tom Marley
1885 John Emery	1936 David Colling	1987 Lindsay Hannen
1886 Steve Murphy	1937 Andrew Cain	1988 Alan Bell
1887 Stephen D. Hewett	1938 Ian Tait	1989 Alexander Gilbert

1990 Andrew Maley	2039 Peter Major	2088 Mark Field
1991 Barney Roddy	2040 Bill Fairman	2089 Julian Field
1992 Glyn Williams	2041 Graham Todd	2090 Andrew Snowdon
1993 Denis Godfrey	2042 Michael J. Robinson	2091 In memory of John Machin
1994 P. B. Groves	2043 Scott Phillips	2092 Stephen Galloway
1995 Victoria Groves	2044 Steve O'Brien	2093 Kenneth Carmichael
1996 Steve Glen	2045 Tony Hannah	2094 Alexander Walker
1997 Mr John Ranson	2046 Carol Maughan	2095 Alan David Moore
1998 Paul Ranson	2047 John Pearson	2096 G. A. Bosomworth
1999 Julie Morton	2048 Lou Jordan	2097 Adrian Devine
2000 Richard Cox (Consett)	2049 Stephen J. Hatton	2098 Michael Pringle
2001 Geoff Atkinson	2050 Andrew Tippins	2099 J. G. Davies
2002 Gary Myles Coates	2051 Anthony Hughes	2100 Steven Telford
2003 Margaret Taylor	2052 John Addleton	2101 Eleanor Storey
2004 Ian Hogg	2053 William S. Welbury	2102 John Michael Cairns
2005 Roger Tames	2054 W. Gubb	2103 Peter Deacon
2006 The Back Page	2055 Steven Mountford	2104 Polly Nicolson
2007 Andrew Bell	2056 Andrew Dodds	2105 Geoffrey McGill
2008 Jayne Barrass	2057 Ben Slack	2106 David Small
2009 Mrs Maureen Barrass	2058 Ray Hannam	2107 Stuart Potter
2010 Dave Hudson	2059 Derek Grey	2108 Stephen Peter Willey
2011 Alan 'Cass' Campbell	2060 David Miller	2109 D. MacLaren
2012 Joseph Mitchinson	2061 Ken Claxton	2110 Jim Hennessey
2013 Jason K. Cordey	2062 Joseph D. Anderson	2111 David Evemy
2014 Kevin Keegan Gilfillan	2063 W. Bailey	2112 Andrew Conway
2015 Gary Conway	2064 Peter O'Shaughnessy	2113 I. K. Marr
2016 Mrs Sandra Johnston	2065 Andrew Evans	2114 Richard Stephenson
2017 Robert Baillie	2066 Warren Hendon	2115 Steven Walker
2018 Bruce Anthony Renwick	2067 Layman Layton	2116 Roberta Louise Connolly
2019 Colin Grey	2068 Jared Robinson	2117 Peter Cunningham
2020 Harry Grey	2069 William Marsh	2118 James & Terry McHugh
2021 Kevin Patrick Richardson	2070 Lee Wilkinson	2119 Andrew Stephenson
2022 J. B. G. Arthur	2071 Natasha Johnstone	2120 E. McDougal
2023 Andrew Boodhun	2072 David Ward	2121 Keith Talbot
2024 Alf Mercer	2073 Ronald Ward	2122 Keith M. Main
2025 Geoff Wilkinson	2074 Christopher Williams	2123 David Atkinson
2026 Anthony Curtis	2075 Edwin Sharratt	2124 John Miller
2027 Ivan Carr	2076 Chris Buckham	2125 Sean Lynch
2028 Iain & Moyra Scott	2077 Thomas Buckham	2126 Bryce John Martin
2029 William Lee	2078 David Jakeman	2127 Colin Leggatt
2030 George Legg	2079 S. Gardner	2128 D. Runciman
2031 Jonathan Connell	2080 Robert Morrison	2129 John James Connor
2032 Craig William Henderson	2081 Jeanne Morrison	2130 Mrs Lynne Brown
2033 Ian Taylor	2082 Alan Cooke	2131 John V. Potts
2034 James Peter Hall	2083 Kenneth Farms	2132 R. Stannard
2035 Roland Glenn Bloomfield	2084 Edward Farms	2133 Nigel Maddison
2036 Clare Erskine	2085 John S. Walker	2134 Mr G. P. Bell
2037 Anthony Matthew	2086 K. M. Thompson	2135 Mr D. A. Lloyd
2038 Simon Cox	2087 Thomas Baxter	